Crossing Cultural Boundaries in East Asia and Beyond

East and West

CULTURE, DIPLOMACY AND INTERACTIONS

Edited by

Chuxiong George Wei (*Hong Kong Shue Yan University*)

VOLUME 10

The titles published in this series are listed at *brill.com/ewcd*

Crossing Cultural Boundaries in East Asia and Beyond

Edited by

Reiko Maekawa
Darwin H. Stapleton
Roberta Wollons

BRILL

LEIDEN | BOSTON

Cover illustration: Utagawa, Yoshitora. *Bankoku zukushi—Amerikajin.* Japan, 1860. [Japan: Yamadaya Shōbei] Photograph. https://www.loc.gov/item/2002700301/. Public Domain.

Library of Congress Cataloging-in-Publication Data

Names: Stapleton, Darwin H., editor. | Maekawa, Reiko, 1952- editor. | Wollons, Roberta Lyn, 1947- editor.
Title: Crossing cultural boundaries in East Asia and beyond / edited by Darwin H. Stapleton, Reiko Maekawa, Roberta Wollons.
Description: Leiden ; Boston : Brill, [2021] | Series: East and West : culture, diplomacy and interactions, 2467-9704 ; volume 10 | Includes bibliographical references and index.
Identifiers: LCCN 2021001682 (print) | LCCN 2021001683 (ebook) | ISBN 9789004434455 (hardback) | ISBN 9789004435506 (ebook)
Subjects: LCSH: East and West. | Cultural relations. | Boundaries–Social aspects. | East Asia–Relations–Western countries. | Western countries–Relations–East Asia.
Classification: LCC CB251 .C75 2021 (print) | LCC CB251 (ebook) | DDC 909–dc23
LC record available at https://lccn.loc.gov/2021001682
LC ebook record available at https://lccn.loc.gov/2021001683

Typeface for the Latin, Greek, and Cyrillic scripts: "Brill". See and download: brill.com/brill-typeface.

ISSN 2467-9704
ISBN 978-90-04-43445-5 (hardback)
ISBN 978-90-04-43550-6 (e-book)

This book is printed on acid-free paper and produced in a sustainable manner.

Contents

PART 2
And Beyond

Preface

This volume is a result of two conferences held at the Graduate School of Human and Environmental Studies, Kyoto University. The first one, held in November 2005, was part of the project "Socio-cultural Studies on Émigré Intellectuals in America" funded by the Japan Society for the Promotion of Science. This project, which I had the pleasure of initiating, focused on the variety and complexity of intellectual transformations that individual exiled intellectuals underwent as a result of the hybridization of European and American ideas. Exchanges of ideas as well as individuals often had far-reaching and often unexpected consequences. Those who participated in this project, both faculty members and graduate students, decided to host an international conference. The main guests were Dr. Darwin Stapleton, Executive Director of the Rockefeller Archive Center, and Dr. Roberta Wollons, Professor of History at University of Massachusetts Boston. Dr. Stapleton talked about how the Rockefeller Foundation supported émigré scholars in the 1930s, as revealed by the wealth of archival material placed in the Rockefeller Archive Center. Dr. Wollons probed into the plight of Jewish refugees and their successful or not so successful careers. I also gave a brief presentation on German social scientists who fled from Nazism and worked for the US Office of War Information and the Office of Strategic Services during the war. This first conference made such a strong impression on a group of students who participated in it that very soon excellent international students started to work on PhDs in the Graduate School of Human and Environmental Studies of Kyoto University. Most contributors to this volume are recent or past PhD-holders of this program, who now pursue their intellectual endeavors in various academic institutions around the world.

To follow up on this first conference, another one, entitled "Crossing Boundaries," was held in September 2014. This conference came out of the three-year project, "Refugee Intellectuals in Postwar America: Crossing of Borders and Transfusion of Ideas," which started in 2009 and ended in 2011. As the leader of this project, funded by the Japan Society for the Promotion of Science and supported by Kyoto University, I tried to explore how refugee scholars who fled the spread of fascism in Europe in the 1930s and 1940s transplanted their ideas and thoughts into American soil through the personal and intellectual networks formed between them and American intellectuals during and after the Second World War. Special attention was paid to how they crossed disciplinary borders and came to their academic or creative maturity, transforming themselves from refugees into cosmopolitan scholars in the US, just as they crossed national, linguistic, and cultural borders in their personal lives. To explore this theme of crossing personal and intellectual borders, I continued to exchange ideas with Dr. Stapleton and Dr. Wollons as well as with my graduate students. The 2014 conference became a lively venue for stimulating discussion among participants. Those who served as commentators and mediators, namely, Andrew Elliott, who specializes in Japan's cultural and diplomatic relations with America and England and Daniel Milne, who writes and teaches on tourism and its political and cultural implications, as well as Donna Stapleton, whose unique experience as a social worker excited many students interested in education, and Dr. Stapleton and Dr. Wollons, constituted a core group of what would become this volume. Later we invited Elena Baibikov, Helena Grinshpun, and Mariko Mizuno, my former students, to join our project. Their respective expertise—Elena's years of experience as a translator of modern Japanese literature into Russian, Helena's extensive research in Japan and Israel about different types of cultural adaptation, and Mariko's sharp insight into the personal and intellectual dilemmas of Japanese intellectuals who crossed the Pacific in the late nineteenth century, made them appropriate additions to this volume. After the conference we continued to discuss the concept of "border" and "boundary" and their multi-fold implications and their positive and negative undertones. While the definition of "border" or "boundary" can be anything but simple, we decided to go ahead with case studies of border crossings with each person's unique perspective.

What came out of these stimulating conferences and mutual discussions is this volume. I might say that it is a product of intellectual and personal exchanges of international (British, American, Australian, Israeli, Japanese) students and teachers who almost by chance encountered each other in Kyoto, the ancient capital of Japan. It would be our greatest pleasure if this volume could contribute in even a small way to the development of border studies as well as Asian studies. Finally, this book is dedicated to the late Professor Morrell Heald, my PhD advisor at Case Western Reserve University and a former colleague of Dr. Stapleton and Dr. Wollons. Dr. Heald's unwavering faith in me helped me regain my confidence.

Reiko Maekawa

Acknowledgements

This volume draws on the research and knowledge of not only the authors and editors,* but also on that of archivists, librarians, other scholars, and a variety of mentors, collaborators, and colleagues. The authors and editors take this opportunity to recognize some of those who have made this volume possible.

Elena Baibikov expresses her sincere gratitude to everyone who contributed to this volume. She very much appreciates the help of Dr. Celia Martin De Leon (Universidad de Las Palmas de Gran Canaria) at the initial stage of this project. She also acknowledges the assistance of the secretary of the Moscow Guild of Literary Translators, Ms. Olga Drobot, who was instrumental in connecting her with the Guild's members. She is also deeply grateful to her respondents whose information was critical to her chapter.

Andrew Elliott thanks Sani Kanemoto, Mei Kibe, Yasuyo Matsuda, Rie Nōmi, Moe Okura, and Midoriko Yamagata for their very helpful suggestions about Perry-related materials at an early stage of his research. He thanks Eleanor Yamaguchi for help in identifying a 2channel figure in the Perry meme. He thanks all the editors of this volume, especially Professor Reiko Maekawa for her consistent support and guidance since first welcoming him into her *kenkyūshitsu* as a master's student many years ago.

Helena Grinshpun thanks the Japanese Government (MEXT) Scholarship, Kyoto University, and the Graduate School of Human and Environmental Studies there for making her research possible. She extends her gratitude to Professor Brian Masaru Hayashi and Professor Reiko Maekawa for their ongoing support and inspiration.

Reiko Maekawa thanks the Japan Society for the Promotion of Science for funding the projects that became the basis of this volume, and the Dean of the Graduate School of Human and Environmental Studies of Kyoto University for providing the facilities and staff necessary for international conferences. She thanks Professor Tadashi Wakashima and Professor Mikiro Kato for joining the two projects on refugee scholars. Her sincere gratitude goes to the late Dr. Ken Rose, the former Assistant Director of the Rockefeller Archive Center, for his constant support and guidance over many years.

Daniel Milne greatly appreciates the work of the editors in putting the project together, along with the referees for providing invaluable feedback.

* Note: This section observes Western name order, i.e., given name first, followed by the family name.

Many of the ideas his chapter draws on were honed through co-editing the *Japan Review*'s special issue, "War, Tourism, and Modern Japan" (2019). He thanks his co-editors Andrew Elliott and John Breen for their collaboration. His chapter in this volume benefitted from the generous support of a grant from the Japan Society for the Promotion of Science. He dedicates his chapter to Professor Reiko Maekawa for her many years of insightful guidance, generosity, and inspiration.

Mariko Mizuno thanks Kumi Itsumi and Mitsuru Suda for helping her to find Kyūin Okina's materials. (Itsumi is the third daughter of Okina, and Suda is a grandson of Okina.) She also thanks Mutsuko Shimoyama for showing her Issō Shimoyama's letters to Shirō Shimoyama, his younger brother.

Darwin Stapleton thanks the staff of the Rockefeller Archive Center not only for assistance with the research that undergirds his chapter in the volume but also for years of support in many other scholarly endeavors. He also is greatly appreciative of the China Medical Board's support, which made it possible to work in the archives of the Peking Union Medical College (Beijing). He is grateful for Professor Reiko Maekawa's invitation to participate in the conference that led to the present volume, and for the editorial collaboration of both Professor Maekawa and Professor Roberta Wollons.

Donna Stapleton acknowledges the Case Western Reserve University School of Applied Social Science that taught her to see and identify social problems, and to develop policies and implement programs to ameliorate those concerns. She thanks the school staff involved in the *Puentes* project, especially Laura Raynolds, Vicki Rashbaum, and Diana Planells-Bloom, who joined together to present materials and programs that welcomed and celebrated new community immigrants.

Roberta Wollons wishes to thank Prof. Reiko Maekawa for organizing the original conference that led to this volume. She would also like to acknowledge the international scholars who have contributed to the field of border studies and expanded the field from nation-state studies to ideas about the individual experiences that challenge and expand cultural understanding.

The editors wish to express thanks to Brill for initial consideration of this volume, and then for continuing contacts and editorial support. Our appreciation goes to our original editor Lauren Bissonnette, and recently to Elizabeth You and Qin Higley who have been equally supportive of our work. Finally, the comments and suggestions of anonymous reviewers contributed substantially to improving the volume.

Illustrations

Notes on Contributors

Elena Baibikov
PhD (2008), Kyoto University, Associate Professor of Russian Studies at Kobe City University of Foreign Studies. She has several scholarly publications in translation studies and many published translations of Japanese literature into Russian. She has also compiled and edited an anthology entitled *Mir v kaple dozhdya* (Inostrannaia Literatura, 2012).

Andrew Elliott
PhD (2011), Kyoto University, is an Associate Professor in the Department of International Studies, Doshisha Women's College. Recent publications include a co-edited special issue of *Japan Review* (with Daniel Milne) on war, tourism, and modern Japan (2019).

Helena Grinshpun
PhD (2009), Kyoto University, is currently teaching at the Asian Studies Department of the Hebrew University of Jerusalem. She is a Research Fellow at the Harry S. Truman Institute for the Advancement of Peace. Her publications include a monograph on coffee and cultural change in Japan, and a number of chapters and articles on consumption, material culture, and urban space in Japan and Israel.

Donna Heckman Stapleton
is a social worker with a Master of Science in Social Administration from Case Western Reserve University (1979). She developed programs and services for public school systems and hospitals, and has taught at three colleges and universities.

Reiko Maekawa
PhD (1985), Case Western Reserve University, is Professor Emeritus of International Studies at Kyoto University, Japan. She has published monographs and many articles on American culture and Japanese-American cultural exchanges, including "The Allied Occupation, the Cold War, and American Philanthropy: The Rockefeller Foundation in Postwar Japan" in *Philanthropy and Cultural Context: Western Philanthropy in South, East and Southeast Asia in the 20th Century*, edited by Soma Hewa and Philo Hove (University Press of America, 1997).

Daniel Milne
PhD (2016), Kyoto University, is a senior lecturer at Kyoto University's Institute for Liberal Arts and Sciences. His research focuses on touristic discourses of Japan and Kyoto, and the political and cultural roles of tourism. With Andrew Elliott, Daniel recently co-edited a special issue of *Japan Review* (2019) that traces the relationships between war and tourism in modern Japan.

Mariko Mizuno
PhD (2012), Kyoto University, is Associate Professor at the Institute of Liberal Arts and Sciences, The University of Toyama. Her most recent publication is a chapter in *Imin ga tsumugu nihon: Kousaku suru bunka no hazama de* [Japanese and immigrants: Reclaiming national culture in a global era] (2018).

Darwin H. Stapleton
PhD (1975), University of Delaware, is Executive Director Emeritus of the Rockefeller Archive Center. He taught at Case Western Reserve University and the University of Massachusetts Boston, and was Associate Editor of *The Papers of Benjamin Henry Latrobe*. He has published widely as a historian of technology, science, medicine, philanthropy, and education.

Roberta Wollons
PhD (1983), University of Chicago. Professor of History at the University of Massachusetts Boston. Editor of *Kindergartens and Cultures: the Global Diffusion of an Idea* (2000), and numerous articles and chapters on American women missionary educators in Japan, India, and Ottoman Turkey.

Introduction

Roberta Wollons

The field of borderland studies has matured in the last decade,* spawning a dedicated journal and professional association.[1] The field has come to encompass geographical, racial, psychological, colonial and post-colonial, and theoretical concepts of encounter and transformation. While most works on boundary crossing focus on the politics of geographical borders, migration and immigration, post-colonialism, or theoretical constructs of exchange, recent anthologies focus on groups, categorized by gender, ethnicity, location, or other identities.[2] Numerous academic book series have been established at university presses with "borderland" titles.[3]

The idea of borderlands has captured the imagination not only of scholars, but of fiction writers as well. A search of borderland fiction yields a plethora of titles largely focused on cultural encounters across national borders or within multicultural and fantasy communities.[4] The majority of scholarship, though, continues to be on physical and cultural encounters at the intersection of territorial boundaries.[5]

---

* This section observes Western name order, i.e., given name first, followed by the family name.

1 *Journal of Borderland Studies,* the journal of the Association of Borderland Studies at http://absborderlands.org/journal/ This journal focuses primarily on political and colonial borders.

2 For an example of this genre of border studies, see Clara Román-Odio and Marta Sierra, eds., *Transnational Borderlands in Women's Global Networks: The Making of Cultural Resistance* (New York: Palgrave, 2011).

3 This includes such series as *Borderlands and Transcultural Studies* published by University of Nebraska Press.

4 For an example of this genre, see Héctor Calderón and José David Saldívar, eds., *Criticism in the Borderlands: Studies in Chicano Literature, Culture, and Ideology, Post-Contemporary Interventions* (Durham, NC: Duke University Press Books, 1991); and Thomas F. Monteleone, ed., *Borderlands: an Anthology of Imaginative Fiction* (Hertford, NC: Crossroad Press, 2014).

5 For examples of this genre, see Margaret Regan, *The Death of Josseline: Immigration Stories from the Arizona Borderlands* (Boston: Beacon Press, 2010); Emily T. Yeh and Christopher R. Coggins, eds., *Mapping Shangrila: Contested Landscapes in the Sino-Tibetan Borderlands* (Seattle: University of Washington Press, 2014); Alexander Victor Prusin, *Nationalizing a Borderland: War, Ethnicity, and Anti-Jewish Violence in East Galicia, 1914–1920* (Tuscaloosa, AL: University Alabama Press, 2016); Gregory D. Smithers and Brooke N. Newman, *Native Diasporas: Indigenous Identities and Settler Colonialism in the Americas* (Lincoln, NE: University of Nebraska Press, 2014); Matthew Salafia, *Slavery's Borderland: Freedom and Bondage Along the Ohio River* (Philadelphia: University of Pennsylvania Press, 2013).

 | DOI:10.1163/9789004435506_002

Thomas Nail's influential *Theory of the Border* (2016) and Vladimir Kolossov's "Border Studies: Changing Perspectives and Theoretical Approaches" (2005), offer detailed overviews of the multiple meanings and dimensions of the concept of borders, as understood by contemporary interdisciplinary scholars.[6] *Postcolonial Border and Legacies of Anglo-French Partition in West Africa*, by William F. S. Miles (2015) is an example of how post-colonial scholars have employed borderland theory as a conceptual model to examine political adversaries.[7] Often in border studies, the underlying tension is an imbalance of power, either across borders (whether physical or conceptual) or social (based in racial, ethnic, or religious hierarchies). Within postcolonial models, the dominant mode of inquiry is oppositional—domination versus subjugation, or control versus resistance. Geographically, it has been about the periphery versus the center and the underlying exchanges flowing in both directions, or between groups vying for political or legal power.

Attempts at taking purely theoretical approaches, or seeking a unifying definition of "borders," have been elusive at best. Nail begins the introduction to his book on theory with a broad definition: "The border is a process of social division."[8] He goes on, though, to interrogate the usefulness of a single definition as he delves into the unique aspects of individual border sites and of spatial processes of division. He remains stymied by the practical research questions associated with a unified theory. "Therefore," he ponders, "a significant methodological problem for a theory of the border is how to create a concept of the border that makes sense of multiple different kinds of borders, not just geographical ones."[9] In the end, Nail relies on the history of state and geographical/political borders in Mexico to illustrate the complexity of theorizing the "border." The very complexity and interdisciplinarity of the idea have made the anthology a preferred vehicle for presenting a range of examples around a central theme. Recent examples include Wilson and Hastings' (2012) *A Companion to Border Studies*, which focuses on nation/state borders;

6 Thomas M. Wilson and Hastings Donnan, eds., *A Companion to Border Studies* (Chichester, UK: Wiley Blackwell, 2012); Rogers M. Smith, *Citizenship, Borders, and Human Needs* (Philadelphia: University of Pennsylvania Press, 2011); Jorge Duany, *Blurred Borders: Transnational Migration between Hispanic Caribbean and the United States* (Chapel Hill, NC: University of North Carolina Press, 2011); Thomas Nail, *Theory of the Border* (New York: Oxford University Press, 2016); Vladimir Kolossov, "Border Studies: Changing Perspectives and Theoretical Approaches," *Geopolitics* (2005) 10: 606–652.

7 William F. S. Miles, "Postcolonial Border and Legacies of Anglo-French Partition in West Africa," *African Studies Review* (2015) 58 (3): 191–213.

8 Nail, ed., *Theory of the Border*, 1.

9 Ibid., 10.

Smith's (2011) *Citizenship, Borders and Human Needs*, oriented to Europe and the United States; and Duany's (2011) *Blurred Borders*, which focuses on Caribbean-United States relationships.

The location of power—whether it is ubiquitous and invisible or concentrated and visible—is something we do not ignore in this volume. However, our efforts deal more with significant gray zones or ambiguous areas where cultural mediators and negotiators—boundary crossers—experience unfamiliar forces, and of necessity make their compromises, yield to, or resist those pressures. Our anthology expands the current geography-bound theoretical landscape by moving beyond studies at the intersection of state borders. We offer new perspectives on the extant literature by engaging the individual experience of border-crossing, rather than on broadly-defined political or social groups located at territorial boundaries. Drawing on various examples of individual experiences has allowed us to explore an array of circumstances and attempts to negotiate the discomforts and challenges of expanding personal boundaries. It attends to the intimate experiences of border crossers, whether they are traveling to an unfamiliar cultural location or at the level of ideational, symbolic, and aesthetic interactions, such as encounters in the classroom or the coffee shop or with popular fiction texts. Our central idea is to examine the complexities and ambiguities of cultural negotiation in a variety of commonplace encounters, in settings of everyday life: inside, outside, and on the edges of one's own culture.

At the heart of border studies are the transformations resulting from exposure to other cultural ideas, artifacts, and traditions. This volume uniquely focuses on East Asia as a site of individual experiences of transformation, juxtaposed with complicating examples of cross-cultural negotiators in the United States and Russia. In *The Country and the City*, Raymond Williams describes D. H. Lawrence as a border crosser: "In his own development, which he writes about again and again, he was on a cultural border. The choice was not only between mine and farm, but between both and the opening worlds of education and art."[10] This British example of geographical and cultural transformation of one individual might seem remote from experiences of East Asians, especially the Japanese border-crossers treated in this volume. Yet, as our contributors show in their respective chapters, cross-cultural mobility, regardless of the border-crosser's location at home or abroad, can be a complex exercise in acculturation or dislocation, often compounded by a sense of empowerment or a sense

10 Raymond Williams, *The Country and the City* (New York: Oxford University Press, 1975), 381.

of loss, by divided sympathies, by expanded intellectual horizons, and by an irritated sense of alienation and discrimination. The chapters in this volume illuminate a wide range of experiences by individuals at the edges of cultural borders over time and place. Readers for whom sites of political or national borders are alien territory will easily identify with the intimate and personal experiences of the daily and familiar borderlands presented here.

∴

Both the first and second chapters are concerned with the theme of cultural representation as sites of border crossing. The authors ask how historical figures or specific locations are represented in public media, what goals or intentions affect the way they are represented, who the people responsible for the creation of certain images are, and how these images inform individual memories and relationships to a historical past. These questions form the underlying conditions that make up the experience of cultural border-crossing through popular culture media.

In the first chapter, Andrew Elliott presents us with a complex set of political and cultural border crossings: between the present and the past, and among contemporary expressions of popular memory. He examines representations of the Perry Mission in recent Japanese popular culture. He looks at the way the 1853–4 diplomatic mission to Japan led by U.S. Navy Commodore Matthew Perry is being portrayed and reinterpreted in novels, TV dramas, manga, and anime in twenty-first century Japan. Perry, not well-known in his mother country, is regarded as one of the most important and influential Americans in modern Japanese history. Therefore, as Elliott argues, Perry's latest representations in popular culture are "a fine lens through which to observe changing and competing visions of both Japan's relationships with its external others and, concomitantly, national cultural identity in Japan." Elliott explores the multiple ways in which the figure of Perry was regarded: as a serious threat to Japan's sense of individual and national identity; as a liberator who freed Japan from feudalism and seclusion; or, paradoxically, as a weak and ridiculous figure. In sum, Elliott's chapter considers how the Perry Mission, portrayed as a subversive cultural encounter, has contributed to the myth of modern nation-building and how the modern stylistic iterations of Perry have allowed for a personal reinterpretation of the Japanese self. These moments of reinterpretation are construed here as crossing borders not only between the past and the present, but also among contemporary, constructed national identities.

The second chapter, Daniel Milne's study of three English-language guidebooks on Kyoto written in 1873 and 1895, explores how the guidebook illustrates authoritative voices representing a sense of place to outsiders. Chronologically, Milne's essay is a follow-up to what happened in Japan after the 1853–4 Perry Mission and how Kyoto, the ancient capital of Japan, exemplified the process of modernization. Where Elliott examines the lingering after-effect of the Perry Mission in the Japanese psyche, Milne focuses on the heartfelt efforts on the part of guidebook authors to present the best of traditional Japanese culture while encouraging an imagined traveler to experience Kyoto in transition to modernity. Similar to how Elliott uses representations of Perry, Milne places his readers at the intersection of Kyoto's past and present, and simultaneously between the visitor's expectations and the "modern" city. He compares three English language guidebooks, two written by Japanese authors, Kakuma Yamamoto and M. Ichihara, and one by Francis Brinkley, a well-established Japan specialist from Ireland. Locating the guidebook at the center of an international contact zone between host and guest, and between the authors of guidebooks and the tourists who use them, Milne argues that guidebooks served as mediating bridges, providing access to, and at the same time interpreting, a new experience. His chapter engages the intentions of the guidebook author who is imagining the reader, whether foreign or Japanese, in determining what and how to characterize the ancient city. In Elliot's and Milne's chapters, mass media materials, whether manga or guidebook, serve as a medium or transmitter of cultural representation to "outsiders" who are the intended audience for these popular media. In these two chapters, it is the authors who guide the readers through cultural, historical, and personal border crossing.

Both the third and fourth chapters draw attention to those who physically crossed national, cultural, and linguistic borders and how individuals, with or without institutional mediators, were transformed by their border-crossing experiences. In both chapters, individuals experienced discrimination and their own "otherness" in situations meant to enhance their status as professionals.

The third chapter is Mariko Mizuno's study of Japanese-Americans' quest for an ideal "cosmopolitan" identity in the 1920s and 1930s, focusing on a group of Japanese intellectuals who crossed the Pacific to the United States. Mizuno's subjects are three Japanese intellectuals advocating cosmopolitanism: Kyūin Okina, Riichirō Hoashi, and Issō Shimoyama. Each individual's concept of cosmopolitanism differs from the other, yet each of them sought a universal identity extending beyond the borders of Japan and America. Their experience as a despised and discriminated minority in the United States, Mizuno argues, increased their desire to go beyond the narrow confines of national or ethnic identity to become *sekaijin,* or new cosmopolitans. She also detects an intellectual affinity among these Japanese intellectuals and American intellectuals such as Alain Locke, Horace Kellen, and Randolph Bourne who, around the same time as the Japanese cosmopolitans, advocated cultural pluralism and transnationalism. Each of Mizuno's subjects experienced deep dislocation and identity crises in the act of crossing national and cultural boundaries, driven by a personal vision of cosmopolitanism.

The fourth chapter is Darwin Stapleton's study of the intentional cross-cultural experiences devised by the Rockefeller Foundation for public health fellows who were recruited from China and Japan in the interwar period in the pursuit of global public health hegemony. The Rockefeller Foundation at this time was the largest international philanthropic organization dedicated to the global diffusion of scientific knowledge. Although Stapleton's chapter focuses on one institution's often rewarding and sometimes frustrating efforts to (in its view) upgrade the skills and knowledge of Asian public health experts, it also provides a nuanced look at a group of Chinese and Japanese fellowship recipients who often felt that while in the United States they were treated in ways that were beneath their status or professional dignity. This essay allows us to witness the parallel histories of fellows from two rival countries who individually crossed borders to experience similar situations in the crucial interwar period. In these two chapters, individuals were placed in uncomfortable circumstances with conflictual "others" for larger intellectual and altruistic ends. They represent individuals struggling to cross the boundaries of discord and mistrust for ideas that represent larger global benefits.

The fifth chapter, in contrast, examines familiar trends in internationalization and the commodification of food. In this chapter Helena Grinshpun takes a fresh look at local and personal examples of cultural encounter. Moving away from cultural mediators such as popular media, intellectuals, or foundations, Grinshpun deals with the commonplace commodity of coffee and coffee shops as the sites of imagined border crossing. While drinking coffee in Starbucks in downtown Kyoto, for example, Grinshpun argues that individuals may go beyond the usual confines of national or gender-specific identity and become virtual citizens of the world. Grinshpun demonstrates that in the same manner that Europeans imagined coffee as culturally exotic, Japanese imagined it as an attribute of modernity and a new West-inspired lifestyle during the Meiji Restoration era (1868–1912). She traces changes undergone by Japanese society, from the reforms of modernization to membership in the global village of the recent decades, through a prism of coffee and the coffee house. Instead of looking at macro-scale encounters, such as that between Commodore Perry's black ships and Japan, this chapter looks at rather small-scale individual encounters that nevertheless affect the multifaceted elements of Japanese culture. In other words, she looks at consumers as reinterpreting coffee as cultural commodity and ascribing to it new border-crossing significance.

Moving beyond Asia, Part 2 and the final two chapters embody the experiences of navigating the boundaries between disparate cultures and languages in situations easily prone to misunderstandings. Both the sixth and seventh chapters focus on the theme of mediators who, in their professional capacities, served as bridges between two seemingly separate cultural and linguistic worlds. In the sixth chapter, Donna Heckman Stapleton, from her experience as a social worker, examines the Early Childhood Center in an urban-suburban New York City school, serving as a bridge between the assimilationist intentions of the school and the immigrant families and their children throughout its diverse economic and ethnic community. She argues that American educators including teachers, social workers, and other experts worked together successfully in overcoming linguistic and cultural barriers experienced by the many Latino families whose children participated in the Center. Her focus is on American educators as cultural mediators who, through their professional skills, facilitated the difficult period of transition experienced by immigrant children and their parents. The educators did not necessarily perceive themselves as crossing cultural or linguistic borders, however they became increasingly aware of how language and cultural boundaries acted to facilitate or impair students' development, contrary to the policy driven assumption of universal equality. Stapleton suggests that providing a critical integrative function for immigrant families led educators to their own transformation as cultural negotiators and mediators, prompting them to cross cognitive and institutional borders. Stapleton's work falls within an emerging category of borderland studies located in the classroom.[11]

The seventh and final chapter is Elena Baibikov's study of Russian literary translators as actors situated directly on cultural and linguistic borders. While the sixth chapter focuses on the social worker as a cultural mediator stationed on the borders within communities, this chapter looks at the translators' various self-images as cultural mediators between the Russian mother-tongue and foreign languages. She argues that Russian literary translators see their roles as akin to stage actors, interpreters, and guides. Women are predominant among the translators surveyed by Baibikov, and their professional self-esteem goes hand in hand with their sense of empowerment as female professionals.

11 For an example of classroom studies, see Richard S. Kitchen and Marta Civil, eds., *Transnational and Borderland Studies in Mathematics Education* (London: Routledge, 2011).

Quoting Italo Calvino, who said that "without translation, I would be limited to the borders of my own country," Baibikov suggests that literary translators make it possible for readers of translated works effectively to cross cultural and national boundaries without leaving their own countries.

Taken together, the essays collected in this volume illuminate the individual and intimate negotiations entailed in acts of crossing physical or personal borders, whether they are imagined and reinterpreted by popular culture or guidebook authors, or they are intentionally created by self-conscious mediators such as social workers and literary translators. Institutions such as the Rockefeller Foundation aided individuals who crossed borders to seek intellectual betterment or increase professional skills, and some individuals who ventured into an unknown world out of personal aspirations, with both types experiencing unintended, transformational consequences along the way. While most of the chapters center on East Asia or by East Asians, by providing Russian and American case studies, this volume seeks to universalize the transcultural experiences of individuals. Certainly, crossing borders is an inexhaustible subject and it is hard to generalize from the singular examples of individuals. However, by looking at these complicated experiences through the lenses of representation, mediation, sites of transformation, and commodification of culture, this volume should serve as a useful addition to our understanding of the complex identities created in the world of ubiquitous popular media and the commonplace accessibility of travel.

Bibliography

The Association of Borderland Studies. *Journal of Borderland Studies*. Abingdon: Taylor & Francis. http://absborderlands.org/journal/.

Calderón, Héctor and José David Saldívar, eds. *Criticism in the Borderlands: Studies in Chicano Literature, Culture, and Ideology*, Post-Contemporary Interventions. Durham, NC: Duke University Press Books, 1991.

Duany, Jorge. *Blurred Borders: Transnational Migration between Hispanic Caribbean and the United States*. Chapel Hill, NC: University of North Carolina Press, 2011.

Kitchen, Richard S. and Marta Civil, eds. *Transnational and Borderland Studies in Mathematics Education*. London: Routledge, 2011.

Kolossov, Vladimir. "Border Studies: Changing Perspectives and Theoretical Approaches," *Geopolitics* (2005) 10: 606–652.

Miles, William F. S. "Postcolonial Border and Legacies of Anglo-French Partition in West Africa," *African Studies Review* (2015) 58 (3): 191–213.

Monteleone, Thomas F., ed. *Borderlands: an anthology of imaginative fiction*. Hertford, NC: Crossroad Press, 2014.

Nail, Thomas. *Theory of the Border*. New York: Oxford University Press, 2016.

Prusin, Alexander Victor. *Nationalizing a Borderland: War, Ethnicity, and Anti-Jewish Violence in East Galicia, 1914–1920*. Tuscaloosa, AL: University Alabama Press, 2016.

Regan, Margaret. *The Death of Josseline: Immigration Stories from the Arizona Borderlands*. Boston: Beacon Press, 2010.

Román-Odio, Clara and Marta Sierra, eds. *Transnational Borderlands in Women's Global Networks: The Making of Cultural Resistance*. New York: Palgrave, 2011.

Salafia, Matthew. *Slavery's Borderland: Freedom and Bondage Along the Ohio River*. Philadelphia: University of Pennsylvania Press, 2013.

Saldivar, Ramon. *The Borderlands of Culture: Américo Paredes and the Transnational Imaginary*, Durham, NC: Duke University Press, 2006.

Smith, Rogers M. *Citizenship, Borders and Human Needs*. Philadelphia: University of Pennsylvania Press, 2011.

Smithers, Gregory D. and Brooke N. Newman, eds. *Native Diasporas: Indigenous Identities and Settler Colonialism in the Americas*. Lincoln, NE: University of Nebraska Press, 2014.

University of Nebraska Press. Borderlands and Transcultural Studies (Series).

Williams, Raymond. *The Country and the City*. New York: Oxford University Press, 1975.

Wilson, Thomas M. and Hastings Donnan, eds. *A Companion to Border Studies*. Chichester, UK: Wiley Blackwell, 2012.

Yeh, Emily T. and Christopher R. Coggins, eds. *Mapping Shangrila: Contested Landscapes in the Sino-Tibetan Borderlands*. Seattle: University of Washington Press, 2014.

PART 1

Crossing Boundaries in East Asia

CHAPTER 1

Loss, Liberation, and Laughter

Reimagining the Perry Mission in Recent Japanese Popular Culture

Andrew Elliott

1 Introduction: The Perry Mission and the Textuality of Cross-Cultural Encounter*

Tenpesuto (The Tempest, 2008), a three-part novel (then play, television series, and film) by the Okinawan writer Ikegami Eiichi, deals with the political struggles of the Ryukyu kingdom at the time of the Perry mission.[1] The Commodore's own entrance is deferred until late in the final book, when the fleet anchors in Naha harbor on its way to Japan, but this is clearly intended as the metaphorical storm, foreshadowed in the title, toward which the narrative has been building. The chapter that describes the squadron's arrival begins with a passage excerpted from the official US *Narrative of the Expedition of an American Squadron to the China Seas and Japan* (1856–57) then a translation of this in Japanese, before the reader is taken into the Commodore's cabin as Perry composes his thoughts and his diary at this historic juncture:

> Commodore Perry saluted the Stars and Stripes, his fist clenched tightly. Deep within him, there existed an extraordinary determination to become the American Homer. He thought of himself now like a performer alone on the stage. A scenario was sketched out, but he had yet to inform the other actors what their roles in this story would be, how their lines had already been prepared in compliance with the wishes of the

* Note: This chapter observes Japanese name order, i.e., family name first, followed by the given name.

1 Ikegami Eiichi, *Tenpesuto*, vol. 3 (Tokyo: Kadokawa, 2010). The decision to use the katakana loanword *tenpesuto* as a title, rather than the Japanese word for storm, makes obvious allusion to Shakespeare's *The Tempest* (1610–11), which dramatizes the visit of outsiders to an exotic island and the destructive effects on the native inhabitants. At the time of the Perry mission, the Ryukyu kingdom was under dual subordination as a vassal state of the Satsuma domain that continued to pay tribute to Qing China, though in practice it maintained a large degree of autonomy. In 1879, the Ryukyu kingdom was formally annexed by Japan, becoming present-day Okinawa prefecture.

 | DOI:10.1163/9789004435506_003

> American people. An historic moment such as this, thought Perry, is like the opening night of a play. Albeit an unrehearsed one, that would fail or succeed on the first attempt.[2]

The scene as written is an imaginary one, and the narrative as a whole largely fictional, but Ikegami obviously did his homework in preparation for writing, and these passages neatly encapsulate the important role that texts played at all stages in the actual encounter. Books were ordered to learn about Japan in more detail. Artists, scientists, and writers were employed to record what was found. Attempts were made to limit publications to those presenting Perry in a good light and the expedition itself as an achievement of immense national and international significance. Through its textual representation, a diplomatic mission to effect a treaty thus became something much more: a big budget production entitled "the opening of Japan," starring the United States as bold but benevolent hero, stepping up onto the Pacific as stage, the bearer of ideals of civilization and progress.[3]

Today, considered in the light of subsequent postcolonial theorizing of East-West relations, this benign image is much harder to maintain. Rather, the mission is easily adjudged paradigmatic of a very different kind of cross-cultural encounter: a "clash," to use Walter LaFeber's emblematic term, of diametrically opposed, vastly asymmetrical powers[4]—"the one young, open, expansive, confident; the other the opposite"[5]—that leads to the deployment of indirect control of Japan by the Western powers, as seen in the unequal treaties and conventions of the 1850–60s.[6] As an encounter seemingly carried out in compliance with a pre-written script by a single (i.e., Western) author, the Perry mission thus exemplifies the enormous discursive power of Orientalism to determine the terms of contact between Western nations and non-Western nations in the post-Enlightenment period.[7]

---

2 Ikegami, *Tenpesuto*, 211. Unless noted otherwise, all translations from Japanese are by the author. Macrons are used to denote long vowel sounds, except in words already familiar in English.

3 See W.G. Beasley, "Introduction," in *The Perry Mission to Japan, 1853–1854*, ed. W.G. Beasley, vol. 1 (Richmond: Japan Library, 2002), 20.

4 Walter LaFeber, *The Clash: U.S.-Japanese Relations Throughout History* (New York, W.W. Norton, 1997).

5 Michael Hoffman, "Face to Face From Worlds Far Apart," *The Japan Times*, June 1, 2003, accessed March 12, 2008, https://www.japantimes.co.jp/community/2003/06/01/general/face-to-face-from-worlds-far-apart/.

6 See Inoue Kiyoshi, *Jōyaku kaisei: Meiji no minzoku mondai* (Tokyo: Iwanami shoten, 1955).

7 Edward W. Said, *Orientalism* (New York: Vintage, 1979). As I invoke the concept here, I follow Said and much subsequent Postcolonial scholarship in understanding "Orientalism" in

It is this violence of encounter, on the level of language rather than cannons (though Perry did go on to use that more concrete threat), that *Tenpesuto* so precisely captures in its writing of the fleet's entrance to Naha. Yet at the same time, Ikegami's novel, and its narrative, offer examples of alternative processes of "writing" that undercut both the official US narrative *and* a reductive reading of this encounter in terms of "simple relations of domination and subordination."[8] Intratextually, this happens most obviously in the various Ryukyuan perspectives on Perry's arrival given here, imagining voices unrecorded in contemporary US accounts; and furthermore in the way the Commodore is forced to negotiate with officials in Naha—these other "authors" rework and rewrite Perry's script, opening a space for both direct challenge and indirect circumvention of their intended lines.[9]

More generally, *Tenpesuto* is itself an example of the diverse ways in which texts have played an important role, not just in the United States, but also on the Japanese side of the encounter as well. Upon first appearance, Japanese writers and artists actively and critically responded to the Perry mission in a range of media and in multiple registers.[10] Following this, into the twentieth and twenty-first centuries, modern modes of representation, many of them clearly marked fictional, have taken up the mission; subsequent historical events find themselves enfolded into these images and narratives, and the figure of Perry is often used metonymically, typically as a synecdoche for the West, modernity, and/or the outside world.[11] This reception history, as I explore below, thus works as a particularly fine lens through which to observe changing and competing visions of both Japan's relationship with its external others and, concomitantly, national cultural identity in Japan; at the same time, it reveals much about the multiple voices and multiple agencies at work in cross-cultural encounters more generally.

---

terms of (1) a worldview, means of representation, and way of thinking founded on radical difference between a superior "West" (Occident) and inferior "East" (Orient); (2) a powerful instrument of political control that has supported the establishment, expansion, and maintenance of modern European and American colonial and neo-colonial empires.

8 Steve Clark uses these terms to argue for the complexity of travel encounters. See his introduction to *Travel Writing and Empire: Postcolonial Theory in Transit*, ed. Steve Clark (London: Zed Books, 1999), 3.

9 Ikegami, *Tenpesuto*, 230.

10 See MIT Visualizing Cultures, "Black Ships and Samurai: Commodore Perry and the Opening of Japan (1853–1854)," last modified 2010, http://ocw.mit.edu/ans7870/21f/21f.027/black_ships_and_samurai/.

11 Works not analyzed in this chapter but which are relevant here include Shimazaki Tōson's historical epic *Yoake mae* (*Before the Dawn*, 1932) and a number of postwar television historical dramas such as Mainichi Broadcasting System's *Ryōma ga yuku* (Ryōma is coming, 1968).

2 Overcoming Loss: Fantasy and the Perry Mission

Some of the most compelling images produced by Japanese artists on the occasion of the US fleet's initial appearance are woodblock prints and paintings of Perry in demonic guise: hairy, long nosed, and with fiercely-angled, sometimes blue eyes. As John Dower suggests, such representations were one way of bringing the new and "unknown" into a native realm of signification, thereby making sense of the US fleet's obvious technological superiority and, at the same time, diminishing its status through a process of othering.[12] A similar procedure, though with different import, takes place in three recent *shōnen*, or boys' manga, that dramatize the Perry mission to Japan and/or its immediate effects: Sorachi Hideaki's *Gintama* series (2003–); *Bakumatsu ibun roku code geass: Hangyaku no Rurūshu* (A record of strange tales from the Bakumatsu, code geass: Lelouch's rebellion, 2008), a standalone manga based on the *Code geass* anime series, drawn by Ganjii (also Gun Zi in English), with a story by Ōkōchi Ichirō and Taniguchi Gorō; and Isayama Hajime's *Shingeki no kyojin* (*Attack on Titan*, 2009–).[13]

These are popular manga, as shown by circulation figures and the extensive media-mix of these franchises in anime, film, video games, and figures, and one assumes that an analysis focused on audience reception would find a diverse range of responses, including readers who share the predominant worldviews expressed, and others who negotiate or challenge them.[14] The analysis that follows focuses not on audiences but on character, visual motifs, and particularly narrative. Yet it assumes that the popularity of these manga in Japan is in part due to their oblique engagement with political, social, and historical issues of concern to many people in Japan today, perhaps especially among their ostensible target audience of young men; and that many of these readers find satisfaction in the use of fantasy in these manga, both in the generic sense and as a means to imagine alternatives to events conceived as past or present-day humiliations.

In these texts, criticism of the Perry mission is expressed with little equivocation. *Gintama* (lit., Silver soul) is set in an alternate Bakumatsu period

---

12 See the second chapter entitled "Perry" in John Dower, "Black Ships and Samurai: Commodore Perry and the Opening of Japan (1853–1854)," *MIT Visualizing Cultures*, last modified 2010, https://visualizingcultures.mit.edu/black_ships_and_samurai/bss_essay01.html.

13 The ostensible target audience of *shōnen* manga is young boys and teenagers, in contrast to *shōjo* manga, which are aimed at a female readership of the same age. In practice, both categories of manga are also consumed by older readers, male and female.

14 To give some idea of their popularity, according to approximate circulation figures available online, as of 2018, *Gintama* has 55 million manga in print and *Shingeki no kyojin* has 76 million; while Bandai Visual shipped over a million DVDs and Blu-ray disks of the *Code geass* anime series in 2008.

(1853–68), twenty years after the invasion of space aliens called the *amanto* (lit., heaven people), with whom a craven shogunate then signed unequal treaties; the present is a steampunk world of wooden houses, TVs, swords, and flying vehicles, in which the new *de facto* rulers of Japan "swagger" (*funzori kaeri aruku*) through the streets of a now "rotten" and "dirty" Edo.[15]

Code geass offers an even clearer portrait of Perry as conqueror and *kaikoku* (opening the country) as colonization. This manga takes the characters and basic plot of the *Code geass* science fiction anime—that Japan has been annexed by the superpower Britannia and turned into a territory called Area 11—and adapts it to an alternate Bakumatsu period. Perry himself makes an appearance here as a long-haired, long-nosed, bearded megalomaniac in top hat and tails (figure 1.1); using a combination of gunboat diplomacy and magic "geass" power, he coerces the shogunate into offering up Japan to his control.[16]

The third text, *Shingeki no kyojin*, is ostensibly about a past civilization trying to survive after the appearance of a race of bloodthirsty giants called titans. Nevertheless, the basic narrative frame of a civilization under threat from an outside, alien force corresponds closely with the *Gintama* and *Code geass* stories and might, arguably, similarly evoke *kaikoku* as a violent, forced opening of the country. In that case, *Shingeki no kyojin* places particular emphasis on so-called *sakoku* (closed country) policy as a necessary protective measure. This is embodied in the massive walls that were built, the first volume of *Shingeki no kyojin* reports in its opening, to close off humanity after the initial attack of the titans a hundred years previously. The story kicks off when new more powerful titans suddenly appear, destroying the long-held peace by breaching the exterior wall.[17]

The "Perry figure" is very obviously othered in these texts, invested with great power but demarcated from Japanese, who maintain recognizable, human form. In *Gintama*, the *amanto* come in various shapes, from humanoid aliens to anthropomorphized animals, and except for a few exceptions, tend to be portrayed as arrogant, often violent, outsiders. In *Code geass*, Perry's depiction bears little relation either to images in the historical record or the popular imagination: here, the lack of usual signifiers, like his uniform, and the addition of beard and long hair, make a familiar figure appear strange. Finally, in *Shingeki no kyojin*, the Perry figure, if the colossal titan may be read here so directly, is a massive, sinewy monster, inexplicable in his sudden appearance, violent in his actions, seemingly unable to communicate coherently.

---

15 Sorachi Hideaki, *Gintama*, vol. 1 (Tokyo: Shūeisha, 2004), 8 and 147. This and all subsequent citations to manga are to collected paperback editions.

16 Ganjii, Ōkōchi Ichirō, and Taniguchi Gorō. *Bakumatsu ibun roku code geass: Hangyaku no Rurūshu* (Tokyo: Kadokawa, 2008), 4.

17 Isayama Hajime, *Shingeki no kyojin*, vol. 1 (Tokyo: Kōdansha, 2010), 50–51.

FIGURE 1.1 Commodore Matthew Perry as imagined in *Code geass*' alternate Bakumatsu period. In this scene, Perry is loudly proclaiming the power of his "Knightmare frame" weapon.
SOURCE: GANJII, ŌKŌCHI ICHIRŌ, AND TANIGUCHI GORŌ, *BAKUMATSU IBUN ROKU CODE GEASS: HANGYAKU NO RURŪSHU* (TOKYO: KADOKAWA, 2008), 137

In all three manga, the arrival of these Perry figures signals loss. In *Gintama*, the samurai have allowed "their swords, and their status to be snatched away, throwing away their pride, throwing away everything … but it is not just the samurai, it is everybody who lives in this country."[18] In *Code geass*, after the forced opening, "Japan lost its land, its pride, even the topknot."[19] Similarly, in *Shingeki no kyojin*, the arrival of the titans has brought loss upon loss: of land, the world beyond the "birdcage"[20] in which humanity is trapped; of friends and family; of the potential to realize an alternative future. As Eren, the central character, bewails when trapped within the belly of a titan, "Why is this happening …? Why are they taking our lives and our dreams …?"[21]

18 Sorachi, *Gintama*, vol. 1, 12.
19 Ganjii, *Bakumatsu*, 7.
20 Isayama, *Shingeki*, vol. 1, 1.
21 Isayama, *Shingeki no kyojin*, vol. 2 (Tokyo: Kōdansha, 2010), 181.

The killing of humans by the titans is a bloody and frightfully repetitious act in this work, and a key feature of *Shingeki's* visual and emotional power; many characters (as well as some readers, perhaps) surrender to feelings of despair, exhaustion, and shame (*kutsujoku*), but for Eren, at this key moment, it is anger that is ultimately called forth, leading to a violent and cathartic counterattack against the titans. That this fight can be visualized in explicit, often vitriolic fashion, even in mainstream, popular manga, is arguably one effect of the othering of the "Perry figure" noted earlier; it allows direct expressions of contempt against the foreign. A similar passage from loss to violence is seen in both *Gintama* and *Code geass*: in the former, it is accomplished in the opening sequence with the introduction of Sakata Gintoki, the skilled samurai who vanquishes not only the aliens who have been humiliating the protagonist, but also his Japanese boss who fraternizes with them; in *Code geass*, the shift is apparent in the final defeat of Perry that concludes the story and leads to the reestablishment of Japanese sovereignty.

A fight to win back that which was lost, a hero defending the weak, an invader repelled, and peace established: these are the narrative bare bones of much fantasy, of course. Here, however, they are fleshed out through a (necessarily myopic and nostalgic) contextualization that locates the particular mode of heroism on display as culturally Japanese and historically prewar. This is particularly true of *Shingeki no kyojin*, about which an internet dispute arose after Isayama acknowledged that the model for his character Commander Dot Pixis was Akiyama Yoshifuru, an early-twentieth century Imperial Japanese Army general.[22]

Extratextual revelations aside, the model of heroism dramatized in *Shingeki* is arguably one informed by nostalgia for a prewar militarism of bold, direct action in support of aggressive expansionism.[23] The manga focuses on a vanguard of idealistic and dedicated young officers, fighting not just against the external other of the titans, but also a corrupt and selfish state: as these patriots sacrifice themselves in battle, political, business, and religious leaders are shown to be more concerned with safeguarding their own wealth and power than defending the nation as a whole (figure 1.2 and 1.3).

22 Brian Ashcroft, "A Thousand Death Threats Against a Popular Anime Creator," *Kotoku*, July 1, 2013, accessed August 29, 2015, http://kotaku.com/a-thousand-death-threats-against-a-popular-anime-creato-631792221. The dispute was conducted mainly on message boards, but included death threats against the author on his homepage. It centered on the military record of Akiyama in Korea during the Russo-Japanese War (1904–5).

23 Jason G. Karlin, "Narratives of Heroism in Meiji Japan: Nationalism, Gender, and Impersonation," in *Gender, Nation, and State in Modern Japan*, eds. Andrea Germer, Vera Mackie, and Ulrik Wöhr (New York: Routledge, 2014), 63–4.

今から100年以上前
〝巨人〟という天敵の出現により
絶滅寸前まで追い詰められた人類は
強固な壁を築くことで
安息の領域を手に入れた
特別編 イルゼの手帳
しかしすべての人類が
壁の中だけの世界に
妥協したわけではない

FIGURES 1.2 AND 1.3 Titans, the wall, and the band of young soldiers. The text reads: "A hundred years ago, humankind was driven to the verge of extinction with the appearance of a natural predator (*tenteki*, lit., heavenly enemy) called "titans." Humanity's remnants retreated behind a huge wall, where they created a place of repose (*ansoku no ryoiki*). But not all were content with the world behind the wall. Some dared to go out to where the titans are. They are known as the Survey Corps."
SOURCE: ISAYAMA HAJIME, *SHINGEKI NO KYOJIN*, VOL. 5 (TOKYO: KŌDANSHA, 2011), 3–4

The fascist fascination, to use Susan Sontag's term, that is evident both in *Shingeki*'s fetishization of military iconography and its "assertion of the righteousness of violence"[24] ("you can't win if you don't fight")[25] is not exhibited to the same extreme in either *Code geass* or, particularly, *Gintama*. Nevertheless, in all three manga, it is an outsider band of young, idealistic soldiers or samurai who are valorized as the true defenders of the national body and the last protectors of the national spirit. In *Shingeki*, as suggested, a correspondence is drawn between its protagonists and ultranationalist groups of the 1920s and 1930s. Historically, these ultranationalist groups themselves invoked an even earlier group of outsiders as legitimatization for their anti-state activities: the *shishi* or "men of high purpose" who fought the shogunate to restore imperial power during the Bakumatsu period. In *Gintama* and *Code geass*, it is these earlier radicals who are explicitly cited as models for its "anti-Perry" group of patriots.

Read collectively, it can therefore be suggested that these manga contextualize their fantasies about overcoming invasion and subsequent loss temporally, in three main ways: first, as a defense of Japan against Western powers in the wake of the Perry mission; second, as a prewar defense against "Western" attempts to limit Japanese imperial expansion; and third, as a present-day defense of Japan against what is seen as the continuing intrusion of outside, typically Western, forces. The latter is perhaps best expressed in *Gintama*'s initial depiction of the alien *amanto* who have invaded Japan.

Figure 1.4 shows an image of an *amanto* labeled *ijin*, a word for foreigner that is most commonly applied to Westerners; he is shown wearing a white sushi t-shirt, and holding a folding fan decorated with Japanese flag motif. This proposes, in the first pages of *Gintama*, a correlation between the Perry "invasion" and a more recent touristic "invasion" of young foreign visitors. In contrast, the samurai who have lost their jobs as a result of this influx are shown lining up at "Hello Work" employment offices in search of a job, Bakumatsu forebears of the modern NEET (a young person "Not in Education, Employment, or Training").[26]

---

24 Cited in Peter C. Luebke and Rachel DiNitto, "Maruo Suehiro's *Planet of the Jap*: Revanchist Fantasy or War Critique?," in *Manga and the Representation of Japanese History*, ed. Roman Rosenbaum (New York: Routledge, 2013), 95.

25 Isayama, *Shingeki*, vol. 2, 25.

26 Sorachi, *Gintama*, vol. 1, 8 and 10. The prevalence of "black ship" metaphors in recent Japanese mass media to describe often-threatening foreign imports of various kinds—from American gravure idol female models to Apple and LG smartphones—is picked up by W. David Marx in this short article: "Black Ships," *Neomarxisme*, September 7, 2007, accessed January 24, 2017, http://neomarxisme.com/wdmwordpress/?tag=black-ships.

FIGURE 1.4 The beginning of volume 1 of *Gintama*. The text reads: " 'Samurai nation.' It's been a long time since our country was called that. Once, the samurai dreamt of winning great renown in Edo; now, alien ships fly about its skies. Once, samurai strode confidently through these streets; now, foreigners (*ijin*) swagger about like they own the place."

SOURCE: SORACHI HIDEAKI, *GINTAMA*, VOL. 1 (TOKYO: SHŪEISHA, 2004), 8

These manga present neither an organized political manifesto nor a constructive critique of modern relations with the United States/West; nor do their narratives yield a single, definitive message in regard to cross-cultural encounter.[27] Rather, in ways both explicit and implicit, the Perry mission (or its narrative framework) is used in these three texts as a metonymic target for generalized, perhaps otherwise ineffable expressions of frustration, anger, and animosity toward the United States, the West, or what is implied as a neocolonial Western-led process of globalization. At the root of these emotions, as far as can be judged from the storylines of these manga, is a strong consciousness of victimhood: as a postwar nation without full sovereignty, forced to depend on US military protection; as young people in an unjust and ineffective labor market, forced to depend on parental support or welfare; as men in a world of rapidly shifting gender identities, without the comfort of older modes of masculinities. The formative role played by victimhood in postwar Japanese identity has been well-studied, and analogies might be drawn between these manga narratives and earlier manifestations of the "victim as hero" trope. Yet, as James J. Orr has argued in his monograph on the postwar discourse, "the focus on war victimhood seems more characteristic of the liberal view of war as evil," a view which these manga, with their militaristic storylines, largely repudiate.[28] Rather, I would argue that collective memories of defeat and surrender in the Pacific War, though not irrelevant here, take a backseat to more recent concerns including but not limited to the post-Bubble recession (the "lost decade" or "lost two decades"), economic and cultural globalization, and the rise of China as an economic and military power in East Asia. The generic codes of fantasy, especially the use of physical combat as the typical means of overcoming narrative conflict, allow these texts to imagine dramatic and emotionally satisfying resolutions to these problems, but in so doing they posit a view of global politics as anarchy and a view of cross-cultural encounter as an inevitable clash between competing civilizations.

---

27 As, for example, *Shingeki no kyojin*. Its story (unfinished at the time this chapter was being written) continues to develop in rather complex and unexpected ways, whereby ambivalent, hybrid relations between humans and titans are dramatized instead of a simple dichotomy between heroic, civilized self and savage other as enemy.

28 James J. Orr, *The Victim as Hero: Ideologies of Peace and National Identity in Postwar Japan* (Honolulu: University of Hawai'i Press, 2001), p. 13. Orr addresses previous scholarship on war victimhood consciousness in this book.

3 Empowerment in Encounter: The Perry Mission and Narratives of Liberation

Gintama, Code geass, and *Shingeki no kyojin* exemplify how, from the postwar period, expressions of nationalism have been relegated to the cultural sphere in Japan[29]; furthermore, in their historical revisionism as much as their affective propensities, they share much with the more recent phenomena of popular nationalism or *netto uyoku* (cyber ultranationalist).[30] However, this is not the only way in which the Perry mission has been taken up in twenty-first century popular culture. Indeed, the following texts, though also concerned with tropes of empowerment, reveal the influence of an apparently more progressive politics, and their messages thus appear to differ significantly from those of the manga. In this version of the Perry mission, the arrival of the US fleet in Edo Bay, the negotiations between Perry and the Tokugawa shogunate, and the successful signing of the 1854 Treaty of Peace and Amity (*Nichibei washin jōyaku*)—an event shown to herald the beginning of modern Japan and modern international relations—are represented not as threat or loss but rather as opportunity.

Perry, easily identifiable by his hairstyle and uniform—gold epaulettes on the shoulders, fringes swinging—performs a march-like dance. Other dancers, representing the shogunate, respond initially with shock, fear, and a choreographed show of strength. But, by the end of the clip, amity has triumphed over animosity and all dance in unison as they sing: "By the treaty signed with Perry, Japan entered a new age (*atarashii jidai*)."[31]

The video clip is from *Rekishi ni dokiri* (Startled by history), an NHK Educational TV program broadcast Wednesday mornings during the school year, which picks up famous historical events and personages from the sixth-grade social studies textbook and teaches about them in an entertaining, often light-hearted way (figure 1.5). This video, produced for the national broadcaster using Ministry of Education-authorized teaching materials, arguably reveals much about official discourses on the Perry mission—a sudden and disruptive challenge, no doubt, but one that triggered a successful, and justly celebrated, national rebirth.

---

29 Sabine Frühstück, *Playing War: Children and the Paradoxes of Modern Militarism in Japan* (Oakland, University of California Press, 2017), p. 166.

30 See Tessa Morris-Suzuki and Peter Rimmer, "Virtual Memories: Japanese History Debates in *Manga* and Cyberspace," *Asian Studies Review* 26:2 (2002).

31 "Mashū Perii: Yureru Edo bakufu," *Rekishi ni dokiri*, season 2, episode 13, aired November 6, 2013 (Tokyo: NHK, 2013), Television broadcast.

FIGURE 1.5 Screenshot of NHK's *Rekishi no dokiri* homepage, showing graphics and lyrics from the Perry episode
SOURCE: HTTP://WWW.NHK.OR.JP/SYAKAI/DOKIRI/SHIRYOU/2014_028_02_SHIRYOU.HTML

A similar perspective is seen elsewhere in popular culture, especially in historical fiction about the Bakumatsu period. Television period dramas, particularly NHK's long-running *Taiga dorama* (lit., Great river drama) series, are the most revealing examples of this mode. These drama are annual televisual events, with a single series playing each year, every Sunday evening from January to December, and are targeted at the whole family[32]; other historical drama series, from the public broadcaster or commercial networks, are often much shorter and lack the prestige of NHK's flagship drama series, but have a similar style and often cover similar content. Like all historical fiction, these dramas must strike a balance between fidelity to the historical record and entertainment, a fact that, if obvious to most viewers, does not detract from their power to both set the agenda of *what* from the past is to be considered important and frame *how* this should be perceived. At the time of writing, the

32 "Annual Historical Dramas: 40 Years Sketching the Shape of the Nation," NHK, accessed September 4, 2015, http://www.nhk.or.jp/digitalmuseum/nhk50years_en/categories/p51/.

Bakumatsu period had been the setting for a large number of period dramas since 2000, including five NHK *Taiga* drama series (compared to just eight in the thirty-seven previous years), one series on NHK-BS, and one series on TV Tokyo as part of its *Shinshun waido jidaigeki* (lit., New Spring wide period drama). In these series, though Perry himself is never a central character, the arrival of the US fleet is nevertheless a key moment of narrative disequilibrium, upsetting the status quo and initiating social, political and individual change.

Most explicitly, this is expressed in terms of national destiny (*unmei*), as in *Atsuhime* (Atsuhime, 2008), and/or national history, as in *Ryōma ga yuku* (Ryōma is coming, 2004): "From this moment, Japan's history was thrust completely into the troubled times of the end of the shogunate."[33] In addition, this larger story of the nation is joined—inevitably perhaps, given the biopic format common to these dramas—to an individual story of heroic, personal growth. In *Ryōmaden* (Life of Ryōma, 2010), for example, the black ships' arrival that will take place in episode five is first announced at the very end of episode one, with a brief scene in which the fleet sets a course for Japan. The protagonist Sakamoto Ryōma is here a young man in Tosa, and the existence of the mission is unknown to him; but he is connected to the event via the voice-over narration, given by Mitsubishi founder Iwasaki Yatarō, and the cuts that link young Ryōma on the beach looking out across the Pacific to Iwasaki's remembrances and finally to shots of the approaching ships:

> Ryōma had no idea about anything at that time. No idea that he'd plunge right into the upheavals of the Bakumatsu, that he'd travel all over Japan, ride the oceans, help establish the *Kaientai* [a trading and shipping company], no idea that he himself would become the very cornerstone of the group that gave new life to Japan. The one who first changed Ryōma was ... that man [Perry].[34]

Compared to Sakamoto Ryōma, the connection to the Perry mission of the historical Okatsu/Tenshōin (*Atsuhime*) and Yamamoto Yaeko (*Yae no sakura*, 2013) is far more tenuous—the former was around eighteen in 1853 and living in Kagoshima, the latter twelve and in Aizu. Nevertheless, in their *Taiga*

---

33 Sano Motohiko, "Oto no namida," *Atsuhime*, episode 7, aired February 17, 2008 (Tokyo: NHK, 2008), Television broadcast; Tadano Kenji, Takeda Isao, and Sasaki Junichi, "Shuppatsu (tabibito)," *Ryōma ga yuku*, episode 1, aired January 2, 2004 (Tokyo: TV Tokyo, 2004), Television broadcast.

34 Iwatani Kanako, "Jōshi to kashi," *Ryōmaden*, episode 1, aired January 3, 2010 (Tokyo: NHK, 2010), Television broadcast.

dramas as well, a link is suggested between the arrival of the US fleet and the characters' maturation, not just on an individual level but as strong, independent women who are representative of the new age engendered by Perry. In *Yae no sakura*, the ships that anchor in Uraga bay are given as a sign of a "world on the move" ("sekai ga ugoiteiru"); yet the following scene, showing Yae back in Aizu being told to stop studying and go to the kitchen, reveals the contrast between this promise and her own life as a young girl in the Edo period. Later, parallel editing between Yae's own secretly-pursued education and classes on the black ships being given by Sakuma Shōzan in Yokohama further establish the analogy being made between her unorthodox aspirations and the new opportunities that have opened up in the wake of Perry's arrival.[35] Similarly, in *Atsuhime*, the central character's desire for escape—from the confines of the castle, and from the expectations forced upon her by the Shimazu household to be a passive and ladylike adopted daughter—is interwoven via crosscutting with the apparently corresponding desires of Perry to open the country. For example, one sequence has the official letter passed from Perry to the shogunate paralleled with letters passed between Okatsu and her former family. While, in another example, an analogy is implied between the subsequent transformation of Okatsu into Atsuhime, a bold and confident princess who accepts her destiny but on her own terms, and the path that Japan will also have to follow in accepting Perry's demands for the opening of the country.[36]

By drawing an analogy between an individual story of self-development and national history, these texts present an inevitably heroic Bildungsroman narrative of the modern nation. In contrast to the manga previously analyzed, there is little room for regret or nostalgia here: all the choices made, in that they lead to climactic maturity, are the right choices. Yet interestingly, the specific choices of the hero/heroine in these period dramas mean that disenfranchised groups are thus given leading roles in the national narrative and their empowerment is made a crucial part of its storyline. *Ryōma ga yuku* and *Ryōmaden* both begin with scenes expressing frustration at the restrictions of the Tosa class system for low-ranking samurai such as Ryōma and, in the latter case, Iwasaki Yatarō as well; Tosa is "konmai" (*small* in Shikoku dialect), Ryōma's sister explains, before the scene cuts to the US fleet that will set in motion his

35 Naitō Shinsuke, "Naranu koto wa naranu," *Yae no sakura*, episode 1, aired January 6, 2013 (Tokyo: NHK, 2013), Television broadcast.

36 Sano, "Oto no namida"; Sano Motohiko, "Ohime-sama kyōiku," *Atsuhime*, episode 8, aired February 24, 2008 (Tokyo: NHK, 2008), Television broadcast; and Sano Motohiko, "Atsuhime tanjō," *Atsuhime*, episode 9, aired March 2, 2008 (Tokyo: NHK, 2008), Television broadcast.

physical, social, and psychological travels out from its confines.[37] In *Atsuhime* and *Yae no sakura*, gender not class constraints trouble the protagonists, but again it is the political and social changes initiated by the arrival of the Perry mission that give them the opportunity to escape.

The ten-part television adaptation of Ikegami's *Tenpesuto* uses a similar emancipatory structure in its narrative as well, downplaying some central elements of the novel—criticism of both Japanese policy vis-à-vis Ryukyu/Okinawa and the present-day US military presence, for example—to create a less-complex but more family-friendly drama.[38] The arrival of Perry in Naha brings the female Mazuru, who had been trapped in the women's quarters of the palace, back to power at court, allowing her to effect a transformation once again into Son Neion, the male official who had previously been exiled. Thus overcoming the limitations imposed by gender discrimination, and using her/his linguistic skills rather than the military force recommended by other counselors, Mazuru/Son Neion achieves the diplomatic success that saves the kingdom from US occupation.

The messages transmitted by these texts about the Perry mission and Japan/foreign relations thus diverge sharply from those in the previously analyzed manga. Firstly, the depiction of the time before Perry's arrival—if presumably more glossy than the historical reality—is comparatively unromanticized in these dramas. In *Gintama* and *Code geass*, pre-1853 Japan is a land of harmony between social classes, and between humans and the natural world, ruled over by a benign samurai elite. The "Edo period" here invoked is what Isolde Standish, following work by Carol Gluck and others, refers to as an idealized "time-space configuration." Standish suggests that this "Edo period" needs to be differentiated from the historical period 1603–1867, with which it is commonly used interchangeably as a term to denote the era of shogunate rule that came to an end after Perry's arrival. Rather, she continues, the "Edo period" is a nostalgic construction operating in postwar popular culture as a shelter

37 Iwatani, "Jōshi to kashi."

38 Okamoto Sachie and Kajima Yoshiharu, "Perii to no taiketsu," *Tenpesuto*, episode 8, aired September 4, 2011 (Tokyo: NHK, 2011), Television broadcast. The most notable omission from Ikegami's novel is the violent rape of a Ryukuan high priestess (*noro*) by US Marines in the sacred grounds of a shrine, in which she is reduced to a broken, "childlike" state: Ikegami, *Tenpesuto*, 244–46. The event is very loosely based on the real (William) Board Incident of 1854, described in other recent Okinawan fiction about the Perry mission, but also has obvious resonances with more recent cases of sexual violence against Okinawan women by US military personnel; see Nakahodo Masanori, "Shōkei to chūgi to bōryoku: Perii raikō to Okinawa no sakka (Admiration, Loyalty, and Violence: Perry's Fleet in Okinawan Fiction)," *Nippon tōyō bunka ronshū*, 12 (2006): 82–3.

for dominant discourses of Japanese identity as an unchanging, monocultural whole set apart from the world/modern—an image of Japan that very much fits the representational patterns seen in *Gintama* and *Code geass*.[39] In contrast, the television dramas looked at here refute the notion of Edo as a perfect world, rather depicting pre-1853 Japan as a place of struggle between competing social groups, and a place of oppression for those outside the dominant power structure. As a result, the Perry mission—though occasionally in its visual presentation accompanied by storm clouds and sinister music—functions in the narrative as a liberating event, upsetting the status quo and furnishing new, empowering identities for those previously disenfranchised because of class or gender. In these texts then, the potential for cross-cultural encounter to bring positive change and positive exchange, both on the individual level and the national, is underlined; and, while contact with foreign others may present challenges, these dramas advocate dialogue and negotiation—rather than physical violence, though that does play a role—as the best means to overcome them.

The apparently more liberal approach to international relations manifested in these television period dramas is an effect, I would argue, of a diverse combination of factors: firstly, their production by national broadcasters targeting a wide, mainstream audience; secondly, the choice of internationalist idols Sakamoto Ryōma and Yamamoto Yae as subjects, which in itself is a product of wider cultural movements such as the *rekijo* (history fan girls) phenomenon and events such as the 3/11 earthquake, tsunami and nuclear meltdown[40]; and finally, the ongoing power of *kokusaika* (internationalization) discourse. This discourse continues to promote a process of self-development—particularly, in the post-Bubble period, via English-language study, study abroad, or other international exchange programs—aimed at becoming an (often ill-defined) "internationally-minded" individual/nation.[41] In particular, the influence of

---

39 Isolde Standish, *A New History of Japanese Cinema* (New York: Continuum, 2005), 107. Also Carol Gluck, "The Invention of Edo," in *Mirror of Modernity: Invented Traditions of Modern Japan*, ed. Stephen Vlastos (Berkeley and Los Angeles: University of California Press, 1998).

40 Akiko Sugawa-Shimada, "'Rekijo' and Heritage Tourism: The Sengoku/Bakumatsu Boom, Localities, and Networks," *The Theory and Practice of Contents Tourism* (2015), 21–2; Philip Seaton, "Taiga Dramas and Tourism: Historical Contents as Sustainable Tourist Resources," *Japan Forum* 27:1 (2015): 82–3. For example, Seaton quotes an NHK producer who notes that the decision to focus on the Aizu-born Yae was made only in the wake of the 3/11 disaster, as a means to encourage the disaster-affected areas.

41 Ross Mouer and Yoshio Sugimoto, *Images of Japanese Society* (1986, reprint, New York: Routledge, 2009), 379–80. Similarly, Ulrich Heinze argues for the influence of globalization

kokusaika is suggested in the narrative arcs of the two Ryōma series and *Yae no sakura*, which appear to lead the protagonists from insularism to cosmopolitanism. It can also be seen in the primacy given to English as a tool for intercultural communication: none of the dramas acknowledge the important role that written Chinese played in the treaty negotiations, and only *Ryōmaden* depicts the two-way translation process from Japanese to Dutch to English and back that also took place; *Atsuhime* and *Yae* show Perry speaking English to shogunate officials, while in *Tenpesuto*, English is the "weapon," to use Karen Kelsky's phrase, that helps Mazuru/Son Neion triumph.[42]

These dramas speak the language of international cooperation with great fluency, and appear to champion the value of cosmopolitan identity and cross-cultural flows of goods, ideas, and people. Yet, as Koichi Iwabuchi argued some twenty years previous at the very end of the Bubble period, internationalization in Japan has typically been a counterpart to nationalism, working rather to "emphasiz[e] inter/national differences" than to encourage transnational expansiveness, much less destabilize a dialectic of the nation and its others. And indeed, the incorporation of *kokusaika* discourse into these dramas' narratives of heroic national rebirth appears to corroborate this argument: with the notable exception of *Tenpesuto* perhaps, the Japan celebrated in these texts is very much a ""coherent" national community" that is, in itself, neither multicultural nor global/international.[43] Instead, in these texts, the global/international is an always already outside entity; either it must be successfully incorporated into the national self, or it is a stage onto which the nation, because of an avowed essential difference, must be skillfully translated through a process of managed cultural dissemination.

---

discourse on post-Bubble *shōjo* or girls' historical manga such as *Siebold Oine* (Siebold Oine, 1995), which is also set against a backdrop of *kaikoku* and depicts an educated, independent female protagonist; see "Making *his*tory *her*story: Nelson's Son and Siebold's Daughter in Japanese *Shōjo* Manga," in *Manga and the Representation of Japanese History*, 114–17.

42 The full quotation is "English and other foreign languages are perceived as the single most indispensable 'weapon' (*buki*) in [Japanese] women's battle for advancement in the business world"; Karen Kelsky, *Women on the Verge: Japanese Women, Western Dreams* (Durham, N.C.: Duke University Press, 2001), 100. The analogy I suggest here between Kelsky's internationalist Japanese women and these dramas' protagonists is deliberate: arguably, it is precisely this group of women, at least as ideally imagined as a bridge between Japan and the West, which is being referenced in mainstream media representations of a figure like Yamamoto Yae.

43 Koichi Iwabuchi, "Complicit Exoticism: Japan and its Other," *Continuum: The Australian Journal of Media and Culture* 8:2 (1994), accessed June 13, 2015, http://wwwmcc.murdoch.edu.au/readingroom/8.2/Iwabuchi.html.

There are, as noted, important differences between these texts and the manga read earlier, but it might therefore be suggested that they share a similarly bold vision for Japan, one that in both cases registers the recent resurgence of the right within mainstream politics (most markedly after the victory of the Liberal Democratic Party under Abe Shinzō in the 2012 general election). In short, through their narratives of encounter between Japan and the United States, both sets of texts perform a process of nation building that includes, on the one hand, a policing of Japan's borders, analogous to that achieved through immigration policy or navy boats; and on the other, the explicit promotion of both hard and soft power resources, analogous to new military capabilities and the government-led "Cool Japan" campaign, to underpin a stronger and more forceful international role for the nation.[44]

4 Laughing at (?) the "Neighborhood Foreigner": Parody and Perry

The texts picked up in this final section differ from those analyzed above in being harder to group, in terms of message, medium, and audience. Nevertheless, all use humor in their representations of the mission and, whether consciously or not, play interestingly with the question of Perry's relationship to Japan in ways that the television period drama do not. Unlike those texts, which often kept the Commodore at a distance (silhouetted, in shadow, or offscreen), the following manga, anime, internet memes, and pop songs tend to put him center stage. The first volume of *Gyagu manga biyori* (Gag manga biyori, 2000) has in its first skit, for example, Perry arriving on ships painted not black but white by the crew (figure 1.6), the beginning of a sequence of comical mishaps.[45]

In the popular meme "Perii raikō" (The arrival of Perry, 2000–), first uploaded on the 2channel (2ch) BBS, there is a monologue of Perry helplessly pleading in Japanese to open the country ("Ne, oh kaikoku shite kudasai"),[46] while a story in *Sayonara zetsubō sensei* (Goodbye, Mr. Despair,

---

44 See chapter 2 in Koichi Iwabuchi, *Resilient Borders and Cultural Diversity: Internationalism, Diversity, and Multiculturalism in Japan* (Lanham: Lexington Books, 2015); and Sally McLaren, "Made in Cool Japan: Disasters and Delights," *Griffith Review 49: New Asia Now* (2015).

45 Masuda Kōsuke, *Gyagu manga biyori*, vol. 1 (Tokyo: Shūeisha, 2000), 5.

46 This is just one example of the many versions of the meme available on YouTube, with added visuals: "Perii raikō," accessed September 14, 2015, https://www.youtube.com/watch?v=W5B2icDl28s&list=RDW5B2icDl28s#t=2.

FIGURE 1.6 Perry's entrance scene in the first story in the first volume of *Gyagu manga biyori* (2000). Its initial description of the mission in the somber, serious tone of a conventional historical narrative is soon undercut by a crew member's revelation that they painted the "black ships" white by mistake.
SOURCE: MASUDA KŌSUKE, *GYAGU MANGA BIYORI*, VOL. 1 (TOKYO: SHŪEISHA, 2000), 5

2005) plays on the Japanese homonym *kaikō* ("opening the country" and "establishment of a school") when a Perry lookalike, referred to as a "troublesome neighborhood foreigner" (*komatta kinjo no gaikokujin*), is invited to the school anniversary. The story focuses on his attempt to "open" everything he finds, from library books to a student's fly to the teacher's closed heart.[47]

Most obviously, these and similar texts play with the usual expectations of Perry as a stern, domineering leader, using a variety of methods and modes of humor to ridicule him. Typically, the texts combine farce (as in *Biyori*'s physical slapstick, when Perry is punched by his teenage daughter or knocked overboard by a goat for example), absurdity (as with the *non sequiturs* of the 2ch meme), and irony (as in the ending of the *Sayonara zetsubō sensei* story, described below). Reducing Perry to a figure of fun in this way creates an obvious sense of distance between audience and object that is reinforced elsewhere in the texts as well.

The 2ch meme (figure 1.7), for example, has Perry addressing an unresponsive audience: "Say something. ... you've been silent all this time, come on, that's enough now, say something! ... Am I being ostracized?"[48] While *Sayonara*, in the aforementioned final frame (figure 1.9), depicts this distance visually, showing an exhausted Perry in the background as the two main characters comment on the closure of the shop he owns.[49]

A counter process is also at work in these texts, however, in that, by visualizing Perry so vividly, they draw him out, as it were, from the haughty isolation seen in both the historical encounter and its televisual dramatizations, presenting him as a familiar and, perhaps at times, even empathetic figure: often ridiculous, to be sure, but ridiculously human. This intimacy is suggested through a variety of other means as well. In *Oshare techo* (Fashionable notebook, 2001), an absurdist gag manga in which a brief arrival scene is used as a segue, Perry is introduced not with his official rank of commodore (*teitoku*) but as plain Mr Perry (*Perii-san*).[50] In the 2ch meme, Perry's language is colloquial and inclusive, as in the frequent use of the sentence-ending particle *ne*, an informal means of asking for confirmation or affirmation. In terms of content too, the meme suggests an affinity between Perry and the Japanese audience to whom he speaks, for example, when he mistranslates a contemporary *tanka* verse expressing shock at the black ships' arrival into an English-language declaration of interdependence—"We cannot sleep without you."[51]

47 Kumeta Kōji, *Sayonara zetsubō sensei*, vol. 2 (Tokyo: Kōdansha, 2005), 21.

48 "Perii raikō."

49 Kumeta, *Sayonara*, 31.

50 Nagao Kenichirō, *Oshare techo*, vol. 2 (Tokyo: Shōgakukan, 2001), 175.

51 "Perii raikō." The verse is *Taihei no nemuri o samasu jōkisen, tatta yonhai de yoru mo nerarezu* ("Awakened from a peaceful sleep by Jōkisen tea/After only four cups, the night is sleepless"). It plays on homonymic and other analogies between peaceful sleep/Pacific ocean, *Jōkisen* tea/steamships, four cups/four ships.

FIGURES 1.7 AND 1.8 At the top is a screenshot from a YouTube version of the 2ch Perry meme. In the bottom right-hand corner of the screen, there is an image of Matthew Perry with a moving mouth, taken from Matthew B. Brady's well-known 1856–58 photograph of the commodore (shown bottom). Inside the speech bubble, the words "say something!!!" ("shabette yo!!!") are written. In the top left of the screen are grouped a number of still and silent figures, including from left to right, Doraemon, Tokugawa Yoshinobu, Mori Yashirō, Katsu Kaishū, and Chibi Maruko-chan. I have not managed to identify the last figure on the right. Although two are historical personages directly involved in the emergence of modern Japan, it is otherwise hard to see an underlying rationale in this selection of household cartoon characters, the last shogun, a gaffe-prone former prime minister, and a Bakumatsu and Meiji period samurai and statesman.
SOURCE: HTTPS://WWW.YOUTUBE.COM/WATCH?V=W5B2ICDL28S
GILMAN COLLECTION, PURCHASE, JOSEPH M. COHEN GIFT, 2005. NEW YORK, METROPOLITAN MUSEUM OF ART [PUBLIC DOMAIN]

FIGURE 1.9 The final frame of *Sayonara zetsubō sensei*'s Perry-related story. One character says: "Perry's own store … closed." The other replies: "I wonder what he could have been selling?"
SOURCE: KUMETA KŌJI, *SAYONARA ZETSUBŌ SENSEI*, VOL. 2 (TOKYO: KŌDANSHA, 2005), 31

Most explicitly, "Perii danshingu" (Perry dancing, 2011), a song by the comedy pop group Rekishi, frames the encounter as a disco-inflected sexual liaison, in which the shogunate's evasiveness is nothing more than flirtatious play ("You want us to open the country, right? / Well not yet, wait, wait just a little longer") and the treaty the successful consummation of their desires; in its final line, the song references the same *tanka* as the 2ch meme, the lack of a night's sleep here also taking on new, more risqué significance.[52]

The construction of Perry in these texts as an ambivalent figure, both remote and intimate, is captured well in *Sayonara*'s description of him as a

52 Rekishi, "Perii dansingu," in *Rekishi*, Cutting Edge, 2011. A more recent intervention from the pop world came to my attention after completion of this chapter: the dancer group Egu-Splosion's "Perii raikō" song and video from May 2015. Quite different from the Rekishi song, here Perry is described as *kumo-oyaji* or "old man bear," presumably in reference to his size and/or hairiness) and threatens to "kill" (*koroshimasu*) the shogunate unless they open up. See the group's YouTube channel, https://youtu.be/K3WUeTH1ZdU.

"neighborhood foreigner." In his appearance, of course, but also in his speech Perry is often depicted as an obvious outsider in these stories: *Sayonara* and *Oshare techo* present his speech in a combination of katakana, the script for loanwords, and kanji; the 2ch meme has him speaking in stereotypically Anglicized Japanese. Yet, if representational elements such as these underline Perry's foreignness, it might be suggested that the very ability to represent him in this way as an easy figure of fun also works as evidence of the opposite: Perry as a part of the "neighborhood." Indeed, the gags that define many of these texts depend upon the audience's preexisting knowledge of Perry, which allows the mission and the man to be introduced without long contextual explanations, and furnishes material for instant comic incongruity, the not-black-but-white ships in *Biyori*, for example, or Perry's display of a dried fish (*aji no hiraki*, a horse mackerel that has been cut *open*) in *Sayonara*.

In some ways, all the texts that have been analyzed in this chapter testify to Perry's importance and familiarity in contemporary Japan. Yet the manga and TV dramas picked up earlier show little of the self-reflexivity exhibited in texts such as *Sayonara*, which have minimal interest in Perry as either a real historical personage or a psychologically independent character in a fictional narrative. Rather, they address Perry's role within the contemporary cultural landscape through metafictional strategies, such as Perry commenting on his own public persona (to other characters or, breaking the fourth wall, to readers or viewers). Much more than the actual image of Perry within these works, it is this presupposition of a shared awareness about Perry between text and audience that most radically expresses his identity as a "neighborhood foreigner"; installing Perry as foreign "other" within the national "self," it speaks of a slippage between Japan and non-Japan.

Linda Hutcheon explores a similar relationship between text and reader in her writing on the politics of postmodern parody. Parody, in her definition, sets up a "dialectical relation between identification and distance" for audiences and artists: in that a parody announces itself as artifice, the audience is distanced from the work; yet, in order to make sense of the work, the audience must also engage in a "participatory hermeneutic activity,"[53] interpreting the relationship between the "parodic foreground" text doing the imitating and the "parodied background" text that is being imitated.[54] In this way, parody both keeps the audience at a distance *and* draws them in. For Hutcheon, parody

53 Linda Hutcheon, "The Politics of Postmodernism: Parody and History," *Cultural Critique* 5 (1986/7), 206.

54 Linda Hutcheon, *A Theory of Parody: The Teachings of Twentieth-century Art Forms* (1985, reprint, Champaign: University of Illinois Press, 2000), 31.

should be decoupled from conventional definitions of "ridiculing imitation"; rather, it can also express deference, even love for that being "refunctioned."[55]

The texts under discussion here offer many specific examples of conventional metafictional strategies using parody: *Biyori*, for example, ends on a *Titanic* reference, with Perry and crew performing Leonardo DiCaprio and Kate Winslet's iconic "king of the world" pose in the bow of their ship; the "Baseball Blues" episode of anime series *Samurai chanpurū* (*Samurai Champloo*, 2004–5), where negotiations between Japan and a Perry-esque US naval mission are fought out on the baseball field, parodies a range of Edo-set narratives, including *chambara* sword-fighting duels and the *Kamisori Hanzō* (*Hanzo the Razor*, 1972–74) detective films.[56] In addition, though, the use of Perry more generally may be read as a form of parody in this way as well, whereby the dominant cultural consensus on Perry within Japan works as a background text to be parodied. While ironic, these parodies of the "Perry figure" are far from ridicule, and in some cases may exhibit a respectful, even loving, refunctioning of his most notorious traits: Perry's bluster and threats, his dramatic manipulation of inaccessibility, the seemingly overwhelming desire to open Japan—these are preserved but placed within new contexts.

The texts under discussion here offer an arguably more subversive, more radical imagining of cross-cultural encounter than that of either *Code geass* et al., with their vision of clashing civilizations, or the television period dramas, with their (albeit more nuanced) projections of a revitalized Japan as strong global power. In that the intertextual references made in parody must be meaningful to readers, the participatory activity of interpretation identified by Hutcheon might, of course, be a nationalistic one in this case, with artist and audience consolidated as an in-(on the joke) group pitted in mockery of this foreign other. And certainly, the texts analyzed here explicitly dramatize many of the same anxieties about outside intrusion seen in other depictions of the US mission to Japan: farcical, absurd, or ironic though their modes of representation may be, laughter does not extinguish entirely the variously imagined threat, shock, or disruption (of the foreign, modern, or new) that the Perry figure here also embodies. Nevertheless, following Hutcheon's formulation, rather it might be suggested that, in their use of parody to comment on Japan's past and present, these texts are able "to speak to a [dominant] discourse from WITHIN it, but without being totally recuperated by it."[57] Concretely, this means they can

55 Hutcheon, "The Politics of Postmodernism," 203–4.

56 Watanabe Shinichirō, "Ikkyū Nyūkon," *Samurai Chanpurū*, episode 23, aired February 26, 2005 (Tokyo: Manglobe, 2004), Television broadcast.

57 Hutcheon, "The Politics of Postmodernism," 206.

voice fears about the very real disruptions of modernity and globalization, or dissatisfaction with actual inequalities in political and cultural relations, without recourse to the scapegoating or virulent denigration of, for example, much anti-American discourse. Differently, they can work through the past without recourse to either nationalist nostalgia for a lost golden age or a heroic founding narrative. Or, they are able to voice, through a self-reflexive and metatextual encounter with Perry, both the difference/distance of the foreign and its simultaneous sameness/proximity, an acknowledgement that helps question at least the bipolarizing concept of "Japan" versus "foreign" upon which postwar constructions of Japanese identity as homogeneous and monocultural have been founded.

5 Conclusion

The texts analyzed in this chapter support recent scholarship on the complexity and diversity of cross-cultural encounters generally and as specific, contextualized events.[58] Especially, they reveal the process of negotiation that, while not always made explicit in contemporary depictions, often can be seen to occur in real-life encounters, even in a period characterized by rapid imperial expansion on the part of Western powers, as that in which the Perry mission took place. This chapter has examined this process of negotiation as it is played out in recent pop cultural representations of that "first encounter" between the United States and Tokugawa Japan. It shows not only the extent to which the dominant discourses that organized the initial encounter and its contemporary US representations have subsequently been resisted and reinvented (as indeed they were from the very beginning), but particularly, as James Clifford writes, the potential for "*mutual* exploitation and appropriation" in cross-cultural encounters. Though "relations of equality" may not exist, Clifford's emphasis on mutuality underlines the agency of all parties to "struggle and negotiate" the terms of that relationship.[59]

58 On globalization and transnational flows of Japanese pop culture, see Matthew Allen and Rumi Sakamoto, eds., *Popular Culture, Globalization, and Japan* (Abingdon: Routledge, 2006). For a discussion of Postcolonial theory and cross-cultural travel encounters, see Clark, "Introduction." As an example of this approach for the historical Perry mission and its representations, see the MIT Visualizing Culture module "Black Ships and Samurai," and the accompanying essay by John Dower.

59 James Clifford, *Routes: Travel and Translation in the Late Nineteenth Century* (Cambridge, Mass.: Harvard University Press, 1997), 194–95.

In this textual contact zone, specific images are shared, most obviously Brady's photographic portrait of Perry from the 1850s—this is parodied in Japanese pop texts *and*, taking advantage of its familiarity in Japan, used by the quintessentially American corporation McDonald's in marketing campaigns there (see footnote 61); also, translations of *Gintama* and other texts into English provide evidence of other types of reciprocation taking place. More significant than these examples of exchange, however, is the counterpoint that an analysis of texts from the Japanese side of the Perry encounter provides to the conventional English-language historiography on the Perry mission, which has tended to emphasize the imposition of American or Western norms through (the threat, at least, of) gunboat diplomacy. This chapter builds on recent scholarship by historians such as Michael R. Auslin and John Dower that, without denying the military and other imbalances that structured the encounter, underlines Japanese agency.[60] The right to represent the encounter was claimed on both sides at the time; and, as my chapter has shown, this has continued into the present especially in Japanese popular culture. In particular, the analyses above suggest the diverse ways in which the historical figure of Perry, and the encounter as historical narrative, are mobilized by different groups in Japan for their own agendas, including but not limited to social and political critique, new and old imaginings of national community, self-empowerment and escapism, as well as entertainment, amusement, and commerce.[61]

My readings of these texts thus attest to the possibilities in fiction, especially, for the reimagining of a historical event as a process of creation rather than falsity. Even in the most obviously fantastic of these texts, the arrival of Perry is used to express present-day concerns and to speak to a contemporary world. The variety of ends to which this reimagining is put, as much as the variety of ways in which it occurs, reveals the influence of different genres, media, and modes of representation, as well as the demands imagined of target audiences.

---

60 Michael R. Auslin, *Negotiating with Imperialism: The Unequal Treaties and the Culture of Japanese Diplomacy* (Cambridge, Mass.: Harvard University Press, 2004); Dower, "Black Ships and Samurai."

61 In terms of commercial appropriations, it is worth noting that McDonald's Japan introduced three limited sale berry-flavored drinks in May 2017 that were marketed using an image of Perry taken from Matthew B. Brady's photograph (figure 1.8), which included a moving mouth very similar to that in the 2ch meme. In that it is hard to imagine a similar campaign in the United States, this offers further proof of the remarkable familiarity of the Perry figure in Japan, not to mention the crossover and interplay between different media and different social groups in their mobilization of Perry. Of course, this use of Perry as a marketing tool is also satirized in the final frame (figure 1.7) of the *Sayonara zetsubō sensei* story. See http://www.mcd-holdings.co.jp/news/2017/promotion/promo0519a.html.

In addition, this diversity provides further evidence for the existence of competing visions of cross-cultural encounter and national cultural identity in contemporary Japan, where nationalist messages—if arguably on the increase in certain spheres of the media—are countered by alternative, often critical and transnational perspectives elsewhere, as Ian Condry has argued in relation to the anime *Blood+* and hip-hop.[62]

Yet, even within such diverse visions of Japan's relations with the world as these, there are conspicuous exclusions. Perhaps inevitably, considering their subject matter, the "foreign" in these texts means the United States or, by analogy, the West. Much like the erasure of written Chinese from the negotiation scenes in the television dramas, Japan's relations with China and Korea, for example, play almost no role here. A different reading, focused more on production and consumption, could no doubt present another level of transnational relations for these media—the outsourcing of much anime production to China, or South Korean responses to *Shingeki no kyojin*, for example; this would certainly augment the conceptualization of cross-cultural encounter seen in this chapter, but it would not necessarily be any more representative of dominant discourses on the "international" in Japan which, as Iwabuchi has discussed recently in relation to "Cool Japan," are still overwhelmingly focused on Europe and America.[63] Thus the image conjured up in Rekishi's "Perii danshingu" song, of Perry and the shogunate locked in a sometimes-coy, sometimes-passionate dance, is still, it might be said, a compelling one, even amidst the huge geopolitical shifts of the early twenty-first century; indeed, whatever their politics, what all the texts analyzed herein reveal is the continuing importance of the United States (and the West) within the Japanese cultural imaginary of the nation and the world.

Bibliography

Allen, Matthew, and Rumi Sakamoto, eds. *Popular Culture, Globalization, and Japan.* Abingdon: Routledge, 2006.

Ashcroft, Brian. "A Thousand Death Threats against a Popular Anime Creator." *Kotoku.* July 1, 2013. Accessed August 29, 2015. http://kotaku.com/a-thousand-death-threats-against-a-popular-anime-creato-631792221.

62 Ian Condry, "Youth, Intimacy, and Blood: Media and Nationalism in Contemporary Japan," *The Asia-Pacific Journal* 5:2 (2007), accessed October 10, 2015, http://www.japanfocus.org/-Ian-Condry/2403/article.html.

63 Iwabuchi, *Resilient Borders*, 27.

Auslin, Michael R. *Negotiating with Imperialism: The Unequal Treaties and the Culture of Japanese Diplomacy*. Cambridge, Mass.: Harvard University Press, 1997.

Beasley, W.G. "Introduction." In *The Perry Mission to Japan, 1853–1854*, edited by W.G. Beasley, vol. 1, 1–24. Richmond: Japan Library, 2002.

Clark, Steve. "Introduction." In *Travel Writing and Empire: Postcolonial Theory in Transit*, edited by Steve Clark, 1–28. London: Zed Books, 1999.

Clifford, James. *Routes: Travel and Translation in the Late Nineteenth Century*. Cambridge, Mass.: Harvard University Press, 1997.

Condry, Ian. "Youth, Intimacy, and Blood: Media and Nationalism in Contemporary Japan." *The Asia-Pacific Journal* 5:2 (2007). Accessed October 10, 2015. http://www.japanfocus.org/-Ian-Condry/2403/article.html.

Dower, John. "Black Ships and Samurai: Commodore Perry and the Opening of Japan (1853–1854)," *MIT Visualizing Cultures*, last modified 2010, https://visualizingcultures.mit.edu/black_ships_and_samurai/bss_essay01.html.

Frühstück, Sabine. *Playing War: Children and the Paradoxes of Modern Militarism in Japan*. Oakland, University of California Press, 2017.

Ganjii, Ōkōchi Ichirō, and Taniguchi Gorō. *Bakumatsu ibun roku code geass: Hangyaku no Rurūshu*. Tokyo: Kadokawa, 2008.

Gluck, Carol. "The Invention of Edo." In *Mirror of Modernity: Invented Traditions of Modern Japan*, edited by Stephen Vlastos, 262–283. Berkeley and Los Angeles: University of California Press, 1998.

Heinze, Ulrich. "Making *his*tory *her*story: Nelson's Son and Siebold's Daughter in Japanese *Shōjo* Manga." In *Manga and the Representation of Japanese History*, edited by Roman Rosenbaum, 102–120. New York: Routledge, 2013.

Hoffman, Michael. "Face to Face From Worlds Far Apart." *The Japan Times*. June 1, 2003. Accessed March 12, 2008. https://www.japantimes.co.jp/community/2003/06/01/general/face-to-face-from-worlds-far-apart/.

Hutcheon, Linda. "The Politics of Postmodernism: Parody and History." *Cultural Critique* 5 (1986/7): 179–207.

Hutcheon, Linda. *A Theory of Parody: The Teachings of Twentieth-century Art Forms*. Champaign: University of Illinois Press, 2000 (1985, reprint).

Ikegami Eiichi. *Tenpesuto*, vol. 3. Tokyo: Kadokawa, 2010.

Isayama Hajime. *Shingeki no kyojin*, vols. 1–2. Tokyo: Kōdansha, 2010.

Iwatani Kanako. "Jōshi to kasha." *Ryōmaden*, episode 1. Aired January 3, 2010. Tokyo: NHK, 2010. Television broadcast.

Iwabuchi, Koichi. "Complicit Exoticism: Japan and its Other." *Continuum: The Australian Journal of Media and Culture* 8:2 (1994). Accessed June 13, 2015. http://wwwmcc.murdoch.edu.au/readingroom/8.2/Iwabuchi.html.

Iwabuchi, Koichi. *Resilient Borders and Cultural Diversity: Internationalism, Diversity, and Multiculturalism in Japan*. Lanham: Lexington Books, 2015.

Karlin, Jason G. "Narratives of Heroism in Meiji Japan: Nationalism, Gender, and Impersonation." In *Gender, Nation, and State in Modern Japan*, edited by Andrea Germer, Vera Mackie, and Ulrik Wöhr. 48–67. New York: Routledge, 2014.

Kelsky, Karen. *Women on the Verge: Japanese Women, Western Dreams*. Durham, N.C.: Duke University Press, 2001.

Kiyoshi Inoue. *Jōyaku kaisei: Meiji no minzoku mondai*. Tokyo: Iwanami shoten, 1955.

Kumeta Kōji. *Sayonara zetsubō sensei*, vol. 2. Tokyo: Kōdansha, 2005.

LaFeber, Walter. *The Clash: U.S.-Japanese Relations Throughout History*. New York, W.W. Norton, 1997.

Luebke, Peter C., and Rachel DiNitto. "Maruo Suehiro's *Planet of the Jap*: Revanchist Fantasy or War Critique?" In *Manga and the Representation of Japanese History*, edited by Roman Rosenbaum, 81–101. New York: Routledge, 2013.

Marx, W. David. "Black Ships." *Neomarxisme*. September 7, 2007. Accessed January 24, 2017. http://neomarxisme.com/wdmwordpress/?tag=black-ships "Mashū Perii: Yureru Edo bakufu." *Rekishi ni dokiri*, season 2, episode 13. Aired November 6, 2013. Tokyo: NHK, 2013. Television broadcast.

Masuda Kōsuke. *Gyagu manga biyori*, vol. 1. Tokyo: Shūeisha, 2000.

McLaren, Sally. "Made in Cool Japan: Disasters and Delights." *Griffith Review 49: New Asia Now* (2015): 165–173.

MIT Visualizing Cultures. "Black Ships and Samurai: Commodore Perry and the Opening of Japan (1853–1854)." Last modified 2010. http://ocw.mit.edu/ans7870/21f/21f.027/black_ships_and_samurai/.

Morris-Suzuki, Tessa, and Peter Rimmer. "Virtual Memories: Japanese History Debates in *Manga* and Cyberspace." *Asian Studies Review* 26:2 (2002): 147–164.

Mouer, Ross, and Yoshio Sugimoto. *Images of Japanese Society*. New York: Routledge, 2009 (1986, reprint).

Naitō Shinsuke. "Naranu koto wa naranu." *Yae no sakura*, episode 1. Aired January 6, 2013. Tokyo: NHK, 2013. Television broadcast.

Nagao Kenichirō. *Oshare techo*, vol. 2. Tokyo: Shōgakukan, 2001.

Nippon Hōsō Kyōkai (NHK). "Annual Historical Dramas: 40 Years Sketching the Shape of the Nation." Accessed September 4, 2015. http://www.nhk.or.jp/digitalmuseum/nhk50years_en/categories/p51/.

Nakahodo Masanori. "Shōkei to chūgi to bōryoku: Perii raikō to Okinawa no sakka (Admiration, Loyalty, and Violence: Perry's Fleet in Okinawan Fiction)." *Nippon tōyō bunka ronshū*, 12 (2006): 59–85.

Okamoto Sachie, and Kajima Yoshiharu. "Perii to no taiketsu." *Tenpesuto*, episode 8. Aired September 4, 2011. Tokyo: NHK, 2011. Television broadcast.

Orr, James J. *The Victim as Hero: Ideologies of Peace and National Identity in Postwar Japan*. Honolulu: University of Hawai'i Press, 2001. "Perii raikō." Accessed September 14, 2015. https://www.youtube.com/watch?v=W5B2icDl28s&list=RDW5B2icDl28s#t=2.

Rekishi. "Perii dansingu." In *Rekishi*, Cutting Edge, 2011.

Said, Edward W. *Orientalism*. New York: Vintage, 1979.

Sano Motohiko. "Oto no namida." *Atsuhime*, episode 7. Aired February 17, 2008. Tokyo: NHK, 2008. Television broadcast.

Sano Motohiko. "Ohime-sama kyōiku." *Atsuhime*, episode 8. Aired February 24, 2008. Tokyo: NHK, 2008. Television broadcast.

Sano Motohiko. "Atsuhime tanjō." *Atsuhime*, episode 9. Aired March 2, 2008. Tokyo: NHK, 2008. Television broadcast.

Seaton, Philip. *Japan's Contested War Memories: The 'Memory Rifts' in Historical Consciousness of World War II*. New York: Routledge, 2007.

Seaton, Philip. "Taiga Dramas and Tourism: Historical Contents as Sustainable Tourist Resources." *Japan Forum* 27:1 (2015): 82–103.

Sorachi Hideaki. *Gintama*, vol. 1. Tokyo: Shūeisha, 2004.

Standish, Isolde. *A New History of Japanese Cinema*. New York: Continuum, 2005.

Sugawa-Shimada, Akiko. " 'Rekijo' and Heritage Tourism: The Sengoku/Bakumatsu Boom, Localities, and Networks." *The Theory and Practice of Contents Tourism* (2015): 21–26.

Tadano Kenji, Takeda Isao, and Sasaki Junichi. "Shuppatsu (tabibito)." *Ryōma ga yuku*, episode 1. Aired January 2, 2004. Tokyo: TV Tokyo, 2004. Television broadcast.

Watanabe Shinichirō. "Ikkyū Nyūkon." *Samurai Chanpurū*, episode 23. Aired February 26, 2005. Tokyo: Manglobe, 2004. Television broadcast.

Yamada Takashi. "Rekishi sakuhin ni tai suru shimin ishiki no ikkōsatsu: dai san kai shinpojiumu ankēto kara." In *Taiga dorama to shimin no rekishi ishiki*, edited by Jiddai kōshō gakkai and Ōishi Manabu, 191–196. Tokyo: Iwata shoten, 2013.

CHAPTER 2

Boundaries in the Cross-Cultural Interaction of Tourism

A Comparative Study of Early English-Language Tourism Guidebooks on Kyoto

Daniel Milne

1 Introduction

Tourism has become one of the primary engines for national and cultural border crossing, a locus in which millions of people encounter, conceptualize, and negotiate difference, and in so doing shape their understandings of self and other. From the early nineteenth until the early twenty-first century, guidebooks were the primary printed media used by tourists and other travelers to navigate such crossing of borders, and are still today essential travel items for vast numbers of people.[1] As a prime medium for modern cross-cultural encounters, it is important to understand how guidebooks shape this encounter through defining the people, cultures, and places the visitor will meet, and national, local, and cultural borders that may be traversed. Guidebooks also reflect the larger issues of identity formation central to modern forms of mobility, whether of the migrant or tourist.[2]

Through the analysis of three guidebooks that describe the same city but from significantly different angles, this chapter will explore the mediating role of guidebooks in cross-cultural encounters. Primarily, it will examine how people, organizations, and cities have utilized guidebooks to try to define their identities through the imaginative and physical border crossings of tourism. In so doing, it will focus on the following questions: How do guidebooks represent

1 Ali Behdad, *Belated Travelers* (North Carolina: Duke University Press, 1994).

2 For Nail, the migrant as a symbol of social exile became the defining figure of modern society. Thomas Nail, *The Figure of the Migrant* (Stanford: Stanford University Press, 2015). In discussing the tourist, Bianchi and Stephenson argue that the right to freedom of movement across national borders became a defining element of post-war conceptions of citizenship and identity. Raoul V. Bianchi and Marcus L. Stephenson, *Tourism and Citizenship: Rights, Freedoms and Responsibilities in the Global Order* (Oxon: Routledge, 2014).

 | DOI:10.1163/9789004435506_004

people and cultures to the reader-user,[3] and what patterns of representation, or "discourse," do we find?[4] Specifically, what is the role of Orientalism (defined later) and concepts of temporality (such as "modernity" and "tradition") in such representations? Do these representations vary depending on whether authors are locals themselves, and thus describe the "self," or non-locals who describe the "other"? What do representations in guidebooks reflect about efforts to define identities through local, national, and cultural borders that separate "self" and "other," "West" and "East," "modernity" and "pre-modernity"?

This chapter compares three English-language tourism guidebooks about the Japanese city of Kyoto written by local and non-local authors in the late nineteenth century. It applies theory developed by Edward Said and related theorists about Orientalism, or how Western writers represent non-Western cultures through a temporal lens as historically static, delayed and traditional.[5] This theory about Orientalism seeks to explain how discourses by Western authors have helped spread and maintain the exploitative power of western colonialism and neocolonialism over non-Western nations and peoples. Orientalism is at the center of discussion about Western representations of the non-West in previous studies of guidebooks and related tourism media.[6] Building on these studies, this chapter explores how guidebook authors present and negotiate "borders," primarily those involved in representing identity ("self" and "other", "Western" and "Japanese"), geography ("West" and "East"), and temporality ("modern" and "ancient", "industrial" and "pre-industrial"). Further, through the guidebooks this study considers

3 The term "reader-user" is borrowed from Behdad and highlights how guidebooks are not just designed to be read, but also to be utilized in travel. Ali Behdad, *Belated Travelers*.

4 The concept of "discourse" will be used here to refer to ways of representing the world that are "intertextual," or shared across texts (such as across guidebooks), and are based in institutions of power (such as the institutions of the state). See Michel Foucault, *The Archaeology of Knowledge* (1969; repr., London: Routledge, 2002); Sara Mills, *Discourse* (London: Routledge, 2004).

5 For Said's classic study on this see, Edward Said, *Orientalism: Western Concepts of the Orient*, rev. ed. (London: Penguin Books, 1995). For studies on "self-Orientalism" and other concepts that have helped strengthen our understanding of intercultural encounters see Sadik Jalal al-Azm, "Orientalism and Orientalism in Reverse," in *Orientalism: A Reader*, ed. A. L. Macfie (Edinburgh: Edinburgh University Press, 2000); Mary Louise Pratt, *Imperial Eyes: Travel Writing and Transculturation* (London: Routledge, 1992).

6 See Behdad, *Belated Travelers*; Deborah Bhattacharyya, "Mediating India: An Analysis of a Guidebook," *Annals of Tourism Research* 24, no. 2 (1997): 371–389; Matthew Tegelberg, "Hidden Sights: Tourism, Representation and Lonely Planet Cambodia," *International Journal of Cultural Studies* 13, no. 5 (2010): 491–509; Tom Selwyn, *The Tourist Image: Myths and Myth Making in Tourism* (Chichester: John Wiley and Sons, 1996).

how these borders are defined, negotiated, and how they shift, and what this reflects about the nature of cross-cultural encounters in tourism and the wider modern world.

The particular guidebooks analyzed are for Kyoto, a city that led early efforts to promote international tourism within Japan and that has become one of the country's most popular tourist destinations. They are three of the first English-language guidebooks to Kyoto, one from 1873 and two from 1895. As the first English guidebook exclusively about a Japanese destination, the 1873 guidebook provides an unparalleled insight into how early local writers and promoters of tourism wished to introduce Japanese cities, sites, and cultures to foreign visitors. The 1895 books provide a rare opportunity to directly compare two very similar guidebooks written by local and non-local authors. Analysis of these three guidebooks reveals the ways in which different types of authors struggled to both represent Kyoto's culture to authors themselves and to the world at a moment when the city was gradually opening its strictly controlled borders to international tourism as a way to escape impending national and economic insignificance.

Previous studies have found that nineteenth-century English-language guidebooks represented Japan and its people as essentially ancient and tradition-bound despite the rapid modernization of the Meiji period.[7] Through focusing not only on books by Western but also local writers, however, this study finds that non-Western, local authors also drew on similar orientalist imagery, and sometimes attempted to overcome and challenge it. Further, it finds that representations of a place and its people in guidebooks are not simply a result of an author's national and cultural background, but are connected to other factors such as the anticipated audience and efforts to encourage them to visit, and the influence of wider national and international discourses. This study thus highlights the complexity of and tensions that can exist between representations of self and other when guiding across and traversing the multiple borders of international tourism. It supports the findings of previous research that the temporal divisions accentuated in Orientalism can be seen not only in literature and politics,[8] but also in English-language guidebooks.[9] However,

---

7 Daniel Milne, "Discourses on Japan at the End of the Nineteenth Century in Murray Guidebooks," *Social Systems: Political, Legal and Economic Studies* 16 (2013): 135–152; Keina Nagasaka, "Meiji Shoki ni okeru Nihon Hatsu no Gaikokujin Muke Ryokō Gaidobukku," *Shakaigaku Kenkyūka Kiyo* 69 (2010): 101–115.

8 Said's focus is on these two spheres, though he does touch on guidebooks in Chapter 1, Part IV of his seminal work on Orientalism. Said, *Orientalism*.

9 Behdad, *Belated Travelers*; Bhattacharyya, "Mediating India"; Tegelberg, "Hidden Sights."

it also shows how these can be adopted and adapted, as well as challenged, by non-Western authors.

The major contribution of this study is its enrichment of our understanding of textual mediators of cross-cultural interaction. Previous studies of guidebooks and related media have largely overlooked attempts by non-Western authors, government officials, and intellectuals to shape representations of their own culture.[10] In so doing they have failed to notice the importance of domestic politics, such as Japan's civil war in the case of this study, and discussions regarding modernization, the past, the nation, and Orientalism in the shaping of representations of non-Western cultures. This study reveals the importance of these factors, and through this the complex processes of fashioning representations of self and other across cultural and national borders.

2 Orientalism, Borders, and Guidebooks

This chapter is primarily concerned with how we conceptualize and identify "others," that is people, cities, and cultures perceived as foreign, and "self," or people, cities, and cultures perceived to be similar to ourselves. It is therefore tied up with how discourses (whether written, spoken, performative, or visual) permeate all aspects of our culture (such as literature, media, politics, law, and everyday conversation) and thereby represent the world in ways that help us define borders separating groups to which we belong and those to which we do not.[11] One of the most historically entrenched borders between "self" and "other," and perhaps the most significant in motivating Western international tourism travel, has been that between the West and non-West, or "Occident" and "Orient." This study examines this border through considering representations of Kyoto, Japan (a city in which the author lives), specifically considering how Kyoto was represented in English-language tourism guidebooks when it first opened its physical and legal borders to international tourism.

The work of Edward Said, who has provided the most influential framework for analysis of discourses and representations of non-Western others, will provide a theoretical basis for the chapter's analysis.[12] For Said, a central feature

10 For example, Bhattacharyya, "Mediating India"; Tegelberg, "Hidden Sights"; Selwyn, *The Tourist Image*.

11 For more on the concept of discourse as used in cultural studies, see Foucault, *The Archaeology of Knowledge*; Mills, *Discourse*.

12 Said, *Orientalism*; Edward Said "Shattered Myths," in *Orientalism: A Reader*, ed. A. L. Macfie (Edinburgh: Edinburgh University Press, 2000).

of Orientalism is what he terms "imagined geographies," or concepts of cultural and geographical bordered units such as "the West," "the Orient," or "Asia," and how they are defined, represented, and maintained in Western literature and politics.[13] According to Said, Orientalism and the imagined geographies shaped by it underlie uneven power relationships between many Western and non-Western nations, and further are intertwined with and diffused through Western military, political, and economic institutions and their colonization and exploitation of many non-Western societies.

For Said, Orientalism rests firstly on the designation of the West and the East (Occident and Orient) into opposing and absolute categories with contrasting characteristics, such as the West as developed, dynamic, and superior, and the East as ancient, static, and inferior.[14] The "oriental woman" is central here; she is typically presented as an erotic symbol and target for the assertion of masculine dominance of the West over the Orient. For Said, Orientalism depends on representations that glorify the history and traditions of non-Western societies, and in so doing define these cultures as static and unchanged from ancient history, or as having a glorious past that atrophied over time. Johannes Fabian, whose work brings attention to the importance of representations of time in Orientalism, calls such neglect of the contemporary nature of other cultures the "denial of coevalness."[15]

Said's analysis of Orientalism has been refined by a number of different scholars. Ronald Inden and others have shown that orientalist discourses are diverse and vary depending on the cultures involved, relations between them, and historical contexts.[16] Richard King has found that these discourses are "bi-vocal" or "multi-vocal," meaning that they are not simply imposed on non-Western cultures by Western cultures, but are produced through interaction, negotiation, and struggle across these borders.[17] In the case of Japan, Takami Kuwayama argues that Japanese writers often draw on the work of foreign authors, and vice-versa, in representing Japanese culture to domestic and

---

13 See Chapter 1, Part II: "Imaginative Geography and Its Representations" in Said, *Orientalism*.

14 Said, "Shattered Myths."

15 Johannes Fabian, *Time and the Other* (New York: Columbia University Press, 2002), 25.

16 See Ronald Inden, "Orientalist Constructions of India," in *Orientalism: A Reader*, ed. A. L. Macfie. (Edinburgh: Edinburgh University Press, 2000); Katherine S. H. Turner, "From Classical to Imperial: Changing Visions of Turkey in the Eighteenth Century," in *Travel Writing and Empire*, ed. Steven Clark (London: Zed Books, 1999).

17 See Richard King, "Orientalism, Hinduism and Feminism," in *Orientalism: A Reader*, ed. A. L. Macfie (Edinburgh: Edinburgh University Press, 2000).

international audiences.[18] Marie Louise Pratt's concept of the "contact zone" provides a useful conceptual tool to help understand how cross-cultural interaction is based in multi-directional discourses. Pratt defines the "contact zone" as "social spaces where disparate cultures meet, clash and grapple with each other," and explains that power relations between the negotiating cultures are almost always unequal.[19] Within contact zones, multi-way borrowing and negotiation occurs between cultures, a phenomenon Pratt refers to as "transculturation." Contact zone and transculturation are important conceptual tools in that, rather than positioning intercultural discourses as dominated by one culture in their suppression of another, they recognize the capacity of local people and organizations to help shape discourses about their own culture. The work of Pratt and others show how Orientalism has been used and adapted by non-Western authors for their own ends, a phenomenon known as "self-Orientalism."[20]

Borders that divide and classify, most fundamentally between "self" and "other," are central to cultural and national representations generally, including those of Orientalism. In Orientalism, borders act to separate the two poles of the "West" and "East" and related concepts such as of "modernity" and "tradition," and "superiority" and "inferiority." This is also evident in imagined geographies, which regard not only a dualistic way of seeing the world as "Western" or "Oriental," but involve the creation and maintenance of imaginary borders around geographical, cultural, political, and racially-defined areas of the world. The term "the Orient" thus comes to categorize cultures and peoples of regions as geographically distanced and linguistically and culturally diverse as China, India, Egypt, and Indonesia despite few commonalities existing among them. This is not simply a problem of the imagination however, as such perception of cultural borders, difference, and similarity help shape cross-cultural interaction. The border between West and East also encompasses ideas of temporality, gender, and other defining markers of identity, so that on one side of the border is the modernity, development, dynamism and masculine power of the West and, on the other, the ancient, traditional, undeveloped, static, and feminine passivity of the East. The exotic allure of travel is also based on borders, especially on the possibility of breaching borders between "West" and "East," "rational" and "sensual," and "modern" and "ancient." The work of scholars such

18 Takami Kuwayama, *Native Anthropology* (Melbourne: Trans Pacific Press, 2004).

19 Pratt, *Imperial Eyes: Travel Writing and Transculturation*, 7.

20 See al-Azm, "Orientalism and Orientalism in Reverse"; Grace Yan and Carla Santos, "China Forever: Tourism Discourse and Self-Orientalism," *Annals of Tourism Research* 36, no. 2 (2009): 295–315.

as Pratt reveal how these apparent borders between the West and East, the strength and persistence of which Said perhaps tends to overemphasize, can change, be negotiated, and become fluid.[21] It is therefore essential to understand the role of borders in how we think of ourselves and other people and cultures, and significantly for this study, in how authors and media represent the self and other.

Tourism guidebooks are one of the earliest forms of modern tourism media and have deeply influenced the genre as a whole, including the various electronic tourism media that have risen to dominance over the last decade.[22] The modern guidebook emerged in Europe at the beginning of the nineteenth century and separated from travelogues, which became increasingly subjective and impressionistic, while guidebooks became the dominant objective and informative media for travel.[23] Since this time, they have changed considerably, and today generally incorporate less text and more photographic and other visual materials, and are increasingly found in online and other electronic forms to which users often provide content.[24] Guidebooks of this earlier period were text-heavy and dense books that compiled a great range and depth of information. They also depended almost entirely on one or two authors to provide content, so that their role in mediating the visitor's experiences was much greater than it is today.

Printed tourism guidebooks are unique among printed tourism media—including posters, brochures and postcards—in being designed as a source of information for use both before and during travel, and thus have the potential to directly influence encounters across national, cultural, and other boundaries between tourists and locals.[25] Bhattacharyya brings attention to the role of guidebooks in mediating interaction when explaining that, "the guidebook is a crucial part of the touristic process, because it mediates the relationship between tourist and destination, as well as the relationship between host and guest."[26] Closely tied to this mediating function of guidebooks is their role in the dissemination and development of dominant discourses about a given society. Ali Behdad argues that as mass tourism emerged in the nineteenth

21 Pratt, *Imperial Eyes*.

22 See Sabrina Francesconi, *Reading Tourism Texts: A Multimodal Analysis* (Bristol: Channel View Publications, 2014).

23 James Buzard, "The Grand Tour and After," in P. Hulme & T. Youngs (Eds.), *The Cambridge Companion to Travel Writing* (Cambridge, England: Cambridge University Press, 2005).

24 See Francesconi, *Reading Tourism Texts*.

25 See Wiebke Ramm, "Textual Variation in Travel Guides," in *Discourse and Community*, ed. Eija Ventola (Tübingen: Gunter Narr Verlag, 2000), 147–168.

26 Bhattacharyya, "Mediating India," 372.

century (precisely the period covered in this study), tourism guidebooks took over from travelogues as the "prevalent mode of discourse in orientalist travel literature," which not only helped buttress Western colonialism but the global expansion of Western tourism.[27] Yet Bhattacharyya, Behdad, and others have consistently focused on tourism guidebooks about countries in the Middle East and Asia—the so-called "East"—written by authors from the UK/Europe, North America, and Australia—the "West"—and ignored those written by authors from the Middle East and Asia who represent their own people, nation, and culture.[28]

3 Late Nineteenth-Century Kyoto

Kyoto has been a major political, religious, and cultural center since it was established as the capital of Japan in A.D. 794. Kyoto city and the surrounding area hold some of the most significant historical and cultural sites and properties in Japan, as well as a wealth of modern and natural attractions. For example, according to government statistics, Kyoto has more National Treasures and Important Cultural Properties than any city in Japan apart from Tokyo, and UNESCO has identified seventeen World Heritage Sites in Kyoto.[29]

Into the second half of the nineteenth century, Japan's physical, legal, and political borders severely limited diplomatic, trade, and cultural intercourse with other countries.[30] Changes brought about by the Meiji Restoration (1868) led to the gradual break down of these borders, including that regarding the movement of tourists. Pressure from Western powers, led by America's Commodore Perry, to break down trade barriers helped spark a civil war that converged on the imperial center of Kyoto and eventually brought about the end of more than 250 years of rule by the Tokugawa shogunate, and the establishment of a new government formed around the Meiji Emperor in 1868.[31]

27 Behdad, *Belated Travelers*.

28 As discussed, concepts such as the "West," "East," "Occident" and "Orient" are socially/politically/culturally constructed and have been shaped by relations of colonial domination. The author hopes that this chapter highlights this through considering the transcultural flows of ideas and people across such imagined geographies.

29 Agency for Cultural Affairs, Government of Japan, "Bunkazai," last modified January 1, 2016, http://www.bunka.go.jp/seisaku/bunkazai/shokai/shitei.html.

30 As Hellyer and others have shown, the so-called *sakoku* was not a period of complete isolation but one in which foreign trade continued in certain domains of Japan and was managed by the Tokugawa shogunate. Robert I. Hellyer, *Defining Engagement: Japan and Global Contexts, 1640–1868* (Cambridge: Harvard University Asia Center, 2009).

31 Satoru Fujita, *Bakumatsu kara Ishin he* (Tokyo: Iwanami Shinsho, 2015).

Opposition to the shogunate, especially among the *sonnō jōi* ("revere the emperor, expel the barbarians") movement, focused on the shogunate's handling of foreign relations epitomized by the "unequal treaties" with Western powers, and this resulted in numerous attacks on foreigners in Kyoto and other parts of Japan.[32] This included attacks in Kyoto on prominent Westerners such as British Consular General Harry Parkes and diplomat Ernest Satow on their way to the first meetings with the emperor in 1868.[33] Eventually however, the Meiji government continued Japan's engagement with the West, partly in order to develop a military and economy that could compete internationally.

At the start of the Meiji period, the people of Kyoto were facing a bleak future. Fires from the Kinmonnohen battle of 1864, a major conflict of the civil war, destroyed approximately half of all residential buildings, the vast majority of its economic center, and 253 temples and shrines.[34] The situation continued to deteriorate with the relocation of the imperial residence, imperial court, and institutions of central government to Tokyo, which ended Kyoto's millennium-long history as the imperial center. This resulted in the loss of employment and vital financial support to Kyoto businesses that severely affected the economy. To make matters worse, it endangered the reputation of many of Kyoto's products, which had long benefited from proximity to the emperor.[35] Other early policies of the Meiji government also had devastating impacts on key components of the city's economy. Attempts to divide Shinto and Buddhism, confiscate unused temple land, and strongly associate the emperor with Shinto badly affected Buddhist sects, many of which were centered in Kyoto.[36]

In response, Kyoto's financial and political leaders worked quickly to reshape the city's economy and identity. Located inland, they could not easily achieve this through trade. Instead, they began a number of progressive initiatives. As described later, one of the largest and most successful of which were the Kyoto Exhibitions. These eventually helped revive traditional industries and develop new ones, foremost of which were domestic and international tourism.

---

32 John Black, *Young Japan: Volume II* (London: Trubner, 1881); Elise Tipton, *Modern Japan: A Social and Political History* (Oxon: Routledge, 2008), 32.

33 Ernest Satow, *A Diplomat in Japan* (London: Seeley 1921; reprint, Berkeley: Stone Bridge Press, 2006), 359–361.

34 Takehiro Kobayashi, *Meiji Ishin to Kyōto* (Kyoto: Rinsen Books, 1998), 10–12.

35 Ibid.

36 Ryōji Igeda and Kumiko Harada, *Kyōto no Hyakunen* (Tokyo: Yamakawa Publishing, 1993).

4 Early International Tourism

Restrictions on international tourism into Japan were gradually lifted from 1858 and virtually eliminated by 1874. Most tourists coming to Japan by the end of that period were well-educated and wealthy, and many came from the UK on Thomas Cook's "round the world" tours. Cook was not only one of the founders of the modern travel agency, but he also helped popularize overseas travel through tours to a series of destinations around the world. Cook's tours began in 1872 and visited Japan each year from 1873.[37]

The emperor and imperial court had made Kyoto a potential center for political strife. To avoid foreign influence, barriers for foreign visitors to Kyoto were only gradually lifted after the relocation of the emperor to Tokyo.[38] The first travel visa for Kyoto was issued for the 1872 Kyoto Exhibition, which attracted approximately 770 foreign visitors. Foreign visitors could even submit items for exhibition, indicating that the exhibition's organizers actively attempted to attract and include them.[39] The exhibition the following year attracted 634 foreign and almost 400,000 domestic visitors.[40] One hurdle that may have limited the number of foreign visitors was a requirement that they pay a deposit, a policy aimed at countering the extraterritoriality granted to most Westerners under existing treaties.[41] In addition, many foreign tourists were apprehensive about visiting Kyoto because they feared being the target of the anti-foreign attitudes that had characterized the city in the years before the Meiji Restoration. An 1868 attack by anti-foreign samurai on the parade of the British Consul on route to Britain's first official talks with the Emperor was perhaps the most infamous of a series of well-publicized attacks on foreigners in Kyoto in the years preceding the exhibition.[42] Reflecting that the relative friendliness they met in Kyoto was not what many foreign visitors expected, John Black, an influential journalist and newspaper editor of the period comments that, "Nothing in the shape of a black look or uncivil word was experienced" by foreign visitors to the exhibition.[43]

---

37 Nagasaka, "Meiji Shoki ni okeru Nihon Hatsu no Gaikokujin Muke Ryokō Gaidobukku," 111.

38 Yoshiko Kudō, "Meiji Shoki Kyōto no Hakurankai to Kankō," *Kyōto Kōka Joshidaigaku Kenkyū Kiyo* 46 (2008): 77–100.

39 Black, *Young Japan: Volume 2*, 856.

40 Kudō, "Meiji Shoki Kyōto no Hakurankai to Kankō," 94.

41 Ibid.

42 Satow, *A Diplomat in Japan*, 359–361.

43 Black, *Young Japan: Volume 2*, 856. John Black established, edited, and wrote for the English-language newspapers *Japan Gazette* and *Far East*, and the Japanese-language *Nisshin Shinjishi* in the 1860s and 1870s.

Ultimately, the Kyoto Exhibitions were a catalyst for increasing foreign interest in the city.[44] They were also a turning point for Kyoto's leaders in re-imagining Kyoto as a historic tourist city, and this helped stimulate investment in accommodation facilities and tourism media.[45] In addition, Kyoto's exhibitions were the first in Japan and helped initiate a boom in exhibition-based tourism that attracted millions of domestic tourists throughout Japan until the 1940s. Ruoff has shown how these exhibitions eventually became central to the dissemination and embodiment of nationalistic narratives in the lead up to WWII.[46]

Japanese-language tourism guidebooks for Kyoto have been published since at least the 1650s. The 1780 Kyoto series *Miyako Meishozue* was the most influential in its effective utilization of illustrations, information on the customs and everyday life of Kyoto people, and reference to traditional poetry.[47] Soon after the Meiji Restoration, such Japanese-language guidebooks started to shift to not only include conventional attractions such as temples and shrines, but also more sites connected to the emperor and modernization.

5 Yamamoto Kakuma and the Guidebook for the 1873 Exhibition

Yamamoto Kakuma was one of the most important figures in Kyoto's modernization and author of *The Guide to the Celebrated Places in Kiyoto* (1873).[48] A student of Western science and military technology, Yamamoto came to Kyoto as a leader of Aizu domain's artillery, a key part of the Tokugawa forces in the city and enemy of rebel domains that eventually defeated them. Yamamoto was captured in 1868 and while imprisoned dictated a petition to the new government calling for a non-authoritarian government working for the benefit of citizens through universal education, reformed politics, and industrialization.[49] These ideas were well received and helped him become the central advisor for Kyoto Prefecture between the 1870s and 1890s, during which time Kyoto led the country in many modernizing initiatives, including the establishment of

44 Ibid.

45 Kazuto Kasahara, "Rekishi Kankō Hakurankai," *10+1* 36 (2004): 164–177, 134.

46 Kenneth Ruoff, *Imperial Japan at its Zenith* (New York: Cornell University Press, 2010).

47 Iso Munemasa, *Miyako Meishozue o Yomu* (Tokyo: Tokyo Do Publishing, 1997).

48 While Yamamoto is credited with authoring the guidebook, one of his closest students, the merchant Niwa Keisuke, claimed that he was its chief author and that Yamamoto played a guidance role. See Kobayashi, *Meiji Ishin to Kyōto*.

49 Kakuma Yamamoto, *Kanken* (Kyoto, 1870), accessed January 10, 2016, http://library.doshisha.ac.jp/ir/digital/archive/yamamoto/128/imgidx128.html.

public schools, new forms of energy production, and public transportation. Some of these initiatives were opposed, including by the influential thinker Fukuzawa Yukichi, on the grounds that Kyoto should focus funding on maintaining sites of tradition and history.[50] Later, Yamamoto also became a central Kyoto figure in Western education and private industry.[51]

Published to coincide with the Second Kyoto Exhibition of 1873, Yamamoto's guidebook was both the first English-language guidebook by either a foreign or Japanese author to focus solely on a Japanese destination, and the first book published in Kyoto using any European-language type.[52] In its early use of English to welcome foreign visitors, the guidebook was a symbol of the triumph of those in Kyoto, including Yamamoto, who wanted Japan to break down its political and cultural barriers and learn from and interact with the West.[53] The pocket-size guidebook consists of forty-six copperplate prints, which, as seen in figure 2.1, have a brief, five to twelve-line written description of different tourist sites in Kyoto city and its surrounds.[54]

Yamamoto's guidebook includes very minimal descriptions of contemporary local people. The most frequent descriptions of people are historical figures such as the eminent monks, emperors, shoguns, and other national leaders who founded sites. Written references to other locals are typically very brief, for example Niyakuoji is described as having "three waterfalls to which many people go to cool themselves in summer," and Arashiyama (figure 2.1) as, "many person go and feast there looking upon the fine flowers in spring."[55] Such descriptions convey the popularity of the site among locals and indicate local customs that visitors might be interested in joining, while also giving an impression of safety following the political unrest of the period. Illustrated depictions of local people are also generally minimal. Of the forty-eight pages, only the illustrations for "Earthenware of Kiyomizu" (see figure 2.2), "Nishijin," and people washing dye from textiles in "Kamogawa river" have people as a key

50 Kobayashi, *Meiji Ishin to Kyōto*, 180.

51 Yamamoto helped found and later became president of Doshisha University and headed the Kyoto Industrial Council from 1885.

52 Kyoto Prefectural General Archives, "Yamamoto Kakuma to Kyōto Hakurankai," last modified April 1, 2013, http://www.pref.kyoto.jp/shiryokan/documents/dayori175.pdf.

53 Kobayashi, *Meiji Ishin to Kyōto*, 104.

54 Despite the importance of Yamamoto and the guidebook in the history of international tourism in Japan, this is perhaps the first attempt at an in-depth scholarly analysis of the book.

55 Kakuma Yamamoto, *The Guide to the Celebrated Places in Kiyoto* (Kyoto: Niwa, 1873. Reprint, Kyoto: Doshisha University, 1981), 7, 33. Citations refer to the Doshisha University edition.

FIGURE 2.1 Arashiyama
SOURCE: KAKUMA YAMAMOTO, *THE GUIDE TO THE CELEBRATED PLACES IN KIYOTO* (KYOTO: NIWA, 1873), 36, INTERNATIONAL RESEARCH CENTER FOR JAPANESE STUDIES, OVERSEAS IMAGES OF JAPAN DATABASE, ACCESSED JULY 29, 2019, HTTP://SEKIEI.NICHIBUN.AC.JP/GAI/EN/TOP/

element. All represent people making their products in traditional kimono-like attire. While people are prominent, the products they make and their non-industrialized, hand-made nature is the primary focus, providing a clear representation of traditional concepts of Japan. In addition, there are five other illustrations in which people are depicted walking around sites, though these mostly emphasize the size of buildings or objects, such as the great bell at Daibutsu and the pagoda of Tōji (see figure 2.3).

In comparison to this guidebook, earlier Japanese-language guidebooks on Kyoto are a valuable resource for learning about local people and their culture, as seen in *Miyako Meishozue* of 1780 and *Karaku Meishozue* of 1864.[56] Depictions of bridges are a good example of this; while frequently featured in these Japanese-language guidebooks as places crowded by many types of

56 International Research Center for Japanese Studies, Miyako Meishozue Database, accessed January 10, 2016, http://www.nichibun.ac.jp/meisyozue/kyoto/c-pg1.html.

FIGURE 2.2 The Earthenware of Kiyomizu
SOURCE: YAMAMOTO, *THE GUIDE TO THE CELEBRATED PLACES IN KIYOTO* (1873), 20

FIGURE 2.3 Tōji pagoda
SOURCE: YAMAMOTO, *THE GUIDE TO THE CELEBRATED PLACES IN KIYOTO* (1873), 32

FIGURE 2.4 Sanjō Bridge in Yamamoto's 1873 guidebook
SOURCE: YAMAMOTO, *THE GUIDE TO THE CELEBRATED PLACES IN KIYOTO* (1873), 5

people entering and leaving Kyoto, in Yamamoto's guide the Sanjō Bridge is deserted (see figures 2.4 to 2.6). In addition, unlike these earlier texts, Yamamoto's guidebook includes no depiction of festivals, areas of dining, drinking, shopping, accommodation, or entertainment. For example, figure 2.7 shows a detailed depiction of people enjoying Ikesu, a lively dining and entertainment district of Edo-period Kyoto. This comparison indicates that while Kyoto's living, present culture found in festivals, dining, and entertainment, and the opportunity to cross regional cultural borders to engage with these, were clearly major attractions to visitors from other parts of Japan during the Edo period, through his guidebook Yamamoto was less inclined to encourage cultural border crossing by foreign visitors. This may have been a consequence of the anti-foreign violence that occurred in the city less than a decade before the publication of this guidebook.

In Yamamoto's guidebook, Kyoto is described as having "remained without particular change" since being founded at the start of the Heian period in 794.[57] Despite his claim, Kyoto's city layout, culture and political nature had in fact

57 Yamamoto, *The Guide to the Celebrated Places in Kiyoto* (1981), 3.

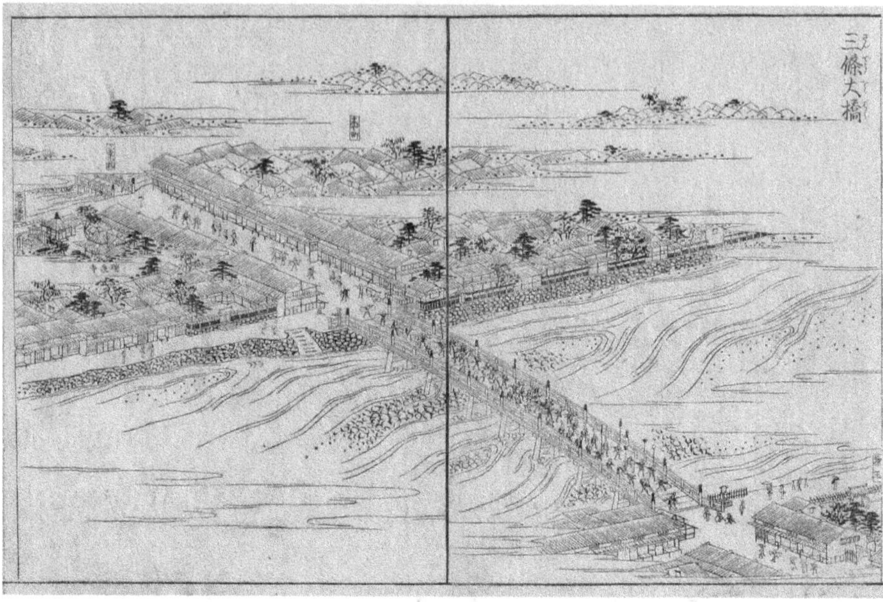

FIGURE 2.5 Sanjō Bridge in Akizato's 1780 guidebook
SOURCE: RITŌ AKIZATO, *MIYAKO MEISHOZUE* (NANIWA, 1780), 33

greatly evolved over the centuries, most notably in the decade immediately before the book's publication.[58] This representation of an unchanging Kyoto is bolstered by the complete absence of markers of modernization and westernization in the guidebook. This is remarkable given that Kyoto was undergoing a period of rapid modernization with the direct advice of the guidebook's author. By this time, Kyoto had founded Japan's first modern elementary school system, built one of the first modern post offices, and started the first modern exhibitions.

6 Tradition and Modernization

Why, at a time in which Kyoto was undergoing a remarkable period of modernization partly led by Yamamoto, does this guidebook portray Kyoto as unchanging and focus almost exclusively on Kyoto's ancient history? Further, why does

58 Matthew Stavros, *Kyoto: An Urban History of Japan's Premodern Capital* (Honolulu: University Hawaii Press, 2014).

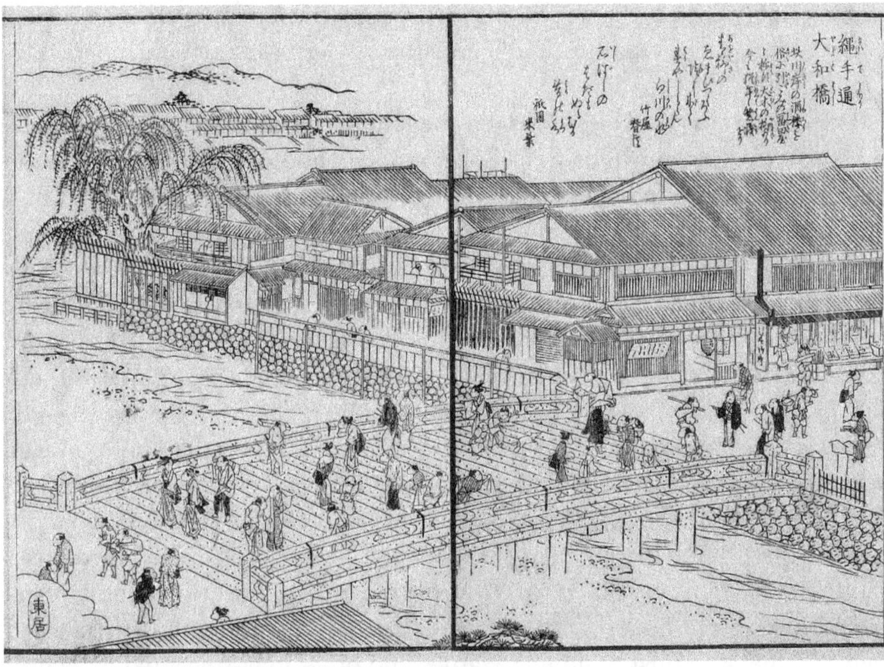

FIGURE 2.6 Yamato Bridge in Akatsuki's 1864 guidebook
SOURCE: KANENARI AKATSUKI, *KARAKU MEISHOZUE* (KYOTO, 1864), 34

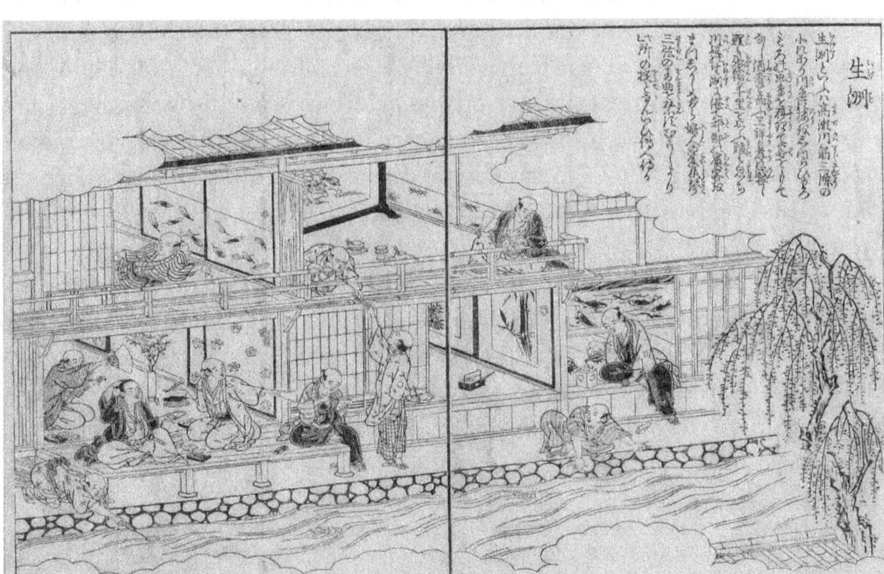

FIGURE 2.7 Ikesu in Akizato's 1780 guidebook
SOURCE: AKIZATO, MIYAKO MEISHOZUE, 30

Yamamoto's guidebook have striking similarities to orientalist representations, which also focus on tradition and ignore the modernization and dynamism of non-Western cultures?

One answer to these questions may be found in Kyoto's recent political turmoil. As explained previously, the Kinmonnohen battle of 1864 resulted in the destruction of approximately half of the city, a battle that was one part of a civil war in which Kyoto became the center for the anti-foreign, anti-shogun movement that resulted in violence directed at Western foreigners. Within this context, the author's representation of Kyoto as ancient and immutable can be understood as an attempt to draw attention away from this recent history and present Kyoto as a stable city in which historical sites could be enjoyed without the discord and conflict that trouble most rapidly-modernizing cities.

As work by Stefan Tanaka indicates, discussions among Japan's political, administrative, and business leaders engaging with Western discourses regarding tradition and modernization may also have influenced Yamamoto's guidebook.[59] Soon after the 1868 Restoration, the Meiji government introduced a number of policies aimed at reducing the political power of Buddhism, including a law to divide it from Shinto that resulted in the destruction and sale of many Buddhist buildings, statues and other long-treasured objects.[60] Kyoto, home to the headquarters of many major Buddhist sects, was no exception to this and even introduced a prefectural law in 1871 that attempted to ban popular customs considered superstitious, many of which had Buddhist roots such as the *Okuribi* bonfires and worship of neighborhood-based *Jizō* statues.[61] However, in mid-1871 the Meiji government issued a decree for the preservation of historical objects (*kyūbutsu*) that explicitly recognized the importance of preserving the past in order to understand the modernizing present.[62] This led to an official survey of historical treasures that covered many parts of Japan, but especially focused on the former capitals of Nara and Kyoto.[63]

The 1871 survey demonstrates that by the time of the publication of Yamamoto's guidebook, the compilation of information about and preservation of historical buildings and objects was seen to be valuable in itself, and further, that it was seen as an important point of reference for the country's modernization. According to Stefan Tanaka, Machida Hisanari led the survey

59 Stefan Tanaka, *New Times in Modern Japan* (Princeton: Princeton University, 2004).
60 Kobayashi, *Meiji Ishin to Kyōto*, 148–149.
61 Igeda and Harada, *Kyōto no Hyakunen*.
62 Tanaka, *New Times in Modern Japan*, 31–32.
63 Ibid.

after touring Europe where he had "recognized the continuity between modern society and its past."[64] The survey team also included Ninagawa Noritane, an official in the exhibitions section of the Education Ministry, who in a draft of the survey wrote how a foreigner complained that Japanese were overly attracted to novelty at the expense of their past.[65] Machida and Ninagawa demonstrate how important ministry officials connected to exhibitions were knowledgeable of and highly attentive to thinking in the West regarding tradition and modernity.

It is highly likely that the opinion held by these men was known, and perhaps even shared, by Yamamoto and other leaders of Kyoto's exhibitions. Such knowledge of the expectations of the guidebook's target readership (Western travelers) is likely to have encouraged the author to focus on Kyoto's history and tradition. For the guidebook's author, showing a knowledge of and appreciation for preserving the city's history and tradition was a way of representing Kyoto's people as civilized moderns worthy of being visited from afar. However, importantly, the author did not introduce symbols of the city's rapid modernization.

The guidebook's focus on an unchanged tradition and silence regarding modernization makes it a case of self-Orientalism, in which—unlike orthodox Orientalism—authors typically do not represent the "Orient" as inferior or degenerate but strategically utilize Orientalism to portray their own culture in a positive light.[66] This self-Orientalism occurred because the author was conscious of needing to reassure cautious visitors that Kyoto was safe and unchanging, while simultaneously engaging with Western discussions about the past and modernization, and wanting to meet the orientalist expectation of visitors. As Neil Harris points out in regard to the 1893 World's Columbian Exhibition in Chicago, the Japanese pavilion in this later exhibition also portrayed Japan as tradition-oriented, rather than as a modern society.[67] Perhaps from the Kyoto Exhibitions of the 1870s until this time, therefore, there was an understanding among Japanese exhibition officials that a modern nation should value its traditions, and further, that Japan's foreign diplomatic interests

64 Ibid, 31.

65 Ibid, 32.

66 Sadik Jalal al-Azm, for example, explains how the notion of essential differences between the West and Orient have been utilized by both Arab nationalists, who seek to lionize the "Arab mind," and Islamic revivalists, who attempt to portray Islam as the generator of change in the Middle East. Al-Azm, "Orientalism and Orientalism in Reverse."

67 Neil Harris, "All the World a Melting Pot? Japan at American Fairs, 1876–1904," in *Mutual Images: Essays in American-Japanese Relations*, ed. Akira Iriye (Cambridge, MA: Harvard University Press, 1975).

could best be served through complying with the orientalist expectations of foreign Western audiences.

7 The 1895 Fourth National Exhibition

The success of the exhibitions of Kyoto and other regions, along with that of exhibitions internationally, encouraged Japan's government to begin their own national exhibition, which was first held in 1877 in Ueno Park, Tokyo. City government and industry leaders were confident they could build on their experience of the Kyoto Exhibitions and hold the next national exhibition in Kyoto. However, their petitioning attempts failed to secure both the 1881 and 1890 national exhibitions, which were again held at Ueno Park, prompting them to rethink their approach.[68] For the 1895 national exhibition, these city leaders proposed that Kyoto host a national exhibition celebrating 1,100 years since Emperor Kanmu transferred the capital to Kyoto. This proposal was eventually accepted by the national government.

The key to the success of Kyoto's 1895 proposal was its reference to imperial history. Japan's new leaders utilized Emperor Meiji, as well as the narrative of the unbroken imperial line, in order to unite the country and justify their rule.[69] Unlike the early 1870s, when regional differences were widely recognized and the "building" of modern Japan was in its early days, by the 1890s the Meiji government consciously attempted to build patriotic nationalism through recourse to ideas of a common tradition and history.[70] Imperial history was a central theme in the unprecedented upsurge in domestic tourism that began around this time.[71] Kyoto's proposal also fit the reputation of the city as both a center of tradition and innovation.[72] The 1895 exhibition was held in a site adjoining the newly constructed Biwako Canal, a symbol of the city's modernization, and visitors were transported there using Japan's first commercial tram line that ran on energy from Japan's first hydroelectricity plant. This exhibition also drew on international trends, such as the 1893 World's Columbian Exhibition in Chicago that likewise utilized history by celebrating the four

68 Kobayashi, *Meiji Ishin to Kyōto*, 176.

69 John Dower, "The Meiji Emperor and Invention of the Modern Emperor System," *MIT Visualizing Cultures*, accessed January 10, 2016, http://ocw.mit.edu/ans7870/21f/21f.027/throwing_off_asia_01/toa_vis_01.html.

70 Tanaka, *New Times in Modern Japan*, 37.

71 Ruoff, *Imperial Japan at its Zenith*.

72 Kobayashi, *Meiji Ishin to Kyōto*.

hundredth anniversary of Columbus's arrival in the Americas. Ruoff has demonstrated how imperial history was heavily utilized in Japanese-language guidebooks and advertising media for national exhibitions of the period, and, as will be shown, this was also the case for English-language guidebooks published for the 1895 Kyoto National Exhibition.[73]

The Miyako Odori, a dance and theatrical performance that features *geiko* and *maiko* (local dialect for "geisha" and "apprentice geisha"), had started in conjunction with the First Kyoto Exhibition of 1872 and became a major feature of the 1895 exhibition. While the Miyako dance was founded on traditional local dance and music styles of the Gion district, it also drew on contemporary European performance, such as the simultaneous dancing of a large number of performers in Paris's cancan dances.[74] This was done as an attempt to appeal both to the tastes of foreign and domestic audiences.[75]

Visitor numbers to Kyoto's exhibitions gradually declined over the 1880s, and then surged after the First Sino-Japanese War (1894–1895). In the run-up to the 1895 exhibition, nationalistic sentiment and pride were sweeping Japan in response to successes in this war and the long-awaited revision of unequal treaties with Western powers. Peace meetings to end the war with Qing China were initiated in late March of 1895, and the Treaty of Shimonoseki was signed on April 17, two weeks after the exhibition began. These military and diplomatic victories benefited Kyoto's exhibition by increasing interest in its imperial theme and encouraging a positive outlook about the nation's economy among Japanese.

The exhibition was a huge success and drew 1,136,000 visitors,[76] more than three times the city's population and the largest attendance for any exhibition in Japan at the time. Though it is not clear how many visitors were non-Japanese, the exhibition did gain the attention of influential foreign authors, such as the writer Lafcadio Hearn and German-born historian Ludwig Riess.[77] The Kyoto City Council commissioned two separate English-language tourism guidebooks for the exhibition, one compiled by a Japanese author, another by an Irish author. Clearly informed by Murray's *A Handbook for Travelers in*

73 Ruoff, *Imperial Japan at its Zenith.*

74 Mariko Okada, "Before Making Heritage: Internationalisation of Geisha in the Meiji Period," in *Making Japanese Heritage*, ed. Christoph Brumann and Robert A. Cox (London: Routledge, 2010), 31–43.

75 Ibid.

76 Shinya Hashitsume, *Nihon no Hakurankai* (Tokyo: Heibansha, 2005).

77 Kobayashi, *Meiji Ishin to Kyōto.*

Japan, the dominant English-language guidebook series on Japan at the time,[78] both guidebooks are lengthy (over three hundred pages), text-heavy, use a dry and objective tone, and include extensive detail. Because these guidebooks share the same destination, year of publication, guidebook style, and context in which they were commissioned and produced, they provide a rare opportunity to accurately compare early Japanese and foreign-authored representations of Kyoto.

8 Ichihara's *The Official Guide-Book to Kyoto and the Allied Prefectures of 1895*

The Official Guide-Book to Kyoto and the Allied Prefectures of 1895 was compiled by a Japanese author named M. Ichihara and published by Meishinsha, a fledgling Japanese publishing company based in Nara, a city about forty kilometers south of Kyoto. Meishinsha won the book's contract by a popular vote conducted among the members of the Kyoto City Council, who commissioned the book as part of an attempt to attract and inform foreign visitors.[79]

Like Yamamoto's guidebook, Ichihara's is almost devoid of reference to or depictions of local people. For example, readers are told in the book's preface that Japan has long been "celebrated for its natural beauty as well as for its interesting people," but this explanation of Japan and Japanese people is not expanded upon.[80] While recognizing international interest in Japanese people, therefore, the guidebook does not develop its own clear portrait of them.

In general, local people are portrayed as a group, with little individualizing characteristics and details. For example, in explaining the exhibition the guidebook states:

> ... this date has been chosen for the commemoration of an event so worthy of being celebrated by all loyal Japanese, but especially by the people of Kyoto who remember what their city owes to the far-sighted Emperor by whom it was founded. ... Hence it was that the people of Kyoto with one voice proposed the observance of this anniversary ...[81]

78 The 1894 edition was the most recent at the time. See Milne, "Discourses on Japan at the End of the Nineteenth Century in Murray Guidebooks."

79 Ichihara, *The Official Guide-Book to Kyoto and the Allied Prefectures*, preface.

80 Ibid., preface.

81 Ibid., 56.

This section portrays the exhibition as emerging from the will of all Kyoto's people in honor of the founder of the city, emperor Kanmu, and the city's imperial legacy. This is however simply an effort to draw on patriotism centered on imperial history because, as explained previously, the exhibition was not driven by a grass-roots movement but by Kyoto's business and political leaders, who utilized this imperial legacy in order to gain the approval of the national government.

The guidebook's focus on history and the imperial line does to some degree represent local people and Japanese culture indirectly. For example, it includes over fourteen pages of lists and historical accounts of the 122 emperors and shoguns since the founding of the nation in 660 BC. The first thousand years of lineage is today considered to be predominantly mythical, and was even in doubt among many Japanese scholars at the time.[82] Through this list, the guidebook presents Kyoto as central to Japanese history and culture, and the imperial line as unbroken and ancient. As Ruoff explains, tracing its roots to 660 BC presents the imperial line as longer than, and thereby as superior to, Christianity, and as predating China's and Korea's influence on Japan.[83] Further, through emphasizing the antiquity of the imperial line, and the unity of local people around it through their devotion to Kanmu, locals are represented as united, faithful, and loyal to their emperor, city, and nation.

While traditions and history are central to Ichihara's guidebook, the nation is also presented through modernization and contemporary international developments. For example, it is stated in the preface that, "Japan … is now drawing the attention and admiration of the whole world on account of the wonderful progress made in recent years. Especially have the brilliant victories gained in the war with China added to her fame."[84] Here, "wonderful progress" refers to Japan's modernization and westernization, including the successes of its modernized military. Later, Kyoto's modernized industries and products are positively described. Ichihara does not, therefore, present Kyoto's culture simply as traditional and static, but as successfully modern and dynamic. Through this, Ichihara provides a more nuanced and heterogeneous representation of Kyoto than those offered in Yamamoto's guidebook, which focused on history and tradition. In adopting a national-imperial narrative, as seen in the fourteen-page lists of emperors and defining the exhibition as an "event so worthy of being celebrated by all loyal Japanese, but especially by the people of Kyoto who remember what their city owes to the far-sighted Emperor," it

82 Ruoff, *Imperial Japan at its Zenith*, 2–3.

83 Ibid., 3.

84 Ichihara, *The Official Guide-Book to Kyoto and the Allied Prefectures*, 39.

frames Kyoto through nationalistic discourses prevalent within Japan at the time.[85]

Later in the guidebook, the site chosen for the exhibition is described as "flourishing in the reigns of the Emperors Shirakawa and Toba," and as a "beautiful place with its views of … the 'Thirty-six peaks of Higashiyama,' " while "the new Biwako Canal that flows before the grounds greatly adds to the beauty and advantage of the site."[86] This description neatly combines the three-pronged representation of the city provided throughout the guidebook of Kyoto's imperial tradition, natural attractions, and modernization.

A comparison of the Yamamoto and Ichihara guidebooks reflects shifts in discourses regarding tradition and modernization between the 1870s and 1890s. Yamamoto's guidebook demonstrates the newly emerged perspective that protecting tradition is both integral to being modern and helps people understand the modernizing present. Yamamoto's guidebook did not draw on nationalistic discourses because in the early 1870s the heritage of Buddhist temples and other historic places were still connected to the local area and had not yet been greatly exploited by the national government in nation building. This began to change around the late 1880s however, so that by the 1890s Kyoto's leaders realized they could benefit from making their own local history a national history through reference to the imperial line. Unlike Yamamoto's guidebook, Ichihara's made direct reference to modernization, both at the national level in their war with China, and at the local level with the Biwako Canal and street trams. This indicates another shift in thinking regarding tradition and modernization after 1873.

From the late 1880s, leading Japanese intellectuals increasingly saw the West as threatening, and became critical of Western thought, which they saw placed itself at the center of world culture and looked down on the East (and Japan) as backward and oriental.[87] The intellectual Miyake Setsurei and others attempted to define modernization not as blind imitation of the West, but as improvement of the nation through rejecting biases and superstitions while building on what was valued from the past.[88] These intellectuals developed perspectives of a Japanese culture as unified, ancient and untouched by the changes of history that attempted to make them equal with, and sometimes superior to, the West. They sheared everyday practices, art, buildings,

85 Ibid., 56.

86 Ibid., 53.

87 Kenneth Pyle, *The New Generation in Meiji Japan* (Stanford: Stanford University Press, 1970). Tanaka, *New Times in Modern Japan*, 93.

88 See Tanaka, *New Times in Modern Japan*, 97.

and other objects and customs of their local context and filled them with national significance.[89] The Meiji government supported this effort as it helped build a concept of a unified Japanese nation and people by providing a shared national past that acted as an important reference point for a unified present and collective future.[90] From early on, the history of the imperial line, which the Meiji government was ostensibly built around, became a significant aspect of such nation building.[91] Likewise, the Japanese pavilion at the 1893 World's Exhibition in Chicago presented a unified nation, however it was focused primarily on symbols of Japanese tradition and largely ignored modernization.[92] This variance with Ichihara's guidebook indicates that success in the Sino-Japanese War (1894–95) provided Japanese leaders with the confidence to present Japan and Kyoto as modern, and therefore as equal with the West. Japan's newly conceptualized history provided a foundation for this modernization that was independent of the West, positive, and uniquely Japanese. Thus, through its nationalistic narrative, frequent recourse to imperial histories, and inclusion of symbols of modernity, Ichihara's guidebook reflects both the redefinition of local histories as national ones and a newfound confidence in Japan's modernization. Through this, the guidebook challenges the boundaries of Orientalism that posit the "West" as "modern" and "East" as "pre-modern."

9 Brinkley's *The Kyoto Industrial Exhibition of 1895*

Francis Brinkley, author of *The Kyoto Industrial Exhibition of 1895*, was a well-established, skilled, and experienced Japan-specialist from Ireland who arrived in Japan in 1867 on commission as a commander in Japan's Royal Artillery. Brinkley's interests and expertise included both traditional Japanese culture and contemporary politics. Brinkley was the owner and chief editor of the Tokyo-based *Japan Mail*, considered the most influential

89 Miyake Setsurei and Okakura Kakuzō were key intellectuals here. See Tanaka, *New Times in Modern Japan*, 93–110.

90 It is important to remember that Japan was not exceptional in such "nation building" but that reimagining the past has been a tool for the establishment of modern nations worldwide. For a classic study on this see Eric Hobsbawm and Terence Ranger, *The Invention of Tradition* (Cambridge: Cambridge University Press, 1984).

91 Ruoff, *Imperial Japan at its Zenith*.

92 Neil Harris, "All the World a Melting Pot? Japan at American Fairs, 1876–1904."

English-language newspaper in East Asia.[93] Brinkley was also a correspondent for *The Times* (UK), and after the guidebook's publication wrote a number of highly regarded books about Japan, such as a co-compiled Japanese-English dictionary, a ten-volume collection of photographs of Japan, and a twelve-volume series on the history and arts of Japan and China. Brinkley was known both for his pro-Japan stance and for encouraging Anglo-Japanese relations, for which he was later awarded the Third Order of the Sacred Treasure by Emperor Meiji.[94]

Brinkley's guidebook contains a number of descriptions that go beyond superficial generalizations of "the people" to represent specific groups of people, especially the *maiko* (and geisha) of the Miyako Odori dances. Including an eight-page article from *The Times* by Henry Spencer Palmer, a correspondent also based in Japan, there are ten pages devoted to the dances, more than to any other single site or event. Drawing on Palmer's article, Brinkley's book frames the dances as traditional and ancient by linking the ancestry of the Miyako dance back to "the Sun Goddess, regarded as the ancestress of the Imperial family."[95] Continuing, it then describes geisha as "bewitching and exquisitely dressed lasses, who wait upon the guests with the prettiest air imaginable, and afterwards entertain them with music, singing and dancing." In this excerpt from Palmer, the text makes repeated references to the youthful and artistic nature of the dancers and musicians involved:

> In person the Maiko are the prettiest little specimens of budding Japanese girlhood, rosy-lipped and black-eyed, with comely and delicate features, tiny hands and feet, and an air of graceful modesty and innocence rarely seen on any stage.[96]

They are then described as, "a pretty picture ... a reproduction in flesh and blood of the typical Japanese beauty of our fans and screens."[97] Here, "our" refers to the collections of Japanese art and other items that were popular in the UK, continental Western Europe, and the US at the time. Such representations, as Ian Littlewood argues, depicts Japanese women as "beautiful butterflies"; as

93 Robert Burton, "Early Photography of Japan," *Harvard College Library*, last modified April, 2012, https://library.harvard.edu/sites/default/files/static/collections/epj/tourist_photography.html.

94 Ian Nish, *The Anglo-Japanese Alliance: The Diplomacy of Two Island Empires 1884–1907*, rev. ed. (London: Bloomsbury Publishing, 2012).

95 Brinkley, *The Kyoto Industrial Exhibition of 1895*, 14.

96 Ibid., 17.

97 Ibid., 18.

physically small and delicate, and as obedient to the desires of men.[98] In addition, comparing them with works of art presents them as static, unchanging, passive and silent, descriptions that fit Said's conception of Orientalism.

Men are also described in the section from Palmer. The Japanese man, the passage states, "never dances himself" but "befitting Oriental dignity, he prefers to have his dancing done for him ... by the prettiest girls in the land."[99] In a typical example of the "imagined geographies" of Orientalism, the passage depicts all men of the culturally, linguistically, and politically diverse "Orient" as homogenous, while again calling on orientalist tropes of exotic and submissive oriental women.

As in the Yamamoto and Ichihara guidebooks, Brinkley describes Kyoto as a "citadel of tranquility" and largely unchanged from ancient times despite a long history of transformation and conflict.[100] Again, as in the Ichihara volume, Brinkley portrays the imperial line as the backbone of Kyoto's stability, highlighting the importance of the discourse to the exhibition, and suggesting the possibility that exhibition leaders required guidebooks they commissioned to include such an explanation.

Brinkley's evaluation of modern industrial developments in Kyoto is at times positive. Rather than mocking Japanese engineering as inferior copies of the West, or criticizing modern development as incompatible with the city's tradition, as others had,[101] the writer praises the Biwako Canal as a "specimen of modern Japanese engineering skill."[102] Building from this, Brinkley presents a dual vision of Kyoto as both more historical than European cities such as Paris and London, while also being modern: Kyoto is both "a centre of art and industry, and ... the time-honoured capital of imperial and feudal Japan."[103]

While Brinkley praises some aspects of Kyoto's modernization, however, this is contradicted by his representation of Kyoto's culture as endangered by modernization. Kyoto is described as "nestling among hills of the softest possible contours, brooded over by a wonderful crystalline atmosphere, and resonant with the gurgle of limpid streams that babble under its bridges and beside its thoroughfares."[104] This idyllic scene, however, is at risk as, "a ruder civilization has disturbed the quiet current of old time."[105] This passage depicts the city

98 Ian Littlewood, *The Idea of Japan* (Chicago: Ivan R. Dee, 1996).
99 Brinkley, *The Kyoto Industrial Exhibition of 1895*, 14–15.
100 Ibid., 3.
101 Kobayashi, *Meiji Ishin to Kyōto*, 180.
102 Brinkley, *The Kyoto Industrial Exhibition of 1895*, 7.
103 Ibid., 10.
104 Ibid., 11.
105 Ibid., 11.

as harmonized with nature, but undergoing transformation from a calm and unchanging temporal realm of "old time" to a swiftly moving, turbulent and roaring "modern time." Later, in reference to Japanese art, Brinkley presents Kyoto and Japan as the last bastion of a world before capitalism and industrialization, writing that "this creator of marvels and despiser of profits, survives in Japan alone."[106] In a similar vein, the Palmer passage questions "how many years ... are likely to elapse before the chaste Miyako-Odori ... will give place to violent muscular achievements such as those with which troops of bounding, perspiring, and half-nude damsels charm the senses of theatre-goers in the West?"[107] These are all clear attempts by the author to attract foreign visitors to Kyoto before the forces of modernization change it irreparably, a strategy common even today in tourism advertising for pristine beaches and so-called "tribal tourism." This representation of Kyoto's culture as under threat by impending modernization is misleading, however, as Kyoto was already a leader in modernization within Japan. In addition, the Miyako dance was heavily inspired by Western forms of performance and organization. Again drawing on Palmer, Brinkley then expands from fear for the continuation of the Miyako dances and art to predict the passing of all of "old Japan." The guidebook questions whether, "is it possible to hope that this and other emblems of Japan's ancient and refined civilization can long survive the overwhelming tide of change and progress which is sweeping over the land? It is to be feared that all are doomed."[108] Brinkley's representation is therefore orientalist in its temporal framing of an imagined, glorified past that is antithetical to modernization. This creates a border separating an oriental past from a Western modernity.

While Brinkley's guide applauds some aspects of Kyoto's modernization, this is contradicted through an orientalist representation seeking to draw visitors to Kyoto before the weaker, tradition-based culture is inevitably corrupted by modernization. Research shows that Murray's handbook, the dominant English-language guidebook series of the period on Japan, utilized similar representations in portraying Japanese culture.[109] Brinkley's representation of Kyoto as under threat by modernization, therefore, is not exceptional, but part of more widespread orientalist discourses about Japan in English-language tourism media of the period. This would likely have encouraged foreign visitors to come to Kyoto, who perhaps would have readily accept the idea that they were not simply crossing national borders but one of a small number of

106 Ibid., 112.

107 Ibid., 19.

108 Ibid., 19.

109 Milne, "Discourses on Japan at the End of the Nineteenth Century in Murray Guidebooks."

lucky people who in visiting Japan, the last bastion of pre-modernity, could cross the border between the Western present and oriental past before that border permanently and irreversibly closed.

10 Comparisons

In their representations of Kyoto, its people and culture, the three guidebooks deal with the boundaries between self and other, East and West, past and present, tradition and modernity in diverse and complex ways. These differences reflect the development of new concepts of modernity and tradition, as well as understandings of how to disentangle these concepts from Western orientalist thinking that confined Kyoto and Japan to the static, tradition-directed Orient. Soon after the Meiji Restoration, Buddhist buildings, practices and articles, once a source of political and religious power, came to be reevaluated as out of date objects of superstitious belief that hindered modernization.[110] This was a point in which certain practices and objects of everyday life were reclassified as part of the pre-modern, feudal past, and divided from their modern equivalents. Influenced by thought regarding Western modernization and orientalist expectations of Japan, the past came to be reimagined as something that should be preserved and an important reference point for modernization.

By presenting Kyoto as tradition-oriented and unchanging, Yamamoto's 1873 guidebook engages with these discourses emphasizing the importance of tradition. Through omitting any reference to the rapid modernization of the city, in which Yamamoto himself was a key figure, it adopts an Orientalism that ignores the contemporary nature of Kyoto. However, the more condescending aspects of Orientalism that represent non-Western cultures as barbaric or inferior are not present. Yamamoto did not blindly adopt Orientalism in this guidebook therefore, but adapted and utilized it in similar ways to the "self-Orientalism" of other national contexts in order to portray Kyoto in a positive light believed to be attractive to foreign visitors.[111] Yamamoto did not attempt to represent Kyoto in a way that breached the borders of the "imagined geographies" of the ancient and unchanging Orient however. At this point, Kyoto's leaders were focused on regional redevelopment, and not devoted to nationalistic goals of putting Japan on equal footing with Western powers by breaking

110 Tanaka notes that this process is part of the experience of modernization worldwide. Tanaka, *New Times in Modern Japan*, 31–32.

111 Al-Azm, "Orientalism and Orientalism in Reverse." Also see Yan and Santos, "China Forever."

free of the orientalist mold. They therefore did not see the chance of being thought of as oriental as problematic.

The lack of representations of local people and culture in Yamamoto's guidebook, as highlighted in their comparison with Japanese-language guidebooks of the Edo-period, may also have been due to new ideas of the past. As evident in Kyoto city's attempt to ban Buddhist practices in 1871, there was a distinction made between objects of tradition, such as temple buildings, statues, and traditional craft pieces, which could readily be controlled by assigning them to the past as historical treasures, and some customs of the masses, which were thought to be superstitious, irrational, vulgar and, in the case of red-light and other areas of entertainment, immoral by Western standards, and therefore as antithetical to modernization. By not informing visitors of places where they might encounter such customs, the author may have hoped to hide these from Western eyes.

An additional reason that Yamamoto's guidebook did not present the local life of the city and portrayed Kyoto as traditional and unchanging can be found in Kyoto's unstable recent history, particularly the destruction of much of the city and its experience of anti-foreign violence. In the end these fears proved to be unfounded, as publications from the time show,[112] however considering the prominent position of some of those attacked it is understandable that some visitors might be concerned even though the civil war had ended. By representing Kyoto as traditional, tranquil, and stable Yamamoto attempted to circumvent these fears and encourage foreign readers to visit Kyoto.

Ichihara's guidebook presented not only Kyoto's history and tradition, but also symbols of modernization. The city's imperial legacy was used to draw this past and present together as well as show the popular support and strength of the nation. Again, the guidebook drew strongly on discourses defining the past, but this time to ones that gave local Kyoto sites and objects national significance and symbolized the nation's cohesion and unity over hundreds of years. Success in the First Sino-Japanese War provided an opportunity to demonstrate that Japan was equal with the Western powers and worthy of equal treatment. This provided the confidence for Japan to promote itself beyond the boundaries of Orientalism, as founded on a long, illustrious, and unique Japanese history, but also as dynamic and independently modern.

Brinkley's guidebook draws on orientalist imagery of Kyoto as a place in which visitors can cross borders between the rational and modernized West and the sensual and pre-modern Orient. Crossing from Western modernity to a

112 See Black, *Young Japan: Volume 2*, 856.

pre-modern, pre-industrial oriental past, the visitor could experience travel to an imagined time before industrialization. Through the Miyako Odori dances and local women, the visitor could become an oriental him or herself and experience the erotic Orient in which women were submissive objects for male display. Though some symbols of the city's modernization were presented in a positive light, modernization was generally represented as an immanent threat to the city, and used to encourage readers to visit Kyoto soon before this "oriental paradise" was ruined. Unlike the Ichihara guidebook, in which modernization and national tradition were in harmony, Brinkley's guide depicted modernization as a threatening, Western force opposed to Kyoto's oriental culture. This strategy to attract visitors is informed by orientalist discourses in which Kyoto's culture is treated as existing in a temporal vacuum of "tradition" and not coeval with "modern" and dynamic Western cultures.

11 Conclusion

This study confirms the criticisms of Said's theory of Orientalism provided by Pratt and others that while power inequalities help shape cross-cultural interaction, there is never a one-way imposition of ideas about cultural others or uncritical reception of these ideas.[113] Through analysis of three guidebooks and the "contact zones" of tourism, this study shows how interaction across national and cultural borders can be mediated through texts that vary greatly depending on the historical context, intellectual, national, and other discourses, the background of the author, and their expectations of their readership. The authors of all three guidebooks did their best to try to appeal to the desires of the readership in an effort to attract them to Kyoto while also attempting to present Kyoto, and for the 1895 books, the Japanese nation, in the most positive light. This included attempts at self-representation for the Japanese-authored textbooks, which involved "transculturation" in their adoption, adaptation, and criticism of discourses from the West and the opinion of Western expatriates. Yamamoto's guidebook attempted to show the people of Kyoto (and, in effect, Japan) as modern by displaying respect for their past, while seeking to allay the fears of foreign visitors through representing the city as peaceful and unchanged, and did this through employing self-Orientalism. Ichihara's guidebook strived to break down orientalist barriers between a

113 Pratt, *Imperial Eyes: Travel Writing and Transculturation*. Also al-Azm, "Orientalism and Orientalism in Reverse."

modernized West and pre-modern Kyoto and Japan. Brinkley's guidebook, which provided a portrait of an oriental other, drew on Orientalism in presenting Kyoto's (and Japan's) culture and (Western) modernity as incompatible.

Boundaries and shifts among them, especially between the self and other, West and East, present and past, and modern and ancient, were found to be central points of definition, redefinition, and negotiation in cross-cultural interaction and mediation. Shifts in understanding among Japanese intellectuals around ideas of the past, tradition, and modernity, as well as Japan's position in the world, greatly influenced the conception of these boundaries among local and national leaders and these leader's representations of Kyoto.

Comparative study of guidebooks and other mediators of cross-cultural encounters can expand our understanding of how international and domestic politics, historical legacies, discoursal shifts, ideas of self and other, power politics, and other factors influence interaction across national and cultural borders. This study has been an attempt to use tourism as a lens to further our understanding of the complex ways in which cross-cultural interaction is negotiated, mediated, and experienced, and to better appreciate the history on which today's national and cultural borders are built.

Bibliography

Agency for Cultural Affairs, Government of Japan. "Bunkazai." Last modified January 1, 2016. http://www.bunka.go.jp/seisaku/bunkazai/shokai/shitei.html.

Akatsuki, Kanenari. *Karaku Meishozue*. Kyoto, 1864. International Research Center for Japanese Studies, Miyako Meishozue Data Base. Accessed January 10, 2016. http://www.nichibun.ac.jp/meisyozue/kyoto/c-pg1.html.

Akizato, Ritō. *Miyako Meishozue*. Naniwa, 1780. International Research Center for Japanese Studies, Miyako Meishozue Database. Accessed January 10, 2016. http://www.nichibun.ac.jp/meisyozue/kyoto/c-pg1.html.

Arayama, Masahiko. "Meijiki ni okeru Eibun Nihon Ryokō Annaisho no Kankō." *Ōsaka Daigaku Nihongakuhō* 10 (1991): 123–140.

Al-Azm, Sadik Jalal. "Orientalism and Orientalism in Reverse." In *Orientalism: A Reader*, edited by Alexander Lyon Macfie. Edinburgh: Edinburgh University Press, 2000.

Behdad, Ali. *Belated Travelers*. North Carolina: Duke University Press, 1994.

Bhattacharyya, Deborah. "Mediating India: An Analysis of a Guidebook." *Annals of Tourism Research* 24, no. 2 (1997): 371–389.

Bianchi, Raoul V., and Stephenson, Marcus L. *Tourism and Citizenship: Rights, Freedoms and Responsibilities in the Global Order*. Oxon: Routledge, 2014.

Black, John. *Young Japan: Volume II*. London: Trubner, 1881.

Brinkley, Francis. *The Kyoto Industrial Exhibition of 1895*. Tokyo: Japan Mail Office, 1895.
Burton, Robert. "Early Photography of Japan." *Harvard College Library*. Last modified April, 2012. https://library.harvard.edu/sites/default/files/static/collections/epj/tourist_photography.html.
Butler, Richard, and Wantanee Suntikul, eds. *Tourism and War*. London: Routledge, 2013.
Buzard, James. 'The Grand Tour and After.' In P. Hulme & T. Youngs (Eds.), *The Cambridge Companion to Travel Writing*. Cambridge, England: Cambridge University Press, 2005.
Dower, John. "The Meiji Emperor and Invention of the Modern Emperor System." *MIT Visualizing Cultures*. Accessed January 10, 2016. http://ocw.mit.edu/ans7870/21f/21f.027/throwing_off_asia_01/toa_vis_01.html.
Fabian, Johannes. *Time and the Other*. New York: Columbia University Press, 2002.
Foucault, Michel. *The Archaeology of Knowledge*. 1969. Reprint, London: Routledge, 2002.
Francesconi, Sabrina. *Reading Tourism Texts: A Multimodal Analysis*. Bristol: Channel View Publications, 2014.
Fujita, Satoru. *Bakumatsu kara Ishin he*. Tokyo: Iwanami Shinsho, 2015.
Harris, Neil. "All the World a Melting Pot? Japan at American Fairs, 1876–1904." In *Mutual Images: Essays in American-Japanese Relations*, edited by Akira Iriye. Cambridge: Harvard University Press, 1975.
Hashitsume, Shinya. *Nihon no Hakurankai*. Tokyo: Heibansha, 2005.
Hellyer, Robert I. *Defining Engagement: Japan and Global Contexts, 1640–1868*. Cambridge: Harvard University Asia Center, 2009.
Hobsbawm, Eric and Terence Ranger. *The Invention of Tradition*. Cambridge: Cambridge University Press, 1984.
Ichihara, M. *The Official Guide-Book to Kyoto and the Allied Prefectures*. Nara: Meishinsha, 1895.
Igeda, Ryōji and Kumiko Harada. *Kyōto no Hyakunen*. Tokyo: Yamakawa Publishing, 1993.
Inden, Ronald. "Orientalist Constructions of India." In *Orientalism: A Reader*, edited by Alexander Lyon Macfie. Edinburgh: Edinburgh University Press, 2000.
International Research Center for Japanese Studies Digital Archive. *Miyako Meishozue Data Base*. Accessed January 10, 2016. http://www.nichibun.ac.jp/meisyozue/kyoto/c-pg1.html.
Kasahara, Kazuto. "Rekishi Kankō Hakurankai." *10+1* 36 (2004): 164–177.
King, Richard. "Orientalism, Hinduism and Feminism." In *Orientalism: A Reader*, edited by Alexander Lyon Macfie. Edinburgh: Edinburgh University Press, 2000.
Kobayashi, Takehiro. *Meiji Ishin to Kyōto*. Kyoto: Rinsen Books, 1998.
Koshar, Rudy. *German Travel Cultures*. Oxford: Berg Publishers, 2000.
Kudō, Yoshiko. "Meiji Shoki Kyōto no Hakurankai to Kankō." *Kyōto Kōka Joshidaigaku Kenkyū Kiyo* 46 (2008): 77–100.
Kuwayama, Takami. *Native Anthropology*. Melbourne: Trans Pacific Press, 2004.

Kyoto Prefectural General Archives. "Yamamoto Kakuma to Kyōto Hakurankai." Last modified April 1, 2013. http://www.pref.kyoto.jp/shiryokan/documents/dayori175.pdf.

Laderman, Scott. *Tours of Vietnam*. Durham: Duke University Press, 2009.

Lisle, Debbie. *Holidays in the Danger Zone*. Minneapolis: University of Minnesota, 2016.

Littlewood, Ian. *The Idea of Japan*. Chicago: Ivan R. Dee, 1996.

Mills, Sara. *Discourse*. London: Routledge, 2004.

Milne, Daniel. "Discourses on Japan at the End of the Nineteenth Century in Murray Guidebooks." *Social Systems: Political, Legal and Economic Studies* 16 (2013): 135–152.

Munemasa, Iso. *Miyako Meishozue o Yomu*. Tokyo: Tokyo Do Publishing, 1997.

Nagasaka, Keina. "Meiji Shoki ni okeru Nihon Hatsu no Gaikokujin Muke Ryokō Gaidobukku." *Shakaigaku Kenkyūka Kiyo* 69 (2010): 101–115.

Nish, Ian. *The Anglo-Japanese Alliance: The Diplomacy of Two Island Empires 1884–1907*. Rev. ed. London: Bloomsbury Publishing, 2012.

Okada, Mariko. "Before Making Heritage: Internationalisation of Geisha in the Meiji Period." In *Making Japanese Heritage*, edited by Christoph Brumann and Robert A. Cox. London: Routledge, 2010.

Pratt, Mary Louise. *Imperial Eyes: Travel Writing and Transculturation*. London: Routledge, 1992.

Pyle, Kenneth. *The New Generation in Meiji Japan*. Stanford: Stanford University Press, 1970.

Ramm, Wiebke. "Textual Variation in Travel Guides." In *Discourse and Community*, edited by Eija Ventola. Tubingen: Gunter Narr Verlag, 2000.

Ruoff, Kenneth. *Imperial Japan at its Zenith*. New York: Cornell University Press, 2010.

Said, Edward. *Orientalism: Western Concepts of the Orient*. Rev. ed. London: Penguin, 1995.

Said, Edward. "Shattered Myths." In *Orientalism: A Reader*, edited by Alexander Lyon Macfie. Edinburgh: Edinburgh University Press, 2000.

Satow, Ernest. *A Diplomat in Japan*. London: Seeley, 1921; Reprint, Berkeley: Stone Bridge Press, 2006.

Selwyn, Tom. *The Tourist Image: Myths and Myth Making in Tourism*. Chichester: John Wiley and Sons, 1996.

Smith, Valene, ed. *Hosts and Guests*. Philadelphia: University of Pennsylvania Press, 1989.

Soyama, Takeshi. *Shokuminchi Taiwan to Kindai Tsurizumu*. Tokyo: Seikyusha, 2003.

Stavros, Matthew. *Kyoto: An Urban History of Japan's Premodern Capital*. Honolulu: University Hawaii Press, 2014.

Tanaka, Stefan. *New Times in Modern Japan*. Princeton: Princeton University, 2004.

Tegelberg, Matthew. "Hidden Sights: Tourism, Representation and Lonely Planet Cambodia." *International Journal of Cultural Studies* 13, no. 5 (2010): 491–509.

Tipton, Elise. *Modern Japan: A Social and Political History*. Oxon: Routledge, 2008.

Turner, Katherine S. H. "From Classical to Imperial: Changing Visions of Turkey in the Eighteenth Century." In *Travel Writing and Empire*, edited by Steven Clark. London: Zed Books, 1999.

Yamamoto, Kakuma. *Kanken*. Kyoto, 1870. Accessed January 10, 2016. http://library.doshisha.ac.jp/ir/digital/archive/yamamoto/128/imgidx128.html.

Yamamotoa, Kakuma. *The Guide to the Celebrated Places in Kiyoto*. Kyoto: Niwa, 1873. Reprint, Kyoto: Doshisha University, 1981.

Yan, Grace, and Carla Santos. "China Forever: Tourism Discourse and Self-Orientalism." *Annals of Tourism Research* 36, no. 2 (2009): 295–315.

CHAPTER 3

Seeking the Ideal Identity

Cosmopolitanism Advocated by Japanese Americans

Mariko Mizuno

1 Introduction*

In today's globalized world, people who live in more than one country and culture are receiving attention in both the media and higher education. As they begin to ask where they belong while they are gradually settling in a new society, they may face an identity crisis. Japanese Americans are not excepted from such an experience. Japanese began to immigrate to the United States at the end of the nineteenth century, and struggled with the difficulties of living in a different culture. We can assume that the impact and shock of leaving Japan and confronting a new culture was much more than one might expect today. For those early immigrants, only about fifty years had passed since Japan had reopened to the world and its people began learning about foreign countries.

As for the identity of the people who crossed from Japan to the US, a lot of research in various areas has dealt with the issue. The term "identity crisis" was first created by the prominent developmental psychologist, Eric Erikson (1902–1994), who focused on the issue of personal identity struggles from the adolescent stage to adulthood.[1] His theory influenced other academic fields such as anthropology and sociology, so that considering the issue of identity became a fundamental and natural part of researchers' analyses of either individual or group social experiences, or community or national histories.

In the area of literature and literary history, the issue of identity has been discussed repeatedly as well. The culmination of the discussion was brought about by the significant ethnic cultural and political events of Asian-American movement, which prompted Asian American writers and researchers to ask themselves what their identities were. Being strongly influenced by the civil rights and anti-war movements of the 1950s and 1960s, the Asian-American

* Note: This section observes Western name order, i.e., given name first, followed by the family name.

1 Joan Shelley Rubin and Scott E. Casper, eds. *The Oxford Encyclopedia of American Cultural and Intellectual History* vol.1 (New York: Oxford University Press, 2013), 359.

 | DOI:10.1163/9789004435506_005

movement started at San Francisco State University in the late of the 1960s when students went on a strike to request the establishment of an ethnic studies department to their university.[2] Second and third generation Japanese Americans, or *nisei* and *sansei*, actively began to ask themselves about their identities, and expressed their struggles to seek their clear identities through poetry and novels. This movement in the field of literature was first seen in the publication of *Aiiieeeee!* (1974), in which previously dismissed works such as John Okada's *No-No Boy* (1957), and Toshio Mori's *Yokohama, California* (1949) were reevaluated and introduced to the readers as pioneering works written by *nisei* writers.[3]

The notion of identity was also developed into the theory of ethnic identity from the ethnic studies point of view, a discipline that considered Japanese Americans' unstable and changing ethnic identity.[4] By creating their own ethnic identities, *nisei* and *sansei* emphasized that they were ethnic minorities who had been suppressed and had suffered from the inequality granted by the social majority. They were active in both political and literary venues where they worked to make their voices heard as Asian Americans. In Asian-American literature and criticism, the issues of identity, ethnic identity, and ethnicity have been kept as key concepts in order to appreciate Japanese-American literature, and in almost every work of literature the identities of the writers and protagonists are analyzed.[5]

2 Steve Louie and Glenn Omatsu, eds. *Asian Americans: The Movement and the Moment* (Los Angeles: UCLA Asian American Studies Center Press, 2006), xv–xxv; Daryl Joji Maeda, *Rethinking the Asian American Movement* (New York: Routledge, 2011), 9–51.

3 Frank Chin et al., eds. *Aiiieeeee!: An Anthology of Asian American Writers* (Washington, D.C.: Howard University Press, 1974).

4 Maigreishon Kenkyūkai, ed. *Esunishiti wo toinaosu: Riron to henyō* [Reclaiming ethnicity: Theories and changes] (Nishinomiya: Kwansei Gakuin University Press, 2007). In this book, Fumisato Minamikawa summarizes the theoretical backgrounds of ethnicity and ethnic identity in the US and develops an idea of how ethnic identity should be understood and described. Among numerous references, he emphasizes the importance of the following works as basic frameworks of descriptions of ethnicity: Werner Sollors, *Beyond Ethnicity: Consent and Descent in American Culture* (New York: Oxford University Press, 1986); Stephen Steinburg, *Turning Back: The Retreat from Racial Justice in American Thought and Policy* (Boston: Beacon Press, 1995).

5 Elaine H. Kim, *Asian American Literature: An Introduction to the Writings and Their Social Context* (Philadelphia: Temple University Press, 1982); Sau-Ling Cynthia Wong, *Reading Asian American Literature: From Necessity to Extravagance* (Princeton: Princeton University Press, 1993); King-Kok Cheung, *Articulate Silences* (New York: Cornell University Press, 1993); King-Kok Cheung, ed. *An Interethnic Companion to Asian American Literature* (New York: Cambridge University Press, 1997).

Although the Asian-American movement and the field of ethnic studies shed light on the new area of ethnic identity, on the other hand, they lacked the viewpoint of the identity issues faced by first-generation Japanese immigrants, or *issei*, who, in particular, were not allowed to obtain US citizenship because of the exclusive Immigration Act of 1924. After the Asian-American movement, *nisei* and *sansei* could emphasize their citizenships and civil rights in the US. Ultimately, *issei*, who could become naturalized under the enactment of the Immigration and Naturalization Act of 1965 and had the chance to insist that they too belonged in the US, did not throw away their ties with Japan; however, less attention has been paid to their ethnic-identity issues that reflected the ways they struggled and survived in the early immigration era when they began to create Japanese communities and settle in the US.

This lack of awareness of *issei* issues would eventually be covered by Japanese researchers who tried to see Japanese-American history and literature from the beginning of Japanese immigration to the US. Influenced by the Asian-American movement and subsequent research on Japanese-American literature, scholars in Japan also showed their interest in Asian-American and Japanese immigrants' history and literature. For example, the Asian American Literature Association was established in 1989 and played a leading role of this area in Japan.[6] In addition, the new social background, such as seen in the increase in Japanese descendants from South America joining the workforce in Japan, and the increase in the number of Asian and Mexican immigrants in the US after Immigration and Naturalization Act of 1965, prompted Japanese researchers to pay attention to the topic of Japanese emigrants. Therefore, the life experiences of Japanese in America were reinvestigated and evaluated, and their identity struggle was documented in such areas of studies as history, literature, and sociology.[7]

In these studies, the issue of first-generation Japanese Americans' identities have been discussed and analyzed as being complicated, often shifting between Japan and America depending on the circumstances in which each person was involved. Their recognition of identity also varied according to their social status, gender and personality. Whether they got to be American citizens or not also influenced their sense of identity. Generally, it was said that they first recognized their ethnic and cultural features as Japanese, but

6 Teruyo Ueki and Gayle K. Sato, eds. *Nikkei amerika bungaku: Sansedai no kiseki wo yomu* [Reading Japanese American literature: The legacy of three generations] (Tokyo: Sōgensha, 1997).

7 Imin Kenkyū Kai, ed. *Nihon-no imin kenkyū: Doukou to bunken mokuroku* [Immigrants studies in Japan: Trends and bibliography] vol.2 (Tokyo: Akashi Shoten, 2008), 3–6.

gradually acquired their sense of identity as Japanese Americans as distinct from Japanese living in Japan.[8]

In order to cope with such identity crises, some Japanese intellectuals living in the US in the 1920s and 1930s used words such as "world citizen" and "cosmopolitan" to describe themselves. As I show later in this chapter, although the meaning of the phrases varied depending on each intellectual, it was used after their long process of identity seeking. For instance, Riichirō Hoashi (1881–1963),[9] a Japanese student at the University of Southern California, contributed an essay titled "Cosmopolitanism" to the university's Japanese Student Association yearbook, *Japanese El Rodeo*, in 1912. He regarded himself as a cosmopolitan who transcended his nationality and race.[10] The West Coast Japanese-American writer, Kyūin Okina (1888–1973) proposed the idea of *sekaijin*, the world citizen, and publicized it to the readers of Japanese-American writing in 1924. He returned to Japan in the same year, and four years later, he published a book, *Kosumoporitan wa kataru* (A cosmopolitan speaks),[11] which was composed of essays written during his stay in the US and after returning to Japan. This book clearly represented his identity as a cosmopolitan. In addition, haiku poet Issō Shimoyama (1879–1935), described himself as a "cosmopolitan" on one of the pages of letters he sent to his family in Japan in the 1920s.[12] This explicit use of terminology like "cosmopolitan" to reflect identity

8 Minako K. Maykovich, *Japanese American Identity Dilemma* (Tokyo: Waseda University, 1972); Souken Togami, *Japanese American: Ijyū kara jiritsu he no ayumi* [Japanese Americans: A process of immigration to independence] (Kyoto: Mineruva Shobō, 1985); Yuji Ichioka, *The Issei: The World of the First Generation Japanese Immigrants, 1885–1924* (New York: Free Press, 1988); Stephen S. Fugita and David J. O'Brien, *Japanese American Ethnicity: The Persistence of Community* (Seattle and London: University of Washington Press, 1991); Yasuo Sakata, "Conflicting Identities: Issei and Nisei in the 1930's," *Osaka Gakuin University International Colloquium* (1991): 133–160; Yasuko Takezawa, *Nikkei amerikajin no esunishiti: Kyousei syūyou to hosyou undou ni yoru hensen* [The transformation of Japanese American ethnicity: The effects of internment and redress] (Tokyo: Tokyo University Press, 1994); Masako Iino, *Mouhitotsu no nichibei kankeishi: Funsō to kyōchō no naka no nikkei amerikajin* [Another history of relationship between Japan and America: Japanese Americans living in the conflicts and cooperation] (Tokyo: Yūhikaku, 2000); Fumisato Minamikawa, *Nikkei amerikajin no rekishi shakaigaku: Esunishiti, jinshu, nashonarizumu* [Historical sociology on Japanese Americans: Ethnicity, race, nationalism] (Tokyo: Sairyūsha, 2007).

9 *Nihon jinmei daijiten* (Tokyo: Kōdansha, 2015), accessed June 25, 2020, https://kotobank.jp/dictionary/nihonjinmei/.

10 Riichirō Hoashi, "Cosmopolitanism," *Japanese El Rodeo* 1 (July 1912): 15–25.

11 Kyūin Okina, *Kosumoporitan wa kataru* [A cosmopolitan speaks] (Tokyo: Jueikaku, 1928).

12 Issō Shimoyama to his younger brother, Shirō Shimoyama, January 5, 1927. Shimoyama's private collection. I would like to express my gratitude to Ms. Mutsuko Shimoyama for access to this collection.

as represented by the first generation has rarely been examined. Several studies have referred to the identity of cosmopolitanism of the above three Japanese Americans respectively, however, they did not clarify the meaning or the context in which the word was used.[13]

Moreover, there is an interesting fact related to people's identification with cosmopolitanism. American writers and philosophers such as Alain Locke (1885–1954), Horace Kallen (1882–1974), and Randolph Bourne (1886–1918) also presented similar theories which included the idea of cosmopolitanism in the same era. Locke was regarded as the "Father of the Harlem Renaissance," and contributed to the development of African-American literature and art.[14] Kallen was a Jew born in Germany who became an American philosopher advocating cultural pluralism.[15] Bourne was regarded as a leftist intellectual for his radical criticism of liberal intellectuals. He was physically disabled and passed away in his early thirties leaving a number of thought-provoking and progressive works about issues of nation and democracy.[16] Locke wrote a manuscript titled "Cosmopolitanism" (1908),[17] in which he presented a new cosmopolitanism as an alternative to the former one that had been discussed among Western philosophers. Kallen, who was Locke's lifetime friend, published an article, "Democracy Versus the Melting-Pot" (1915),[18] in which he criticized the one national model of Anglo-Saxon culture, and presented the new model of "cultural pluralism." Bourne also had ideas about nations similar to those Kallen presented, and he focused on the importance of transnational

13 Kristina S. Vassil, "Passages: Writing Diasporic Identity in the Literature of Early Twentieth-Century Japanese America." PhD diss., University of Michigan, 2011, Chapter 2; Eiichiro Azuma, *Between Two Empires: Race, History, and Transnationalism in Japanese America* (New York: Oxford University Press, 2005), 5–4; Teruko Kumei, "Amerika gasshūkoku tanshikei bungaku kou: Shimoyama Issō wo chūshin ni" [An analysis on Japanese short poems in the United States: Focusing on Issō Shimoyama], A Presentation in International Research Center for Japanese Studies, July 19, 2014.

14 *Stanford Encyclopedia of Philosophy Online,* s.v. "Alain LeRoy Locke," accessed June 25, 2020, https://plato.stanford.edu/entries/alain-locke.

15 Ayako Uchida, "Tayōsei to chōwa: H. M. Kallen no bunka tagen shugi" [Diversity and harmony: Cultural pluralism of H. M. Kallen], *Amerika Kenkyū* [The American review], no. 29 (1995): 217–228.

16 Mari Jo Buhle, Paul Buhle, and Dan Georgakas, eds. *Encyclopedia of the American Left* (New York: Oxford University Press, 1988), 100–101.

17 Yuri Sakuma, "Amerika kokunai no kosumoporitanizumu: Alain Locke no kosumoporitanizumu kara yominaosu *The New Negro*" [Cosmopolitanism within a nation: Alain Locke's cosmopolitanism and *The New Negro*] *Amerika Bungaku Kenkyū* [Studies in American literature], no.49 (2013): 21–38.

18 Horace M. Kallen, "Democracy versus the Melting-Pot: A Study of American Nationality," *The Nation* 100, no.2591(1915): 217–220.

identities and the ideal state of a modern nation in "Trans-national America" (1916).[19] Regardless of some differences among these American writers, they may have had some intellectual influences on each other, and may have also been influenced by the social situations of America which was thriving as a large multi-ethnic country.

To make up for the lack of attention paid by ethnic studies to *issei* life experiences in the era of early Japanese immigration to the US, and to explore a new and explicitly-named identity instead of being limited to an ambiguous identity expressed in Japanese-American immigrants' studies, this chapter deals with the idea of cosmopolitanism advocated by Japanese Americans around the 1920s and 1930s, and clarifies the ideal identity they sought. As the first step, this chapter focuses on the writer Kyūin Okina, who clearly explained his identity as a cosmopolitan, and considers why he advocated the idea and what, exactly, he meant from the word by analyzing both his personal and social environments.[20] In addition, Okina's idea of cosmopolitanism will be compared with American philosophers' similar ideas of cosmopolitanism and with other Japanese Americans' self-identification as a cosmopolitan. By doing so, this chapter will present the common aspects of their ideas that may have been created in the same social environment, and also the differences of contexts, revealing how ideas of cosmopolitanism were produced. This will lead to an understanding of the trends of thought represented by people who crossed "the border" or by people who were interested in American racial and ethnic issues and the state of America as an ideal nation integrating immigrants in the 1920s and 1930s.

2 Kyūin Okina and His Idea of Cosmopolitan

2.1 *Okina's Background: Searching for His Identity*

Okina was a leading journalist and writer who advocated for the need for Japanese Americans to create their own literature, an "immigrant literature,"

---

19 Randolph Bourne, "Trans-National America," *Atlantic Monthly*117, (July 1916): 86–97; Reiko Maekawa, "Randolph Bourne saikou: Dai ichiji sekai taisenka no amerika chishikijin" [Randolph Bourne reconsidered: An American intellectual under the shadow of World War I], *Amerikashi kenkyū* [Studies of American history], no.27 (July 2004): 20–34.

20 As I explain later, Okina went to the US in May 1907 and returned to Japan in March 1924. It is slightly inaccurate to include Okina in the category of *issei*, based on the fact that the term is used for those who migrated permanently to the US, but I do so because his life and literary activities in America were based on Japanese-American communities and represented the first generation's thoughts and feelings.

in the 1910s and 1920s. He wrote a large number of short stories, several long novels, and literary reviews and essays in order to realize the idea of immigrant literature. In his estimation, one important theme was Japanese Americans' ambiguous identity. Looking back on his life beginning with his boyhood, when he decided to go to the US, he found he had always been considering who he was, where he belonged, and what kind of people Japanese should be in the context of the wider world.

Okina was born in a small village called Rokurōdani in Japan's Toyama prefecture in 1888, twenty years after Japan had initiated the Meiji Restoration that signaled Japan's modern period after a long self-imposed seclusion from the rest of the world.[21] His father was a competent doctor of Chinese medicine, and he educated Kyūin and his older brother very strictly, hoping that they could also become doctors. Kyūin was good at studying; however, when he was in the second year of Toyama Junior High School (currently Toyama Prefectural High School) he was involved in mischief with his friends, and all eight students were expelled from school. In despair, with his father's advice, he went to Tokyo to attend a private school in preparation for entering college. There he met several young students who were daring to go to America to see an advanced culture and learn English. They expected that when they came back to Japan, they could get better jobs and higher status. The atmosphere that prevailed among young men in those days, called *tobei-netsu,* means having "strong zeal for going to America." Because of his unexpected failure in school and the harsh treatment he got from teachers and educators, he was disappointed with rural Japanese society and longed to go abroad in order to seek another identity instead of Japanese. As he explains in *Kosmoporitan wa kataru,* he went to the US in order to become "a cosmopolitan," by which he meant that he would become a stateless and free person without nationality.[22]

In May 1907, Okina arrived in Seattle where he found temporary jobs such as housekeeping and strawberry picking like other Japanese sojourners usually did. However, recognizing that in Seattle he was living in a primarily Japanese district, and was still immersed in Japanese culture, he left for Bremerton,

21 Okina's biographical information comes mainly from the following sources: Okina Kyūin, *Okina Kyūin zenshū* [The complete works of Kyūin Okina], ed. Okina Kyūin et al., vol.2 (Toyama: Okina Kyūin Zenshū Kankōkai, 1972); Kumi Itsumi and Mitsuru Suda, eds. *Okina Kyūin nenpu: 1888–1973* [Chronological record of Kyūin Okina: 1888–1973], 3rd ed. (Tokyo: Okina Kyūin Zaidan, 2020). For more information about Okina and his idea of cosmopolitanism, see Mariko Mizuno, *Nikkei amerikajin no bungakukatsudō no rekishitekihensen: 1880 nendai kara 1980 nendai ni kakete* [The history of Japanese American's literary activities: from the 1880s to the 1980s] (Tokyo: Kazama Shobō, 2013), 67–156.

22 Okina, *Kosumoporitan wa kataru*, 1–9.

Washington, a port city that had a much smaller Japanese population. He became a "school boy," doing housework in the daytime while staying with an American family, and going to school in the evening. Although he left Seattle to distance himself from Japanese people, he soon came to feel very lonely and isolated in an environment dominated by the English language. He realized that his thoughts and feelings were based on Japanese language and Japanese cultural tradition; in order to find out who he was, he started to write short novels in Japanese to ease his isolated feelings. Almost every day, he wrote short stories and sent them to several Japanese-American newspapers published in Seattle. By doing so, Okina became a member of the young Japanese men's group comprised of those who were interested in literature, and they discussed the themes of love and life that were central to modern Japanese literature in that era, especially for young amateur writers. Although he struggled to cope with his life in America, he anticipated that he would go home in the near future and hoped to become a professional writer in Japan.

In 1913, he married a Japanese woman from the same prefecture while he was temporarily in his hometown (figure 3.1). He alone came back to America and began to work at a grocery shop. In 1914, he was asked to be a correspondent of a magazine, *Taiheiraku* (Happy and nonchalant) published by *Saeki Benri-sha* (A limited partnership company headquartered in Hiroshima), then his wife joined him and they started a new life in Stockton, California. Having his own family, he gradually came to settle into Japanese-American society. In 1915, he became a journalist and head of the Stockton branch office of the Japanese-American newspaper, *Ōfu Nippō* (Sacramento Daily News). He also became a leading member of the Japanese American Organization in Stockton. He met a lot of poor Japanese immigrants and invited them to become members of the organization as well. This experience helped him understand Japanese Americans' difficulties and realities, and he came to feel a strong tie with them. He earnestly wrote short nonfiction pieces and serialized novels, titled *Akuno hikage* (The evil shadow, 1915), and *Akaki hi no ato* (The trace of the red sun, 1916) depicting a young Japanese-American man who struggled to live in Japanese-American society, with all of its troubles and agonies, including situations in which he faces racism.

Recognizing his writing talent, Kyūtaro Abiko, a founder of the Japanese-American newspaper, *Nichibei*, invited Okina to head the paper's branch at Oakland in 1918. He edited the literary section and encouraged the readers to write short novels and tanka and haiku poems. He also contributed essays about immigrant literature, and discussed the qualities of literature and the themes that should be included in literature about Japanese immigrant society. By this time, he had recognized himself as a Japanese American,

FIGURE 3.1 Kyūin Okina and his wife, Kiyoko, in Stockton, California around 1915
SOURCE: KYŪIN OKINA, *OKINA KYŪIN ZENSHŪ* [THE COMPLETE WORKS OF KYŪIN OKINA], EDS. KYŪIN OKINA ET AL., VOL.5. (TOYAMA: OKINA KYŪIN ZENSHŪ KANKŌKAI, 1971), III. REPRODUCED WITH PERMISSION

one who had an ambiguous identification with both Japan and America. He insisted that Japanese Americans should have their own literature, one which described their struggles to live in an unfamiliar culture. He regarded Japanese-Americans literature as unique and totally dissimilar to Japanese literature from and circulated in Japan.

In order to create immigrant literature, Okina focused his keen eyes on social and political problems in Japanese-American communities, such as the second generation's education, the collapse of couples and family relationships at home, picture brides that were condemned by mainstream American society, the cultural gaps between the first and second generation, and the continuing anti-Japanese movement in America. In addition, he broadened his knowledge about world politics, criticized Japan from outside, and often wrote his views on Japan for his hometown's local newspaper. In 1921, he went to Washington D.C. to report on the Washington Naval Conference as a correspondent for *Nichibei*.

At the beginning of 1924, he received a letter from his family informing him that his father was in critical medical condition. Okina again had to face his identity problem. Although he had almost made up his mind to stay in America, he decided to go back to Japan to tend to his father. While he was wondering if he should return to Japan completely, he found that his wife was expecting their third child when they were on board the ship. By then, the US

Immigration Act of 1924 had passed the United States Congress and was signed by the president. According to the law, Okina's third child, who would be born in Japan, would not be allowed to enter America, while Okina, his wife, and his first son could return. Okina did not want his family separated, so he decided to settle in Japan with his family.[23]

2.2 *An Answer for His Identity Quest: The Idea of Sekaijin and Cosmopolitanism*

2.2.1 The Idea of Sekaijin

Although Okina's identity quest continued throughout his stay in the US, he reached a tentative answer sometime in the 1920s. This became the most important principle of his lifetime, one which influenced his viewpoints and literary activities in his later life. In 1924, he contributed a series of essays, "Beikoku kara no kansou" (Impressions from America), to a local newspaper in his hometown, *Toyama Nippō*.[24] In the first essay he clearly showed his idea of *sekaijin*, "the world citizen," and the original idea of the word he would use later, "cosmopolitan." In this essay, Okina intended to let people in his hometown know the life and issues of Japanese immigrants in America, and to show critical viewpoints on Japanese society in Japan and the Japanese ways of thinking by comparing them with American society and the moral values represented by democracy, justice, and humanitarianism. He considered social problems in Japan from the standpoint of a Japanese living in America. His idea has two interesting characteristics. The first is that it is based on his experience of leaving his hometown and departing from Japan to live in America in search of liberty and wider society. The second characteristic is that his idea was strongly influenced by his own experience of racial discrimination and the long struggle of Japanese immigrants against the anti-Japanese sentiment in America.

As for the first point, Okina showed how human beings are integrated into societies and how, as they expand their places to live, they are changing their identities. For example, a person like Okina, who is first born in a *mura*, a rural Japanese village, is called a *mura-no mon*, a villager. When he is older, he goes to school in a *machi*, a town outside of the village, and recognizes himself as a *machi-no mon*, a townsman. If he decides to leave his prefecture and enter a college in a larger city like Tokyo, he meets other students from different prefectures. At that time, he first identifies himself as a person from a prefecture,

23 The first daughter, Michiko passed away in 1917 when she was only eleven months old.

24 Kyūin Okina, "Beikoku karano kansou," no.1–12, *Toyama Nippō*, from January 1 to January14 in 1924.

for example, *Toyama mon*, a person from Toyama prefecture. Furthermore, if he endeavors to go to America and meets people from different nations, he regards himself as Japanese. As you can see, when people move to larger societies, their recognition of their identities also changes based on where they live. Okina developed his idea from his experience of leaving his hometown and going to the United States.

In addition, when a person enters the larger society, he first persists in his previous sense of belonging and regards other persons from different places as *yoso-no mon*, outsiders, and tends to exclude them. However, as people from different places are integrated into the same society, they gradually communicate with each other, share the same identity as members of the same society and finally stop excluding each other. In this context, Okina thinks that Japanese people tend to have a narrow mindset and exclude others because they come from different local areas. Therefore, he insists that all Japanese should first acknowledge that they are Japanese, withdrawing any exclusive sense of identity based on their respective local origins such as villages, towns and prefectures. Then he argues that Japanese should throw away such a feeling of excluding others and recognize themselves as *sekaijin* (world citizens) when they leave Japan and go to another country. When they understand the idea of *sekaijin* and behave as if they are truly *sekaijin*, they are also regarded as real human beings who can coexist with other people from different countries.

The important point of Okina's idea of *sekaijin* is that the image is not the universal human being who loses Japanese ethnic identity. He explains an impression that occurred to him when he saw a picture of the staff of the first Japanese Embassy to the United States in 1860, around the end of Edo period. The members in the picture seemed confident and proud of Japan, wearing Japanese traditional kimono in the samurai style. Okina explains their appearance and attitude as an example of Japanese ethnicity and culture in those days. They did not show any timidity or lack of confidence in the land of America, which they regarded as a much more advanced country than Japan, and which they regarded as a powerful imperial country. Their magnificent attitude showed that they were Japanese and at the same time human beings, *sekaijin* who could survive in different countries in harmony with other nations' people. Comparing the attitude of the members of the embassy, he criticized general Japanese people who tended to superficially accept and follow the trend of westernization without noticing the real goodness of Japanese culture.

As the second interesting point, his idea of *sekaijin* is strongly associated with racial issues. In the essay "Beikoku kara no kansou," Okina discusses

Japanese people's racial discrimination against Koreans living in Japan.[25] In 1923, an earthquake caused great damage to the Kanto region that includes Tokyo. In the confusion of the earthquake, a false rumor that Koreans rioted and set fires was circulated. Armed forces were sent out to subdue the riots. From his standpoint as a Japanese living in America, Okina criticized the Japanese who called Koreans "insubordinate Koreans." He felt upset when he read the unpleasant articles full of discriminatory words against Koreans that described the incident in Japanese newspapers published in Japan. He strongly doubted if the confusion was really caused by such "insubordinate Koreans." Over the course of the incident, Okina strongly criticized both the Japanese people who blindly discriminated against Koreans in Japan and the Japanese society which allowed this kind of incident to happen. He pointed out that Japanese people in Japan were obsessed with the idea of excluding others, and therefore they could not communicate with Koreans. To discard that sense of exclusiveness, he concluded that people should adopt the identity of *sekai-jin*. His harsh criticism of Japanese in Japan focused on their having not yet acquired a sense of justice and humanitarianism, generally considered to be seen in America as the ideal that influenced the founding of the country. His notion is clearly based on his experience as a Japanese person who was also discriminated against by Americans.

Among the things he learned from America, the most important is that there are so many different races living in the world. The idea of *sekaijin*, he perceived, was mostly influenced by this recognition of races and his experience of racism. As soon as he arrived and started his life in Seattle in 1907, he found that he was also regarded as "one of the Japanese," who had been harshly judged as an inferior people. In 1906, only one year before his arrival in the US, the San Francisco School Board instituted segregation of Japanese students in the city's school amid the confusion created by the earthquake. This incident caused a deterioration of the relationship between Japan and America. Based on the 1907 Gentleman's Agreement, through which Japan and the US tried to settle the issue of anti-Japanese agitation on the West Coast, the Japanese government stopped issuing passports to Japanese laborers, and in return the California state legislature withdrew its anti-Japanese bills. Despite these measures taken by both governments, anti-Japanese feeling persisted.[26]

---

25 Okina, "Beikoku kara no kansou," no.9, *Toyama Nippō*, January 11, 1924.

26 Iino, *Mouhitotsu no nichibei kankeishi*, 30–34; Toshihiro Minohara, *Cariforuniashū no hainichi undō to nichibei kankei: Imin mondai wo meguru nichibei masatsu, 1906–1921* [Anti-Japanese movement in California and Japan-US relations: Conflicts over immigrants' issues, 1906–1921] (Tokyo: Yūhikaku, 2006), 31–34.

Throughout the ongoing atmosphere of the anti-Japanese sentiment, Okina soon realized that he was one of Japanese immigrants so disdained by mainstream society. He wrote about his inner struggle over racism in his diary.[27] While he was engaged in housework for a Jewish family, he felt that he was regarded simply as a Japanese immigrant who had to put up with the oppressive attitude of the host. In Bremerton, when he went to Union High School, he longed for an American girl in his class. Although he was attracted to her, he felt that she sometimes showed a cold and somewhat discriminatory attitude to Okina. Although it was not certain whether she really took an indifferent attitude because he was Japanese, Okina was sensitive to how he was treated by white people.

Moreover, his experience as a journalist for a Japanese American newspaper gave him many chances to understand Japanese Americans' racial issues. Based on those experiences, and the creation of the works he called *iminchi bungei* (immigrant literature), Okina established the new field of immigrant literature. It described Japanese Americans' struggles to adapt to and merge with American society. One of the points emphasized in his literature was that Japanese in America should write their hope to be treated equally as human beings. He insisted that they had to record their hard and severe experiences and should endeavor to create splendid literary works.

2.2.2 As a Cosmopolitan

When Okina returned to Japan in 1924, he considered his identity again, at which point he began to use another word, "cosmopolitan" instead of *sekaijin*. He published *Kosumoporitan wa kataru* in 1928, which was composed of essays on Japanese and American cultures, Japanese American's living conditions, and his life experience in America. In the preface, "Sokoku ni kaeru ki" (An account of returning to the homeland), he recalls the day he wondered where his home really was, while he was returning from America to Japan on the ship *Siberia*. He asked to himself, "Where is my homeland? Is it America, which made me a strong and healthy adult after seventeen years, or is it Japan, my native country, which raised me in my boyhood?"[28] He considered his identity, and concluded:

> I feel that I am a person who does not have a nation to return to, though I have a nation to go. I will go wherever, but I will not return anywhere.

---

27 Kyūin Okina, *Itsuwarazaru no ki* [A diary: Real confession], December 2, 1909: 4, Okina Kyūin's Library, C-1, Ritsumeikan University.

28 Okina, *Kosumoporitan wa kataru*, 190–191.

> I am a person having no motherland in a general sense, so I cannot go back to anywhere. It is meaningless if I say, 'I will go home.' Even if people regard me as a strange person because I do not have a homeland, their criticism is natural. I myself am my own homeland. If others understand this situation wherever I go, that I have a homeland there, there will be no misunderstanding between us. Namely, I am a person who carries his homeland, that is, a cosmopolitan.[29]

His explanation may be hard to conceive at first glance, but this idea is more understandable if the idea of *sekaijin* is taken into consideration. He says that he himself is his homeland, and he carries his homeland wherever he goes. This idea sounds like the state of diaspora, which is used extensively to explain the situations of immigrants living in other countries. However, what Okina emphasizes here is that he always holds something important wherever he goes, that is, his origin—where he was born and raised—so that his homeland means a kind of local origin, or in other words, his ethnicity, although he did not know or use the word at that time. Therefore, here he means that a cosmopolitan is not just a person who travels as a stateless person but a person who has an explicit ethnicity and homeland.

Thus, he showed that he was a cosmopolitan, and in the collection of essays he presented several comparisons between Japanese and American cultures, and criticized Japanese cultural trends that simply mimicked American ways of living. He thought Japanese people's understanding of American culture was very shallow and that they were just satisfied with accepting and enjoying clothes, foods, and other commodities that originated from America. They did not fully understand what American and Japanese cultures really meant and what each culture's goodness was. Okina also emphasized that without deeper consideration, they just praised anything imported from America, and imitated and copied American designs and styles while withdrawing from Japanese traditional ways and forms of culture.

3 Other "Cosmopolitanisms" in America around the 1920s and 1930s

3.1 *American Intellectuals' Theories Related to Cosmopolitanism*

Okina's idea of *sekaijin* was acquired by his experience of living in America, and he evolved the idea of *sekaijin* into the idea of cosmopolitan. It is not

29 Okina, *Kosumoporitan wa kataru*, 192.

clear how he knew the word "cosmopolitan." Judging from the books known to have been in his personal collection preserved in Toyama city library, and the books and articles that he wrote, there seems to be little evidence showing he had read books or articles relevant to the ideas of cosmopolitanism being discussed in Europe. Thus, presumably, he was less likely deeply influenced by the European idea of cosmopolitanism.

Generally, cosmopolitanism is the idea that regards the world's people as belonging to a single community, regardless of their political affiliation or ethnicity.[30] It is said to have been originated in ancient Greece in the fourth century B.C. A Greek philosopher, Diogenes, who was one of the founders of Cynic philosophy, called himself a "cosmopolites" (a citizen of the world), when he was asked where he was from. He was the first person who showed that his identity was not limited to a particular city in Greece. Later, as the Roman Empire was built and expanded the philosopher Cicero and the emperor, Marcus Aurelius Antoninus created the idea of the world citizen that featured cosmopolitanism with the intent of including the people living in the various areas ruled by the empire. This is regarded as being close to the idea of cosmopolitanism, as it is now generally understood. In the Middle Ages, Christianity prevailed in Europe, so that people from various nations imagined that they were connected to a wide community of Christians. In the eighteenth century, the Enlightenment philosophers deepened the idea of cosmopolitanism from the perspective of morality and politics. Immanuel Kant argued for the establishment of a world citizens' law and of world political institutions that would contribute to the realization of eternal world peace.

At present, there seems to be little proof that Okina really knew the historical development of the idea of cosmopolitanism. However, considering the fact that Japanese writers active in Japanese literary circles used the word cosmopolitan as if they had already knew it when they reviewed Okina's book *Kosmoporitan wa kataru*, it may be assumed that the word was familiar to intellectuals in Japan as well as in America and Europe. During the Taishō era (1912–1926), the active literary group *Shirakaba* had members that included writers and artists such as Saneatsu Mushanokōji and Naoya Shiga. The group published the journal *Shirakaba* (1910–1923) which tried to spread the ideologies of individualism, idealism, and humanitarianism largely influenced by the writings of Leo Tolstoy. They showed the cosmopolitan ideals that transcended narrow Japanese nationalism.[31] Even while in the US and after returning to

30 *Stanford Encyclopedia of Philosophy* s.v. "Cosmopolitanism," accessed June 25, 2020, https://plato.stanford.edu/entries/cosmopolitanism/.

31 *Nihon kindai bungaku daijiten* (Tokyo: Kōdansha, 1984), 1441–1444.

Japan, Okina was highly interested in Japanese literary trends, so it is possible that he knew of the idea of cosmopolitan discussed in *Shirakaba*. Okina also used the word cosmopolitanism in the short story, "Rakujitsu no hikari" (The light of the setting sun) in 1918, so it is plausible that he knew the word and concept itself while he was in America.

It is also difficult to show the exact proof that he knew the works of American intellectuals who engaged the concept of cosmopolitanism. Even though there appears to be little direct connection with the American intellectuals such as Locke, Kallen and Bourne, Okina's idea of *sekaijin* and cosmopolitanism have many similarities and significant differences to compare. According to Yuri Sakuma, Locke presented a new cosmopolitanism, which can be understood as an alternative of the cosmopolitanism discussed in the Western philosophical tradition.[32] Locke criticized the conventional cosmopolitanism that sought unification of the world under the only universal culture, namely Western culture embodied by the imperial countries such as Britain, France and Germany. Therefore, the concept of cosmopolitanism as expressed in the first decades of the twentieth century ironically supported imperialism and colonization of other countries. In order to solve this contradiction, Locke considered and envisioned a new cosmopolitanism that allowed universalism and localism without destroying particular cultures. He also created a new image of the United States that integrated different ethnicities and cultures in the name of "unity through diversity." It was said that Locke acquired this idea after being influenced by pragmatism as theorized by William James; Horace Kallen and Randolph Bourne were influenced as well. In addition, Locke presented his cosmopolitanism in the context of the experiences of African Americans who had been oppressed and who had suffered under racism for a long time, and immigrants who were forced to be assimilated into the predominant Anglo-Saxon culture in America.

Kallen also discussed the ideal state of a nation using the phrase "cultural pluralism."[33] His idea was first presented in his 1915 work, "Democracy versus Melting-Pot," which criticized the theory of Anglo conformity and the notion of the melting pot as the force by which ethnic minorities were to be assimilated into one dominant culture; if they were not successfully assimilated, they were regarded as people who should be excluded from American society. He emphasized the importance of ethnic traditions that helped people maintain their ties to the old world, and explained that people cannot be completely

32 Sakuma, "Amerika kokunai no kosumoporitanizumu," 21–26.

33 Uchida, "Tayōsei to chōwa," 218.

assimilated into one culture. Considering this, the ideal state of the nation is that in which the nation can offer democracy in a way that accepts each ethnicity and connects people in public places. He used the word "democracy of nationalities" and "federation of nationalities" to explain that objective.

Bourne also presented his idea about nation and democracy in "Trans-National America" in 1916.[34] He explained that there were immigrants who were regarded as inferior because they could not be assimilated into American mainstream society. He insisted that such people were also citizens of the United States, that the nation should integrate such minorities, and the experimental nation should be created based on "a new cosmopolitan ideal." Bourne presented his idea with a warning about the atmosphere of discrimination against and exclusion of foreign born people and immigrants, especially Germans, when American intellectuals were inclined to earnestly support America's joining of the war in Europe. He also advocated a new Americanism which was different from the exclusive nationalism that prevailed in Europe. Under this principle, new immigrants would not be isolated through the process of losing ethnic and cultural identity. They would rather be integrated into American society, not by having imposed upon them Anglo-Saxon culture and identity, but by having their ethnicity respected in the process of their education at home and school. In his later works, he harshly criticized modern nations' reliance on war to activate their regimes, even while people living in the nations were forced to take part in those wars and suffer the resulting destruction and damage. As an ideal, he envisioned a form of nation in which different communities could hold on to their own ethnic identities and still be united with each other to make a peaceful nation. He expected the US to become such as the ideal nation he termed "Trans-National America."

As for the philosophical context, the ideas expressed by these American intellectuals and those of Okina do not seem to be the same. The former were influenced by the pragmatism advocated by William James and the cosmopolitanism in the Western philosophical tradition, which Locke criticized, while Okina's thought was less likely to have been influenced by Western philosophy. However, the writers lived in the same era and the same nation, therefore, even if indirectly, these ideas may have been created as the by-products of that era in broader sense. In fact, they raise similar concerns about the issue of immigrants and minorities. In America of the 1910s and 1920s, because of the influx of the new immigrants from southern and eastern Europe, and the strong nationalism forcing American citizens to follow the principle of

34 Bourne, "Trans-National America," 86–97; Maekawa, "Randolph Bourne saikou," 23–26.

one-hundred percent Americanism advocated by the American Legion, the issue of assimilation into America was an important problem. Even though Kallen and Bourne did not mention Japanese American immigrants' issues such as anti-Japanese sentiment, their recognition of the presence of new immigrants and the attitude of the American majority toward them may have include Japanese immigrants' issues. For instance, the immigration laws established in the 1920s targeted not only immigrants from Europe but also those from Japan. Locke was also likely to have had an idea about Japanese people in America, because he mentioned Japanese culture would never be blended when he explained his idea of an ethnic culture. He said Japanese and Western cultures could not be merged, and should develop respectively and independently.[35]

Furthermore, their personal situations as minorities were similar to Okina's situation. Locke's cosmopolitanism was naturally influenced by his background as an African American. Kallen was Jewish, and had been strongly concerned about the racial issues that Jewish people had confronted. Although Bourne was Anglo-Saxon, he was disfigured at birth and had suffered from tuberculosis of the spine when he was young, leaving him with a hunched back—a situation that left him socially vulnerable.

Another thing worth mentioning is that, compared with those ideas espoused by the American intellectuals, Okina's is not as sophisticated. He did not explicitly draw the picture of a democratic America as the other American intellectuals did. He did not criticize the assimilation of Japanese Americans into American society; rather, he had the idea that Japanese people should modify their living conditions in order to be welcomed by American society. In addition, the attitude of and activity involved in being anti-war were different from those notions held by American intellectuals, especially Bourne. Okina advocated cosmopolitanism in 1928, but during the 1930s and 1940s, his voice for resisting World War II was not so strong. He surely held the idea of cosmopolitanism, and knew, at the bottom of his heart, that the war against China and the US was desperate and useless, but officially, he had to behave as if he supported Japan and believed in Japanese victory so as to survive among the atmosphere of all-out war.[36] In spite of several theoretical weaknesses of Okina's cosmopolitanism, it has still common interests in creating an ideal world, one where all people of all ethnicities can coexist by keeping and developing ethnic particularities while living in harmony.

---

35 Sakuma, "Amerika kokunai no kosumoporitanizumu," 24.

36 Itsumi and Suda, *Okina Kyūin nenpu*, 41–58.

3.2 *Cosmopolitanism Referred to by Other Japanese Americans*

In addition to Okina's idea of cosmopolitan, other Japanese American intellectuals used the word cosmopolitan to explain their own identities. Riichirō Hoashi's remarks on cosmopolitanism, as found in his article of the same name that was published in the University of Southern California's *El Rodeo*, are more westernized than Okina's idea.[37] In the article, Hoashi summarizes the history of the advancement of people's rights to liberty and equality, and the sense of the individual. He also generalizes the development of political institutions beginning with households, and leading to clans and tribes, then finally to political states, or the nation. He points out that people have sought unity throughout history, and suggests that gradually the world is reaching toward the unity of all nations. In order to achieve such unity, people need one universal religion and language. However, races cannot be merged with each other, so he thinks that the ideal unity is "not unity in uniformity, but unity in diversity."[38] Hoashi then asks what religion and language will allow people to attain the ideal unity in diversity, and he answers that they are Christianity and English, because the former had already been accepted from Asia to Europe, supported by universal humanitarian moral values, and the latter has various European origins of languages such as Latin, Greek, French, and German, and was already spoken by one fifth of the world population.

From his article, Hoashi's cosmopolitanism appears to be in the context of the idea of cosmopolitanism discussed by the European philosophers. Judging from his words, he was probably a devout Christian, and he might have been influenced by the cosmopolitanism advocated by Kant, because like Kant, he strongly insists on the importance of peace. He also criticizes the contemporary world in which temporary peace is achieved by weapons and balance of powers. In addition, his cosmopolitanism is based on the idea of universalism, which will be achieved by one superior culture. This brand of cosmopolitanism is what Locke critiqued as a vehicle that accelerates imperialism. Although Hoashi points out the importance of diversity, like Locke, Kallen, and Bourne, he finally praises Christianity and English under the strong conviction that they are the only universal religion and language.

On the other hand, Hoashi's cosmopolitanism may also be the result of his own identity crisis brought about by the experience shared by many first generation Japanese Americans. He begins his essay as follows: "Born in Japan and educated in America, we are neither Japanese nor Americans but

---

37 Japanese Student Association of University of Southern California, *Japanese El Rodeo* 1 (June 1912); Hoashi, "Cosmopolitanism," 15–25.

38 Hoashi, "Cosmopolitanism," 22.

are Cosmopolitans; and as Cosmopolitans we may be allowed to express our opinions, freely and frankly, for nothing but Cosmopolitanism can be our ideal since we have transcended the narrow bound of nationality."[39] From these words, we can imagine his struggles of living in the US as a Japanese minority, tackling the restrictions and obstacles which may have prevented him from expressing his opinions freely and honestly.

Issō Shimoyama (1879–1935) also regarded himself as a "cosmopolitan." He came to the US in 1903 from Morioka city in Iwate prefecture. He earnestly worked to earn money to send to his family in Japan. While working hard, he wrote a number of haiku and became a famous poet in Japanese-American literary circles. Shimoyama contracted osteomyelitis in 1920, and suffered from acute pain for the rest of his life. Because of this disease and the suffering it caused him, Shimoyama developed an interest in Christianity and reflected on who he was and what his life meant.[40]

He wrote many letters to his younger brother, Shirō, who was keeping their house in his hometown, from which we can trace his identity quest in America. In the letter dated January 25, 1925, he says that he is a person who was born to deviate from the old Japanese ethical and moral standard, and he will live the rest of his life by the grace of God. In addition, he regarded himself as a person who could not follow the common rules of his Japanese community, saying that he would become a complete "cosmopolitan."[41] He also presents his conception of the world, the hometown, and each person. He thinks that people tend to care where they live, and they are likely to emphasize the differences between people's lives in foreign countries and in their homelands. He disagrees with such a concept of generalizable people, because he thinks that the place where people live is, as it were, just like bits of trash in a space, scattered around. Accordingly, he thinks it is not worthwhile to consider whether a person lives in his hometown or a foreign country. According to Shimoyama, the important thing is the fact that people just live in their proper places in proper ways.[42] From these words, we can see that he was seeking his universal identity, which was "beyond the border" between Japan and America.

39 Hoashi, "Cosmopolitanism," 15.

40 Fumiko Nakagō, "Nikkei issei tachi no jiko hyōgen: Shimoyama Issō to Iseda Hatsue no tanshikei bungaku"[Nikkei Isseis' self-expressions: Issō Shimoyama and Hatsue Iseda's short form poetry], in *Ajia kei amerika bungaku: Kioku to souzou* [Asian-American literature: Threading past, present, and future], ed. Ajia kei amerika bungaku kenkyūkai (Osaka: Osaka Kyouiku Tosho, 2001), 325–350.

41 Issō Shimoyama to Shirō Shimoyama, January 25, 1925.

42 Kumei, "America gasshūkoku tanshikei bungaku kou."

From his remarks, several things can be compared to Okina's idea of cosmopolitanism. Shimoyama's image of cosmopolitanism is different in that he does not necessarily keep in mind his Japanese ethnicity. On the other hand, there is a similarity to Okina's cosmopolitanism. Shimoyama has an image of a human being who lives on the earth, seen with a wider view, as though from space. That broader sense of describing human beings from the standpoint of the earth is similar to Okina's idea. Shimoyama may also have known of the literary trend found in the publication *Shirakaba,* as Okina seemed to have. In truth, Okina and Shimoyama were acquaintances, and it was possible that they shared their knowledge of literary works with each other.

4 After Returning to Japan—The Meaning of Okina's Idea of Cosmopolitan

Okina's cosmopolitanism was not as mature and organized as the theories of the American intellectuals who expanded their ideas to encompass the issue of how the ideal nation should be and what kind of democracy should be performed. However, for Okina, *sekaijin* and cosmopolitanism were very important and they influenced his decision about how he would spend his later life in Japan.

After returning to Japan, he became literally a Japanese living in Japan, however, his identity did not return to that held by a Japanese who had not lived in America. In 1924, he got an editing job at *Asahi* Newspaper, and in 1926, he became the chief editor of *Shūkan Asahi* (The Asahi Weekly). From that time, he engaged more actively in writing, and published a novel *Michinaki michi* (A road without milestones, 1928) and a book of essays *Kosmoporitan wa kataru* (A cosmopolitan speaks, 1928), both of which were written based on his life in America. By publishing the two books, he was welcomed as a unique writer who had experienced living in America and who had the different viewpoints that were expected to influence the Japanese literary world. In 1931, he left *Shūkan Asahi,* using his retirement money to visit America with the artist, Yumeji Takehisa (1884–1934) with the desire to revive Takehisa's work. In addition, he planned to go to India to see historical Buddhist sites and statues and to interview the Nobel prize writer, Rabindranath Tagore (1861–1941). The journey was part of his quest to discover what Japanese identity was by analyzing the origin of the religion that had so influenced Japan, Buddhism, at its source in India. He could not get an explicit answer to that question, but he became more interested in what characteristics Japanese culture had and what kind of role Japan should play as one of many Asian countries in the world.

In 1933, he came back to Tokyo and started a career researching and writing about India and Asian civilizations, and about Japanese culture and religion, including Buddhism.

In 1936, after returning from his travels in America and the research he did in India, he became more interested in his hometown's traditions, history, and folklore. Commuting from Tokyo to Toyama, he published a magazine called *Koshibito* (A man with high aspirations), which explored rural Toyama's folklore. Also, he built a publishing company, *Koshi Shobō*, and started to publish a series of books about world history, *Zusetsu sekai shiwa taisei* (The world history series with illustrations) (1937–1941) edited by Akira Nakakōji. Publishing *Koshibito* and building *Koshi Shobō* was his first practice of the idea of cosmopolitanism. According to his reminiscences, he had a great deal of anxiety about world politics, the deteriorating relationship between Japan and America, and the growing atmosphere of militarism in Japan. He questioned and implicitly criticized the slogan "*chūkun aikoku*" (loyalty to the Shōwa emperor and love for Japanese empire) which was repeatedly advocated by the government in those days. Okina thought that the world needed the policy of loving the world instead of fostering strong nationalism, and devoting oneself to all human beings in a peaceful sense instead of devoting oneself to expressions of loyalty to one emperor. In order to love the world, people should know more about it, he thought, and in order to be devoted to human beings, people must consider themselves and understand who they are. Based on this idea, he started publishing *Zusetsu sekai shiwa taisei*, which would contribute to open people's mind to the world, and he edited *Koshibito*, which would probe into people's origins and ethnicity based on local culture.[43] Although he kept the idea of cosmopolitanism at the bottom of his heart, during the Pacific War, he avoided showing strong anti-war sentiment based on his idea of cosmopolitanism.

As was analyzed, the first generations of Japanese American immigrants like Okina, Hoashi, and Shimoyama represented their ideal identity as a cosmopolitan. Interestingly, American intellectuals such as Locke, Kallen, and Bourne also reached the idea of cosmopolitan while they were considering how human beings should live and what kinds of nations should be realized. Their process of defining their own identities and seeking the ideal nation show how people who crossed national boundaries encountered different cultures and races, and how they dealt with severe social problems such as discrimination, racism, and exclusive nationalism. They sought a universal identity like cosmopolitanism in order to create an ideal world where every person can be treated equally

43 Okina, *Okina Kyūin zenshū* 2, 85.

regardless of their racial and ethnic characteristics. This idea of cosmopolitanism can be compared with the similar ideas today, such as global citizenship, and we can ask what the differences and similarities are. This will lead to understanding and provide a clue to solutions to contemporary issues of people who are crossing borders for various kinds of reasons in today's globalization era.

Bibliography

Azuma, Eiichiro. *Between Two Empires: Race History and Transnationalism in Japanese America.* Oxford: Oxford University Press, 2005.

Bourne, Randolph. "Trans-National America." *Atlantic Monthly* 117 (July 1916): 86–97.

Buhle, Mari Jo., Paul Buhle., and Dan Georgakas, eds. *Encyclopedia of the American Left.* New York: Oxford University Press, 1988.

Cheung, King-Kok. *Articulate Silences.* New York: Cornell University Press, 1993.

Cheung, King-Kok, ed. *An Interethnic Companion to Asian American Literature.* New York: Cambridge University Press, 1997.

Chin, Frank, Jeffery Paul Chan, Lawson Fusao Inada, and Shawn Wong, eds. *Aiiieeeee!: An Anthology of Asian American Writers.* Washington,D.C.: Howard University Press, 1974.

Fugita, Stephen S., and David J. O'Brien. *Japanese American Ethnicity: The Persistence of Community.* Seattle and London: University of Washington Press, 1991.

Hoashi, Riichirō. "Cosmopolitanism." *Japanese El Rodeo* 1 (July 1912): 15–25.

Ichioka, Yuji. *The Issei: The World of the First Generation Japanese 1885–1924.* New York: Free Press, 1988.

Iino, Masako. *Mouhitotsu no nichibei kankeishi: Funsō to kyōchō no naka no nikkei amerikajin* [Another history of relationship between Japan and America: Japanese Americans living in the conflicts and cooperation]. Tokyo: Yūhikaku, 2000.

Imin Kenkyū Kai, ed. *Nihon-no imin kenkyū: Doukou to bunken mokuroku* [Immigrants studies in Japan: Trends and bibliography] Vol.2. Tokyo: Akashi Shoten, 2008.

Itsumi, Kumi, and Mitsuru Suda, eds. *Okina Kyūin nenpu: 1888–1973* [Chronological record of Kyūin Okina: 1888–1973], 3rd ed. Tokyo: Okina Kyūin Zaidan, 2020.

Japanese Student Association of University of Southern California. *Japanese El Rodeo* 1 (June 1912).

Kallen, Horace M. "Democracy versus the Melting-Pot: A Study of American Nationality." *The Nation* 100, no.2591 (1915): 217–220.

Kim, Elaine H. *Asian American Literature: An Introduction to the Writings and Their Social Context.* Philadelphia: Temple University Press, 1982.

Kumei, Teruko. "Amerika gasshūkoku tanshikei bungaku kou: Shimoyama Issō wo chūshin ni" [An analysis on Japanese short poems in the United States: Focusing on Issō Shimoyama]. A Presentation in International Research Center for Japanese Studies, July 19, 2014.

Louie, Steve, and Glenn Omatsu, eds. *Asian Americans: The Movement and the Moment*. Los Angeles: UCLA Asian American Studies Center Press, 2006.

Maeda, Daryl Joji. *Rethinking the Asian American Movement*. New York: Routledge, 2011.

Maekawa, Reiko. "Randolph Bourne saikou: Dai ichiji sekai taisenka no amerika chishikijin" [Randolph Bourne reconsidered: An American intellectual under the shadow of World War I]. *Amerikashi kenkyū* [Studies of American history], no.27 (July 2004): 20–34.

Maigreishon Kenkyūkai, ed. *Esunishiti wo toinaosu: Riron to henyō* [Reclaiming ethnicity: Theories and changes]. Nishinomiya: Kwansei Gakuin University Press, 2007.

Maykovich, Minako K. *Japanese American Identity Dilemma*. Tokyo: Waseda University, 1972.

Minamikawa, Fumisato. *Nikkei amerikajin no rekishi shakaigaku: Esunishiti, jinshu, nashonarizumu* [Historical sociology on Japanese Americans: Ethnicity, race, nationalism]. Tokyo: Sairyūsha, 2007.

Minohara, Toshihiro. *Cariforuniashū no hainichi undō to nichibei kankei: Imin mondai wo meguru nichibei masatsu, 1906–1921* [Anti-Japanese movement in California and Japan-US relations: Conflicts over immigrants' issues, 1906–1921]. Tokyo: Yūhikaku, 2006.

Mizuno, Mariko. *Nikkei amerikajin no bungakukatsudō no rekishitekihensen: 1880 nendai kara 1980 nendai ni kakete* [The history of Japanese American's literary activities: from the 1880s to the 1980s]. Tokyo: Kazama Shobō, 2013.

Nakagō, Fumiko. "Nikkei issei tachi no jiko hyōgen: Shimoyama Issō to Iseda Hatsue no tanshikei bungaku" [Nikkei Isseis' self-expressions: Issō Shimoyama and Hatsue Iseda's short form poetry]. In *Ajia kei amerika bungaku: Kioku to souzou* [Asian-American literature: Threading past, present, and future]. Edited by Ajia kei amerika bungaku kenkyūkai. Osaka: Osaka Kyouiku Tosho, 2001.

Nihon jinmei daijiten. Tokyo: Kōdansha, 2015. https://kotobank.jp/dictionary/nihonjinmei/.

Nihon kindai bungaku daijiten. Tokyo: Kōdansha, 1984.

Okina, Kyūin. "Beikoku Karano Kansou." no.1–12, *Toyama Nippō*, from January 1 to January 14 in 1924.

Okina, Kyūin. *Itsuwarazaru no ki* [A diary: Real confession], December 2, 1909: 4, Okina Kyūin's Library, C-1, Ritsumeikan University.

Okina, Kyūin. *Kosumoporitan wa kataru* [A cosmopolitan speaks]. Tokyo: Jueikaku, 1928.

Okina, Kyūin. *Okina Kyūin Zenshū* [The complete works of Kyūin Okina]. Edited by Kyūin Okina, Kinpei Hieda, Kumi Itsumi and Yoshio Matsuda. Vol.5, Toyama: Okina Kyūin Zenshū Kankōkai, 1971.

Okina, Kyūin. *Okina Kyūin Zenshū* [The complete works of Kyūin Okina]. Edited by Kyūin Okina, Kinpei Hieda, Kumi Itsumi and Yoshio Matsuda. Vol.2, Toyama: Okina Kyūin Zenshū Kankōkai, 1972.

Rubin, Joan Shelley, and Scott E. Casper, eds. *The Oxford Encyclopedia of American Cultural and Intellectual History*. Vol.1. New York: Oxford University Press, 2013.

Sakata, Yasuo. "Conflicting Identities: Issei and Nisei in the 1930's." *Osaka Gakuin University International Colloquium* (1991): 133–160.

Sakuma, Yuri. "Amerika kokunai no kosumoporitanizumu: Alain Locke no kosumoporitanizumu kara yominaosu *The New Negro*" [Cosmopolitanism within a nation: Alain Locke's cosmopolitanism and *The New Negro*]. *Amerika Bungaku Kenkyū* [Studies in American literature], no.49 (2013): 21–38.

Shimoyama, Issō to his younger brother, Shirō Shimoyama. Letters. Shimoyama's private collection.

Sollors, Werner. *Beyond Ethnicity: Consent and Descent in American Culture*. New York: Oxford University Press, 1986.

Stanford Encyclopedia of Philosophy Online, s.v. "Alain LeRoy Locke," accessed June 25, 2020, https://plato.stanford.edu/entries/alain-locke.

Stanford Encyclopedia of Philosophy s.v. "Cosmopolitanism," accessed June 25, 2020, https://plato.stanford.edu/entries/cosmopolitanism/.

Steinburg, Stephen. *Turning Back: The Retreat from Racial Justice in American Thought and Policy*. Boston: Beacon Press, 1995.

Takezawa, Yasuko. *Nikkei amerikajin no esunishiti: Kyousei syūyou to hosyou undou ni yoru hensen* [The transformation of Japanese American ethnicity: The effects of internment and redress]. Tokyo: Tokyo University Press, 1994.

Togami, Souken. *Japanese American: Ijyū kara jiritsu he no ayumi* [Japanese Americans: A process of immigration to independence]. Kyoto: Mineruva Shobō, 1985.

Uchida, Ayako. "Tayōsei to chōwa: H. M. Kallen no bunka tagen shugi" [Diversity and harmony: Cultural pluralism of H. M. Kallen], *Amerika Kenkyū* [The American review], no. 29 (1995): 217–228.

Ueki, Teruyo, and Gayle K. Sato, eds. *Nikkei amerika bungaku: Sansedai no kiseki wo yomu* [Reading Japanese American literature: The legacy of three generations]. Tokyo: Sōgensya, 1997.

Vassil, Kristina S. "Passages: Writing Diasporic Identity in the Literature of Early Twentieth-Century Japanese America." PhD diss., University of Michigan, 2011.

Wong, Sau-ling Cynthia. *Reading Asian American Literature: From Necessity to Extravagance*. Princeton: Princeton University Press, 1993.

CHAPTER 4

Rendering "a Service" yet "Infected with a Foreignness"

The Cross-cultural Experiences of Rockefeller Public Health Fellows from China and Japan in the Interwar Period

Darwin H. Stapleton

This chapter discusses a case of cross-cultural encounters involving public health students and officials in China, Japan, and the United States in the first half of the twentieth century. It focuses on problems of acculturation engendered by the international fellowship program of the Rockefeller Foundation, and in particular the Chinese and Japanese medical and public health officials who accepted the challenge of taking fellowships that required them to leave their home countries for months and years of education in Western nations. With the goal of improving public health in China and Japan, the fellows dealt with problems of language, racial discrimination and varying cultural norms, while being initiated into a growing international public health network that to some degree superseded their national identities. To examine this phenomenon this chapter draws on the rich archival record of the Rockefeller Foundation that documents not only the operations of the Foundation but also frequently reveals the experiences of the fellows.

In the twentieth century public health became an international obsession. On the one hand, scientific and medical researchers had developed the means of identifying the causes of diseases, and in some cases the vaccines and other methodologies to fight them; and on the other hand, the twin factors of global colonialism and rapidly growing international means of transportation made it increasingly clear that public health concerns crossed geographic, social, and political boundaries.[1] The Rockefeller Foundation, established in 1913 with a vision of promoting the improvement of humankind throughout the world, was an exemplar of the global obsession with public health, promoting effective means of disease-control that changed

1 It is appropriate to remember that in the midst of the era that this chapter discusses Paul de Kruif published a best-selling popularized celebration of the rise of scientific medicine: Paul de Kruif, *Microbe Hunters* (New York: Harcourt, Brace, 1926).

 | DOI:10.1163/9789004435506_006

and magnified governmental and social responses to the problems of public health.[2]

This chapter will examine an important element of the Foundation's public health program—the training and educational fellowships it granted to promising new actors in the public health arena—and will focus on fellows from China and Japan from 1916 to the earliest phase of World War II. In doing so, this chapter will consider the boundary-crossing dynamics of the fellowship program, considering the perspectives of the Foundation, and of the Chinese and Japanese fellows, and the implications of those dynamics for global public health in the first half of the twentieth century. While it is not possible to fully understand the goals, motivations, and outcomes of the fellowship program, or of the individual fellows, it is intriguing and illuminating to find hints and expressions of those goals, motivations, and outcomes in the archival record—and to draw on them to better understand the world inherited from them. In the twenty-first century we continue to grapple with the legacies of boundary-crossing that we can see in microcosm in the early twentieth century public health fellowship program. Matters such as nationalism and internationalism, perceptions of race and indigeneity, and elite medical education versus grassroots health delivery remain with us today. The Chinese and Japanese public health fellows bravely tested these boundaries.

In part, this chapter grapples with Michael Kearney's idea, expressed in a classic article on boundary-crossing, that "international migrants [to some degree] escape the impress of the nation-state to shape their identity."[3] The Chinese and Japanese fellows described here are exemplars of modern transnationals who experience the breakdown of the nation-state as the primary determinant of self, and who adopt other signifiers, in this case the language and professional status acquired by the study of Western scientific medicine. This chapter is thus a contribution to the historiography of what Kearney calls the "transnational condition" of individuals whose identities can no longer be accurately inscribed within the typical boundaries of state and culture.[4]

The international fellowship program instituted by the Rockefeller Foundation drew on nineteenth-century establishments of funds to support

---

2 For convenience, the term Rockefeller Foundation will be used herein to include several subsidiary and interrelated entities. The Foundation was established in 1913, and in the same year the International Health Commission (soon renamed the International Health Board) was established.

3 Michael Kearney, "Borders and Boundaries of State and Self at the End of Empire," *Journal of Historical Sociology* 4 (March 1991): 59.

4 Kearney, "Borders and Boundaries," 66.

research and scholarship. The Tyndall Fund, established in 1874 in the United States, for example, provided Americans with support for postgraduate research and travel in Europe.[5] By the early twentieth century the term "fellow" was applied to "holders of certain sums of money for a fixed number of years to be devoted to special study or research."[6] But it was a new enough concept for Americans that in 1902 a major figure in American medical education had to take pains to explain the nature and possibilities of fellowships to one of the trustees of the newly-founded Carnegie Institution of Washington.[7] By the time the Rockefeller Foundation was established, however, its trustees could draw on the experiences of a decade of fellowship and research grant awards by two earlier Rockefeller philanthropies, the General Education Board (1902) and the Rockefeller Institute for Medical Research (1901). Fellowships became a keystone of the Rockefeller Foundation's development of numerous fields of learning, but were particularly important in public health.[8]

In 1915 executives of the Rockefeller philanthropies expressed the view that they "and other public health agencies in the United States [are] handicapped in the development of their programs due to the fact that there [are] no schools where men [*sic*] could receive the special training to equip them properly for the responsibilities of public health workers."[9] From the beginning, fellowships

5 Howard S. Miller, "Science and Private Agencies," in David D. Van Tassel and Michael G. Hall, eds., *Science and Society in the U.S.* (Homewood, IL: Dorsey, 1966), 210–211, and Howard S. Miller, *Dollars for Research: Science and its Patrons in Nineteenth-Century America* (Seattle: University of Washington Press, 1970), 122–123. John Tyndall, who set up the fund, was a British scientist; he had given a series of popular lectures in the United States and used the proceeds of the lecture tour for the fund. In 1884 he endowed a fellowship at Columbia University that supported research in physics: *A History of Columbia University, 1754–1904* (New York: Columbia University Press, 1904), 146.

6 "Fellow" in *The Encyclopedia Brittanica*, 11th ed. (New York: Cambridge University Press, 1910), 10: 243. See also: Darwin H. Stapleton, "Philanthropy," *The Oxford Companion to the History of Modern Science* (New York: Oxford University Press, 2003), 630–32.

7 William Henry Welch to John Shaw Billings, 16 January 1902, in Nathan Reingold and Ida H. Reingold, eds., *Science in America: A Documentary History, 1900–1939* (Chicago: University of Chicago Press, 1981), 11–12.

8 Darwin H. Stapleton, "Malaria Eradication and the Technological Model: The Rockefeller Foundation and Public Health in East Asia," in Ka-che Yip, ed., *Disease, Colonialism, and the State: Malaria in Modern East Asian History* (Hong Kong: Hong Kong University Press, 2009), 74–75. It is notable that in his otherwise valuable book John Farley does not take up fellowships in his history of the International Health Division of the Rockefeller Foundation: John Farley, *To Cast Out Disease: A History of the International Health Division of the Rockefeller Foundation (1913–1951)* (New York: Oxford University Press, 2004).

9 Cited in "Fellowship Report 1931," 9 April 1932, folder 316, box 43, series 100E, Record Group [hereafter RG] 1.2, Rockefeller Foundation Archives [hereafter RFA], Rockefeller Archive Center [hereafter RAC], Sleepy Hollow, New York, USA.

for Chinese students to study in the United States were central to the program. The Foundation's *Annual Report* for 1918 noted that "since 1915 it has been the policy of the foundation to bestow stipends ... in 1918 a total of $55,000 was expended for this purpose. There were sixty-eight fellowships and scholarships ..."[10] It was further noted that sixty-five of the awards were for the support of Chinese medicine and public health. The fellowship program supported about 2000 public health fellows through the next three decades, of which a significant number were awarded to Chinese and Japanese students and officials.[11]

It is possible to make some general observations about how the Foundation viewed and carried out the fellowship program. First, fellows were not selected competitively, but by recommendations made by Foundation officers based in locations around the world in which the Foundation intended to develop programs. The Foundation looked for promising young men and women who were expected to return to their homelands as leaders in the field for which they were trained. One officer deeply involved in the fellowship process recalled that

> According to the system we developed, our fellows were not necessarily recruited among those who had graduated at the heads of their classes ... We chose instead those who had in practical work demonstrated ability and capacity for leadership.[12]

Fellows were awarded tuition and living stipends and sent to selected universities, most frequently those in the United States, Canada, United Kingdom: Johns Hopkins University, Harvard University, the University of Toronto, and the London School of Tropical Medicine and Hygiene were favored destinations for public health fellows. If they were not already fluent in English, fellows often were given language instruction before commencing their studies.

---

10 Rockefeller Foundation, *Annual Report for 1918* (New York: Rockefeller Foundation, 1919), 48.

11 Darwin H. Stapleton, "Fellowships and Field Stations: the Globalization of Public Health Knowledge, 1920–1950," read for the "Explorations in Public Health History" conference, Bellagio conference center, Bellagio, Italy, 27 October–1 November 2003. Note that after ten years of the Rockefeller fellowship program ten percent of all public health fellowships were awarded to China, out of thirty-three nations and colonies awarded fellowships: Rockefeller Foundation, *Annual Report for 1930* (New York: Rockefeller Foundation, 1931), 107.

12 Victor Heiser, *An American Doctor's Odyssey: Adventures in Forty-five Countries* (New York: W.W. Norton & Co., 1936), 279.

Nonetheless, cultural adaptation to Western environments was implicated, and the Foundation tended to view that process ethnocentrically. One officer with twenty years of experience in East Asia had this perspective on the fellows he worked with:

> In the course of many years I interviewed thousands [of prospective fellows] … I always tried to give personal attention to those whose choice had fallen upon American schools, and arranged to have them invited into homes, so that when they returned to their far countries, they would have a broader picture of what we were like.
>
> It was equally necessary to present the habits of the East to our own young staff members, not only to show them how inexorably the Orientals were yoked to their ancient and onerous customs, but that patience must be cultivated before the yoke could be removed.[13]

It is difficult to assess how much this "we-they" view permeated the Foundation, but similar comments can be found throughout the Foundation's archives for this period, and it seems likely that this attitude was felt by prospective fellows from the moment they engaged with the fellowship process.

Finally, it is important to note that an underlying goal of the Foundation, the expansion of Western science-based medicine throughout the world, was clearly expressed in the fellowship program. Fellows were trained at institutions that met the Foundation's standards for teaching "scientific medicine," and usually received intensive laboratory experience. Often they became co-authors of scientific papers coming out of those laboratories. Many fellows were sent to field stations or sites of local public health delivery for substantial periods for practical experience. With that mix of education and training, fellows were expected to be change agents and advocates for the Foundation's approach to public health when they returned to their homelands.

The Foundation's president, George Vincent, gave the anticipated fellowship experience a very positive spin as the program was initiated when he wrote that

> A study of the public health and medical education fields makes it clear that a largely augmented personnel of well-trained and experienced experts is a first requisite. The wise provision of stipends for the training of such persons is a fundamental contribution to the progress in each

13 Heiser, *An American Doctor's Odyssey*, 280.

> nation, and may be means of promoting international understanding and good will.[14]

After fifteen years of the fellowship program in public health, Vincent's successor, Max Mason, offered this evaluation:

> One of the factors in bringing about [social change] represented by the upswing in public health work, especially in Europe, has been the invigorating contacts made by various leaders, young and old, due to fellowships ...[15]

For returning fellows, however, acceptance of Western medicine and science involved a struggle with cultural norms, often with political implications, that were not easily resolved. In a recent work Sean Hsiang-Lin Lei has examined how in the 1920s and 1930s leading Western-oriented public health and medical officials in China (several of whom had been Rockefeller fellows) engaged with practitioners of traditional Chinese medicine regarding the nationalization of medical services. Although "the first generation of biomedically trained Chinese doctors swiftly took over the leadership positions" in the Chinese medical infrastructure, and specifically "assumed the role of the architects and promoters of public health," they did not extinguish the role of traditional medicine in China. The result of that sometimes contentious interplay, Lei argues, was not a victory for scientific medicine, but rather a hybrid of Western and traditional Chinese medicine.[16]

Another episode of cultural dissonance played itself out in Indonesia in the 1930s when it was still a Dutch colony. The Rockefeller Foundation initiated a program there that "focused on health prevention work in rural villages." The program included a school to train rural health workers, and a demonstration program in a town in Java. According to Eric Andrew Stein:

> The Rockefeller Foundation projects, which proposed a model of health education that had the potential to reach the ailing bodies in the remote corners of the [Indonesian] archipelago with a modern scientific

14 George Vincent, "President's Review," in Rockefeller Foundation, *Annual Report for 1918* (New York: Rockefeller Foundation, 1919), 49.

15 Max Mason, "President's Review," in Rockefeller Foundation, *Annual Report for 1930* (New York: Rockefeller Foundation, 1931), 105.

16 Sean Hsiang-Lin Lei, *Neither Donkey nor Horse: Medicine in the Struggle over China's Modernity* (Chicago: University of Chicago Press, 2014), 66–67.

> rationality, enabled doctors and health workers to see their efforts as building Indonesia as a whole, connecting them to the rural masses, for whom their education and elite status placed at a distance. Given the rootedness of Indonesian physicians in Dutch notions of civilization, discipline, and the primacy of science, [however] this distance could only be marginally bridged ...[17]

The subtleties of such history certainly caution us not to ascribe inevitability or even homogeneity to the westernization promoted by the Rockefeller Foundation; and even more relevant to the focus of this chapter, we must understand that the Foundation's fellowship program, in playing out, involved personal and cultural struggles for the fellows.

What were the costs and what were the benefits of boundary-crossing for the Chinese and Japanese fellows? First must be considered the extent to which the fellows were complicit in what some writers have considered to be the Rockefeller Foundation's imperialist project. Edward Berman and David Fisher famously accused the Foundation of being an active and intentional arm of United States' policy of supporting the colonial powers prior to World War II, and of working to suppress nationalist movements throughout the period (1916–1940) being considered in this chapter.[18]

Certainly the Foundation had no apparent qualms about providing fellowships to Japanese public health workers who were destined for positions in the Japanese colonies of Formosa and Korea, and in its zone of control in Manchuria. This was completely in line with the Foundation's strategy of working with numerous elements of the British colonial empire and, not surprisingly, with the Foundation's commitment to American colonial outposts in Puerto Rico and the Philippines. In fact, the Foundation was generally content with the political status quo, and generally was out of sync with the United States government and American public opinion in its relations with Italy, Japan, Germany, and the Soviet Union in the 1920s and 1930s, remaining engaged with those nations even when they veered sharply away from

17 Eric Andrew Stein, "Hygiene and decolonization: The Rockefeller Foundation and Indonesian nationalism, 1933–1958," in Liping Bu, Darwin H. Stapleton and Ka-che Yip, eds., *Science, Public Health and the State in Modern Asia* (London: Routledge, 2012), 52.

18 Edward H. Berman, *The Influence of Carnegie, Ford, and Rockefeller Foundations on American Foreign Policy: the Ideology of Philanthropy* (Albany, NY: State University of New York Press, 1984); Donald Fisher, *Fundamental Development of the Social Sciences: Rockefeller Philanthropy and the United States Social Science Research Council* (Ann Arbor, MI: University of Michigan Press, 1993).

the internationalism favored by the Foundation.[19] It seemed to have political blinders on.

There are two contexts to consider in this regard. First, this study's focus on the Rockefeller Foundation draws on the latest wave of scholarship to come out of the vast archives of the Foundation, and of Rockefeller philanthropy in general.[20] After the opening of the archives in the 1970s, influenced by the politics of the Cold War and the Vietnam War, early scholarship emphasized the Foundation's perceived complicity in the imperial project of the United States.[21] This work emphasized the global power of the Foundation, and its enmeshment with American foreign policy. (Dean Rusk, secretary of state under John F. Kennedy, was previously a President of the Foundation, and John Foster Dulles, secretary of state under Dwight D. Eisenhower, had been a trustee.) Although this view was attacked as simplistic and biased, it long remained a fundamental critique of the Foundation's programs.[22]

In the 1990s, a new generation of scholars, often from less-developed nations, mined the Rockefeller archives to examine the policies and programs of the Foundation from, as it were, the other end of the telescope. In a series of studies focused on the nations and institutions where the Foundation was active, these scholars saw grantees not as mere receivers of the Foundation's largess, but as equal actors who negotiated the terrain of fellowships and grants with their own interests in mind.[23] Although those negotiations did not negate

19 Susan Gross Solomon, "'The Power of Dichotomies': The Rockefeller Foundation's Division of Medical Education, Medical Literature, and Russia, 1921–1925," in Giuliana Gemelli and Roy MacLeod, eds., *American Foundations in Europe: Grant-Giving Policies, Cultural Diplomacy and Trans-Atlantic Relations, 1920–1980* (Brussels: P.I.E. Peter Lang, 2003), 31–51; Paul Weindling, "Modernizing Genetics: The Role of Foundations in International Population Studies," in Gemelli and MacLeod, eds., *American Foundations*, 167–170; Farley, *To Cast Out Disease*, 242–253; Darwin H. Stapleton, "Internationalism and Nationalism: the Rockefeller Foundation, Public Health, and Malaria in Italy, 1923–1951," *Parassitologia* (2000) 42: 127–134.

20 The archives of the Rockefeller Foundation, as well as the archives of the Rockefeller family, and other Rockefeller philanthropies and institutions, are held at the Rockefeller Archive Center, Sleepy Hollow, New York, USA (www.rockarch.org).

21 Robert F. Arnove, ed., *Philanthropy and Cultural Imperialism* (Bloomington, IN: Indiana University Press, 1982); Berman, *The Influence of Carnegie, Ford, and Rockefeller Foundations on American Foreign Policy*; Fisher, *Fundamental Development of the Social Sciences*.

22 Martin Bulmer, "Philanthropic Foundations and the Development of the Social Sciences: A Reply to Donald Fisher," *Sociology* 18 (1984): 572–77. See also: Donald Fisher, "Philanthropic Foundations and the Social Sciences: A Response to Martin Bulmer," *Sociology* 18 (1984): 581–87.

23 For example: Robert E. Kohler, *Partners in Science: Foundations and Natural Scientists, 1900–1945* (Chicago: University of Chicago Press, 1991); Marcos Cueto, ed., *Missionaries of*

the power of the Foundation, or avoid its sometimes deleterious effects, they frequently redirected the Foundation's efforts in ways that more closely met the needs of the local institutions and client nations.

More recently scholarship has returned to the question of the Rockefeller Foundation's global mission, trying to make sense of the Foundation as an element of the twentieth-century trend toward internationalism and, even, Americanization. This theme tends to emphasize the Foundation's substantial contributions to improved global health, welfare, and education, accepting at face value the Foundation's proclaimed mission—"For the wellbeing of mankind throughout the world."[24] John D. Rockefeller's personal philanthropic interests are shown to underpin the Foundation's sense of purpose.[25]

Finally, this study fits a recent trend that puts American history in more general postcolonial and transnational frames. While "historians have long served nationalist ends by treating the nation as the dominant analytical unit," historians are increasingly adopting trans-national perspectives that recognize the flows of people, goods, and ideas that shape history.[26] Borders are porous and, in the true sense, artificial—constantly violated by migrations, transfers of technology, religious missionaries, warfare, and popular culture, among others. The fellowship program of the Rockefeller Foundation is another example of that porosity, and one that, examined in detail, helps better understand its meaning for individuals and institutions.

In consideration of this historiography, it is most effective to consider the Rockefeller fellowship program as a complex, negotiated web of relationships. While it may have been Rockefeller-funded, the program was welcomed by

---

Science: The Rockefeller Foundation and Latin America (Bloomington, IN: Indiana University Press, 1994); Soma Hewa, *Colonialism, Tropical Disease and Imperial Medicine: Rockefeller Philanthropy in Sri Lanka* (Lanham, MD: University Press of America, 1995); Shirish Kavadi, *Rockefeller Foundation and Public Health in Colonial India, 1916–1945: A Narrative History* (Mumbai and Pune, India: Foundation for Research in Community Health, 1999). See also: Shirish Kavadi, "'Parasites Lost and Parasites Regained": Rockefeller Foundation's Anti-Hookworm Campaign in Madras Presidency," *Economic and Political Weekly* (January 13, 2007): 130–37.

24 Ludovic Tournès, "La foundation Rockefeller et la naissance de l'universalisme philanthropique américain," *Critique international* (avril–juin 2007) 35: 173–97.

25 Soma Hewa. "The Protestant Ethic and Rockefeller Benevolence: The Religious Impulse in American Philanthropy," *Journal for the Theory of Social Behavior* 27 (1997): 419–52; Soma Hewa, "The Protestant Personality and Higher Education: American Philanthropy Beyond the 'Progressive Era'," *International Journal of Politics, Culture and Society* 12 (1998): 135–163.

26 Kristin Hoganson, "Twenty Years since the Imperial Turn: Time for Trans-imperial Histories," *The American Historian* 3 (February 2015): 36.

Chinese and Japanese officials. A statement in 1929 by J.A. Lin, a Chinese public health official, is representative of their general attitude:

> I was very pleased to learn from Dr. [John] Grant that twelve fellowships are to be given to physicians from China for the study of public health in the United States. At this period in China this decision will have very far-reaching significance.
>
> The demand for trained men [*sic*] in Public Health has so greatly increased that it is impossible for us to meet the need. The Foundation, in helping us through these fellowships, renders a service for which we cannot be grateful enough.[27]

As Chinese and Japanese fellows crossed cultural and national boundaries to study abroad, they and their host institutions faced several issues. Most obvious was language: with few exceptions the Rockefeller Foundation officers sent the fellows to English-language institutions, primarily in the United States, but also in Canada and the United Kingdom. The Foundation even considered sending Japanese fellows first to the Peking Union Medical College in Beijing, where English was the language of instruction, before they undertook their full fellowships.[28]

Language clearly proved to be the most difficult transitional problem for the fellows. Although the fellowship selection process took language preparation into account, there was an apparent difference between adequate knowledge of English as a written language, and capabilities with spoken English as a student in the classroom and the laboratory. Foundation officers were particularly concerned that fellows do well in laboratory settings, as many of them were being sent to research-intensive universities such as Harvard and Johns Hopkins.[29] The Foundation had some understanding of the situation, and had at least one English-language tutor in Baltimore who prepared the students who were sent to Johns Hopkins University.

While it appears that the majority of fellows fared well, the fellowship records are full of complaints of inadequate language skills, particularly for the Japanese fellows: as early as 1925, one Rockefeller officer referred to "Japanese fellows with whom there have been difficulties because of lack of English."[30]

27 J.A. Lin to Victor Heiser, July 30, 1929, folder 355, box 43, series 601, RG 1.1, RFA.

28 Excerpt from W. S. Carter diary, March–April 1929, folder 64, box 9, series 609, RG 1.1, RFA.

29 See comments on some fellows' research abilities: fellowship cards for Unichi Miura, Haruo Mizushima, Keizo Nobechi, Kiyoshi Saito, fellowship recorder cards, RFA.

30 R.M. Pearce to N. Gist Gee, May 1, 1928, summary of letter, folder 63, box 6, series 609, RG 1.1, RFA.

A few years later another foundation officer commented that "The [Japanese] men who are [in the United States] now have great difficulty in understanding [English] and sorely try the patience of those with whom they come in contact."[31] In light of many other positive assessments of the abilities of Japanese fellows, it is possible that these perspectives derived in part from preconceived ideas of their poor language skills.[32]

In fact, Foundation officers and fellowship mentors generally ranked the Chinese fellows as more able than the Japanese fellows, making comments such as "the Japanese are notoriously poor linguists," and that "of the two nations [China and Japan] they [Chinese fellows] are the better linguists."[33] This discrepancy may have had its basis in the recruitment of Chinese fellows from the network of missionary schools in China that taught English, while Japan had few similar institutions. Moreover, the flagship Rockefeller organization in China, the Peking Union Medical College, carried out its instruction in English, and a significant number of fellowships were granted to faculty and recent graduates of the College, a guarantee that those fellows had strong English capabilities.

While English ability was at least capable of assessment, another quality of Chinese and Japanese fellows—what may be characterized as cultural adaptation—was equally important in the views of Foundation officers and the fellows' mentors as they discussed the fellows' accomplishments. One fellow, a nurse sent to Simmons College in Boston, was described initially as "being given a great deal of special attention on account of difficulty in becoming adjusted to [a] new country and new work." But eight months later it was reported that she was a "very satisfactory student."[34] Many of the fellows were reported to have adapted well to the circumstances of a different culture.

Some, however, clearly had difficulty with transition to American, Canadian, or British cultural norms and expectations, although comments in the archival record were frequently made by observers who did not have first-hand knowledge of China or Japan. Nevertheless, the record suggests that for some Japanese fellows the American expectation of forthright communication was

---

31 Victor Heiser to John Grant, August 19, 1931, folder 559, box 79, China Medical Board Inc. Archives, RAC.

32 Fellow Hiroto Yoshioka, who studied at Johns Hopkins in 1937–38, was described as having "a much better command of English than most of [the] Japanese fellows." Fellowship card for Hiroto Yoshioka, fellowship recorder card file, RFA.

33 John B. Grant to Victor Heiser, December 14, 1930, folder 64, box 9, series 609, RG 1.1, RFA; G.S. Parkinson to A.J. Warren, October 14, 1938, folder 64, box 9, series 609, RG 1.1, RFA.

34 Fellowship record for Masae Ando, 1927–28, fellowship recorder card file, RAC.

a stumbling block: one can see in that the circumambulations of Japanese language were often retained in English conversations, one mentor complained of a Japanese fellow's "evasiveness" and another mentor referred to a Japanese fellow as "something of a sphinx."[35] These kind of perspectives probably reinforced one Rockefeller officer's judgment that it was unusual for Japanese fellows to mix easily with those of other cultures.[36] One Japanese fellow was simply described as "not likeable."[37]

Class distinctions were also problematic. The Rockefeller Foundation booked travel for the fellows, and found that, in particular, Japanese fellows were offended by being offered accommodations below first class. According to one Foundation assessment regarding travel plans, "Japanese, particularly of the official class, feel that they have a certain status to maintain ... and will [not] take kindly to second class accommodations."[38] Yet this situation applied more generally to East Asian fellows, who recognized that perceptions of race were important in the West: they may have seen any class distinction as a racial slight.

Racism did, in fact, become apparent in certain circumstances. The Rockefeller imprimatur may have insulated the fellows from the usual conventions of American racism, such as segregated housing and transportation in university settings, but the Foundation seemed blissfully unaware of potential issues when planning to send the fellows into the deep South for malariology studies at Rockefeller-funded stations in Leesburg, Georgia and Andalusia, Alabama.[39] In the first two years of operations at Andalusia, 1923–24, four Chinese fellows were trained there. A Japanese fellow arrived in 1926, whom the Director of the station described as "lazy, [and] superficial," derogatory terms commonly used to describe African-Americans in that era. The same fellow received positive comments from other observers of his fellowship work.[40]

35 Fellowship record for Takashi Hirayama, 1931–32, fellowship recorder card file, RAC; "Comments on Ability and Work of Japanese Fellows," November 22, 1934, folder 64, box 9, series 609, RG 1.1, RFA.

36 O'Brien diary entry, November 22, 1934, excerpt in folder 64, box 9, series 609, RG 1.1., RFA.

37 Fellowship card for Kiyoshi Saito, fellowship recorder cards, RFA.

38 Summary of message from unidentified Rockefeller Foundation official, October 30, 1930, folder 64, box 9, series 609, RG 1.1, RFA.

39 "Report 1. Fellowships," November 20, 1926, folder 63, box 9, series 609, RG 1.1, RFA. The reference is on page 3.

40 "Annual Report of the Training Base of the International Health Board, Andalusia, Alabama," 1923, folder 28, box 4, series 201, RG 5.2, RFA; W.G. Smillie, "Second Annual Report of the Training Station of the International Health Board at Andalusia, Alabama," 1924, folder 28, box 4, series 201, RG 5.2, RFA; W.G. Smillie to F.F. Russell, December 29, 1924, folder 26, box 4, series 201, RG 5.2, RFA; fellowship recorder card for Kiyoshi Saito, 1926, fellowship card file, RFA.

The Foundation itself was permeated with racial perspectives common to the social theories of the era. For example, it clearly was aligned with eugenics in its support of the Brush Foundation, in Cleveland, Ohio, which was investigating supposed characteristic racial distinctions in human physiology. More famously, the Foundation provided research funding to a German institution, the Kaiser Wilhelm Institute, well into the 1930s, until it became an instrument of Nazi propaganda. Sometimes the expressions of racism were more than theoretical: one prominent Rockefeller public health officer, Louis Hackett, laced his correspondence with views of South Americans and others that were virulently racist; another public health officer assigned to Puerto Rico in the 1930s had a private letter containing racist comments about the residents of the island published in a newspaper.[41]

Chinese and Japanese fellows would certainly have been aware of discriminatory American policies and practices leveled not only against African-Americans, but also against East Asians. Japanese fellows knew of the "antagonistic attitude of many Americans," and were aware that "Japanese fellows ... do not have in the U.S. as friendly a reception as fellows from other countries." Many Japanese fellows expressed a preference for placements in Germany, "where they [were] treated as equals," rather than in the United States.[42] Almost all Chinese and Japanese fellows coming to the United States arrived on the West coast, where they likely immediately were aware of well-established discrimination against Chinese and Japanese immigrants, and, as public health observers, may have seen how frequently government officials associated disease with East Asian populations.[43] Then the Immigration Act of 1924 and related legislation effectively stopped Chinese and Japanese immigration (although it did not impinge on the fellowship program). Official American attitudes toward Chinese and Japanese were all too clear. Occasionally reactions to these antagonisms boiled to the surface. One prospective Chinese fellow was reported to be "very anti-foreign, [and] especially

41 Farley, *To Cast Out Disease*, 80–82. See the Lewis W. Hackett Papers, RAC.

42 Excerpt from Richard M. Pearce's interview with Dr. Rudolph Teusler, May 26, 1928, folder 63, box 9, series 609, RG 1.1, RFA; Excerpt from E.R. Embree letter, June 1, 1922, folder 63, box 9, series 609, RG 1.1, RFA; Alan Gregg to W. A. Sawyer et al., December 6, 1937, folder 64, box 9, series 609, RG 1.1, RFA.

43 Jeannie Natsuko Shinozuka, "From a 'Contagious' to a 'Poisonous Yellow Peril'? Japanese and Japanese-Americans in Public Health and Agriculture, 1890s–1950," doctoral dissertation, University of Minnesota, 2009, 185–86, 190.

anti-American," but was nonetheless awarded a fellowship "because of his qualities of leadership."[44]

In the face of these circumstances, some fellows were very well-received. Hirotoshi Hashimoto was a fellow at the Mayo Clinic in Rochester, Minnesota, who was appreciated both professionally and personally. His supervisor remarked that Hashimoto "has won a place in [our] hearts" and "made a host of friends."[45] Public health nurses, who were almost always women, were praised in terms suggesting that subservience was valued by the Rockefeller Foundation officers. Japanese public health nurses, in particular, were described as "most responsive and cooperative," "interested and alert," and "very discreet."[46] In American culture "getting along" with others was highly valued, and was viewed as an essential element of the fellowship process.

Clearly, the fellowship experience varied widely and is difficult to assess with a degree of certainty. We can say that Chinese and Japanese fellows faced significant linguistic and cultural obstacles as they crossed boundaries of class, race, and education. No doubt those obstacles were too daunting for some, and the accounts of those who failed to complete their fellowships, or who completed them without receiving a certificate or a diploma from their residential institutions, suggest that the difficulties of boundary-crossing were substantial.

Nonetheless, all of the Chinese and Japanese fellows who completed their fellowships were subsequently followed intently by the Rockefeller Foundation, as the archival record demonstrates. The Foundation proudly noted the positions they held, the promotions they received, their publications, and their roles in developing public health programs and institutions—even after World War II. Some were provided further career support, such as a second fellowship, or research grants. Equally important, the Chinese and Japanese fellows became part of an informal, but substantial international network of public health officials. After the fellowships were completed they were equipped with the shared language of scientific medicine and, moreover, shared a common understanding of the Rockefeller approach to public health that can be characterized as "demonstrate, educate, collaborate and estimate."

---

44 John B. Grant to Victor Heiser, July 16, 1929, folder 354, box 43, series 601, RG 1.1, RFA. The May Fourth Movement, beginning in 1919 in China, had an anti-imperialist and nationalist focus that influenced the views of many young Chinese intellectuals.

45 Fellowship recorder card for Hirotoshi Hashimoto, 1923–24, fellowship recorder card file, RFA; "Comments on the Ability and Work of Japanese Fellows," November 22, 1934, folder 64, box 9, series 609, RG 1.1, RFA.

46 Fellowship recorder cards for Yoshi Kitade, Kimiko Michibe, and Kikue Shimizu, fellowship card file, RFA.

They also had visited other Rockefeller sites throughout the world, and attended global public health conferences under Rockefeller auspices. Often they published their fellowship research in Rockefeller-related journals.[47] One Chinese fellow, Oo-keh Khaw, a parasitologist from Peking Union Medical College, traveled throughout Europe in 1933, visiting public health projects. Everywhere he encountered Rockefeller-trained workers.[48] His reception in Spain was typical:

> One of the Divisional Inspectors—a Rockefeller Foundation Fellow of Johns Hopkins—came with me, so that besides being received with kindness—hospitality everywhere—I saw not only anti-malaria work but other public health activities as well. The latter are receiving feverish attention and are carried out in approved American style as most of the heads [of public health units] are R[ockefeller] F[oundation] fellows.[49]

Returning Chinese and Japanese fellows usually took the government and institutional posts that they were expected to take when their fellowships were granted, although some of them soon moved on to better-paying business or private positions. Returning to their native culture certainly had its difficulties, mainly because of the elite training the fellows had received. John Grant, a Rockefeller Foundation officer who was very supportive of Chinese students, nonetheless remarked:

> Our criticism of the returned fellow is chiefly that he not only entirely lacks the spirit of service upon his return which is essential for work in China today, but that he becomes infected with a foreignness that is hardly compensated [for] by his increased technical knowledge.[50]

---

47 Stapleton, "Malaria Eradication and the Technological Model," 73–77. For a specific example of the effect of Rockefeller fellowships, and publications by recipients of fellowships, see: Darwin H. Stapleton, "'An International Contribution to Medical Education': The Global Context of the Peking Union Medical College," in Mary Brown Bullock, ed., *The Legacy of PUMC: Centennial Essays* (Beijing: Chinese Academy of Medical Sciences and Peking Union Medical College, 2017), 23–29. Note that this chapter appears in Chinese in the same volume, pages 3–18.

48 O.K. Khaw to Roger Greene, August 6, 1933, volume 1312, Peking Union Medical College Archives.

49 O.K. Khaw to Roger Greene, June 6, 1933, volume 1312, Peking Union Medical College Archives.

50 John B. Grant to Victor Heiser, August 5, 1932, folder 355, box 43, series 601, RG 1.1, RFA.

Several years later Grant reported that Chinese fellows were viewed as "spoil[ed]" by their training in the United States.[51]

For the Chinese and Japanese fellows an additional, probably unanticipated, kind of boundary-crossing problem soon appeared. The Japanese invasion of China in 1937 soon caught up many of them in the circumstances of unrelenting warfare. In Japan the war changed the mission of public health work from the development of a more effective delivery of services to the support of an increasingly strident and militaristic state. In China the war completely disrupted plans for a national health service, compelling massive relocations of professional cadres: the Peking Union Medical College was cut off from communication with "Free China." Not surprisingly, the Chinese fellows caught in the United States after the US entered the war were very reluctant to return to China.[52]

One group of Rockefeller fellows surfaced in south-central China along the Burma Road. Amazingly, in that remote region, where they attempted to develop an antimalarial program for the Chinese soldiers, they established communication with the Rockefeller Foundation and obtained some financial assistance for their efforts. Much of this team eventually migrated to Taiwan and helped establish an antimalarial program there that became a global model for public health programs in less-developed nations.[53] Other Chinese fellows emerging from the chaos of the Second Sino-Japanese War made other choices. Some, such as C.C. Chen, emigrated and had long careers outside of China. Some fellows eventually chose to join the administration of the Peoples Republic of China and became key figures in Chinese public health for decades afterward.[54]

Former Japanese fellows also had a shattered nation to help repair. Those who survived the war appear to have been able to put their prewar training and experience to work rather quickly. No doubt their capacities in English gave them a favorable hearing from the postwar American administrators in charge of their nation. One former Rockefeller nursing fellow reported at the end of World War II that "I am very well and still at the Tokyo Health Center."[55] Others became instructors or officers in reconstituted universities and institutes.

51 R.A. Lambert interview of John B. Grant, June 16, 1945, folder 350, box 43, series 601, RG 1.1, RFA.

52 R. A. Lambert to Joseph Beach, April 14, 1942, folder 350, box 43, series 601, RG 1.1, RFA.

53 Stapleton, "Malaria Eradication and the Technological Model," 79–82.

54 Mary Brown Bullock, *An American Transplant: The Rockefeller Foundation and the Peking Union Medical College* (Berkeley, CA: University of California Press, 1980), 215–226.

55 Fellowship recorder card for Masae Ando, fellowship recorder card file, RFA.

Conclusion

Although this study has not focused on the consequences of the fellowship program for China and Japan, it is fair to assume that the results were similar to those found by other historians who have looked at the Rockefeller program. A scholar of the history of public health in Mexico has commented that "many of the lasting changes in the conceptualization and practice of public health in Mexico were effected through the grants the R[ockefeller] F[oundation] offered to individual health professionals to study in the U.S."[56] Similar consequences of Rockefeller public health fellowships were experienced in Columbia.[57] Another scholar, assessing the important effects of the Rockefeller Foundation globally in the interwar period, and referring to the fellowship program, pointed to "scientific tourism" as a "central element in the Rockefeller strategy."[58]

Clearly the Chinese and Japanese fellows who were drawn into the Rockefeller public health project were trained at the highest levels of Western public health, and returned to positions of importance. They were expected to make substantial contributions. But in the process they experienced collisions of culture that shaped their lives. The Chinese and Japanese public health fellows discussed in this chapter were enmeshed in the Rockefeller Foundation's plan to globalize public health norms and strategies through training and education that was based on Western science and technology.

The fellowship program required participation in a process that crossed cultural boundaries of language, behaviors, and professional expectations. This process was often painful: there was the necessity of communicating in English; there was racial discrimination to observe or experience; there were cultural misunderstandings to overcome. For all fellows these obstacles were substantial, and for some they were overwhelming. For those who passed through the fellowship process and re-entered the public health bureaucracies of China and Japan, they became instrumental to the globalization of public health—participants in a process that after World War II created the World Health Organization which depended on an international understanding of

56 Anne-Emmanuelle Birn, "Public Health or Public Menace? The Rockefeller Foundation and Public Health in Mexico," *Voluntas* 7 (1996): 49.

57 Paola Mejía Rodríguez, "De ratones, vaunas y hombres: el programa de fiebre amarilla de la Fundación Rockefeller en Columbia, 1932–1948," *Dynamis: Acta Hisp. Med. Sci. Hist. Illus.* (2004) 24: 153.

58 Tournés, "La foundation Rockefeller," 190. Translation by the author.

goals and strategies significantly fostered by the public health fellowship program of the Rockefeller Foundation.

Bibliography

Publications

Arnove, Robert F., ed. *Philanthropy and Cultural Imperialism.* Bloomington, IN: Indiana University Press, 1982.

Berman, Edward H. *The Influence of Carnegie, Ford, and Rockefeller Foundations on American Foreign Policy: The Ideology of Philanthropy.* Albany, NY: State University of New York Press, 1984.

Birn, Anne-Emmanuel. "Public Health or Public Menace? The Rockefeller Foundation and Public Health in Mexico." *Voluntas* 7, no. 1 (1996): 35–56.

Bullock, Mary Brown. *An American Transplant: The Rockefeller Foundation and the Peking Union Medical College.* Berkeley, CA: University of California Press, 1980.

Bulmer, Martin. "Philanthropic Foundations and the Development of the Social Sciences: A Reply to Donald Fisher." *Sociology* 18 (1984): 572–77.

Columbia University. *A History of Columbia University, 1754–1904.* New York: Columbia University Press, 1904.

Cueto, Marcos, ed. *Missionaries of Science: the Rockefeller Foundation and Latin America.* Bloomington, IN: Indiana University Press, 1994.

De Kruif, Paul. *Microbe Hunters.* New York: Harcourt, Brace & Co., 1926.

Farley, John. *To Cast Out Disease: A History of the International Health Division of the Rockefeller Foundation (1913–1951).* New York: Oxford University Press, 2004.

"Fellow." *Encyclopedia Brittanica.* 11th ed., 10: 243. New York: Cambridge University Press, 1910.

Fisher, Donald. *Fundamental Development of the Social Sciences: Rockefeller Philanthropy and the United States Social Science Research Council.* Ann Arbor, MI: University of Michigan Press, 1993.

Fisher, Donald. "Philanthropic Foundations and the Social Sciences: A Response to Martin Bulmer." *Sociology* 18 (1984): 581–87.

Heiser, Victor. *An American Doctor's Odyssey: Adventures in Forty-five Countries.* New York: W.W. Norton & Co, 1936.

Hewa, Soma. *Colonialism, Tropical Disease and Imperial Medicine: Rockefeller Philanthropy in Sri Lanka.* Lanham, MD: University Press of America, 1995.

Hewa, Soma. "The Protestant Ethic and Rockefeller Benevolence: The Religious Impulse in American Philanthropy." *Journal for the Theory of Social Behavior* 27, no. 4 (1997.): 419–452.

Hewa, Soma. "The Protestant Personality and Higher Education: American Philanthropy Beyond the 'Progressive Era'." *International Journal of Politics, Culture and Society* 12, no. 1 (1998): 135–163.

Hoganson, Kristin. "Twenty Years since the Imperial Turn: Time for Trans-imperial Histories." *The American Historian* 3 (February 2015): 36–38.

Kavadi, Sirish. *Rockefeller Foundation and Public Health in Colonial India, 1916–1945: A Narrative History.* Mumbai and Puna, India: Foundation for Research in Community Health, 1999.

Kavadi, Sirish. " 'Parasites Lost and Parasites Regained' ": Rockefeller Foundation's Anti-Hookworm Campaign in Madras Presidency." *Economic and Political Weekly*, January 13, 2007, 130–137.

Kohler, Robert. *Partners in Science: Foundations and the Natural Scientists, 1900–1945.* Chicago: University of Chicago Press, 1991.

Lei, Sean Hsiang-Lin. *Neither Donkey nor Horse: Medicine in the Struggle over China's Modernity.* Chicago: University of Chicago Press, 2014.

Miller, Howard S. *Dollars for Research: Science and its Patrons in Nineteenth-Century America.* Seattle: University of Washington Press, 1970.

Miller, Howard S. "Science and Private Agencies." In *Science and Society in the U.S.*, edited by by David D. Van Tassel and Michael G. Hall, 191–221. Homewood, IL: Dorsey, 1966.

Reingold, Nathan, and Ida H. Reingold, eds. *Science in America: A Documentary History, 1900–1939.* Chicago: University of Chicago Press, 1981.

Rockefeller Foundation. *Annual Report for 1918.* New York: Rockefeller Foundation, 1919.

Rockefeller Foundation. *Annual Report for 1930.* New York: Rockefeller Foundation, 1931.

Rodríguez, Paola Mejía. "De ratones, vaunas y hombres: el programa de fiebre amarilla de la fundación Rockefeller en Columbia." *Dynamis: Acta Hisp. Med. Sci. Hist. Illus.* 24 (2004): 119–155.

Shinozuka, Jeannie Natsuko. "From a 'Contagious' to a 'Poisonous Yellow Peril'? Japanese and Japanese-Americans in Public Health and Agriculture, 1890s–1950." PhD diss. University of Minnesota, 2009.

Solomon, Susan Gross. "'The Power of Dichotomies': The Rockefeller Foundation's Division of Medical Education, Medical Literature, and Russia, 1921–1925." In *American Foundations in Europe: Grant-Giving Policies, Cultural Diplomacy and Trans-Atlantic Relations, 1920–1980*, edited by Giuliana Gemelli and Roy MacLeod. Brussels: P.I.E. Peter Lang, 2003.

Stapleton, Darwin H. "Fellowships and Field Stations: The Globalization of Public Health Knowledge, 1920–1940." Paper presented at the "Explorations in Public History" conference, Bellagio Conference Center, Bellagio, Italy, October 27–November 1, 2003.

Stapleton, Darwin H. " 'An International Contribution to Medical Education': The Global Context of the Peking Union Medical College." In *The Legacy of PUMC: Centennial*

Essays, edited by Mary Brown Bullock, 19–36. Beijing: Chinese Academy of Medical Sciences and Peking Union Medical College, 2017.

Stapleton, Darwin H. "Internationalism and Nationalism: the Rockefeller Foundation, Public Health and Malaria in Italy, 1923–1951." *Parassitologia* 42 (2000): 127–134.

Stapleton, Darwin H. "Malaria Eradication and the Technological Model: The Rockefeller Foundation and Public Health in East Asia." In *Disease, Colonialism, and the State: Malaria in East Asian History*, ed. Ka-che Yip, 71–84. Hong Kong: Hong Kong University Press, 2009.

Stapleton, Darwin H. "Philanthropy." In *The Oxford Companion to the History of Modern Science*, 630–632. New York: Oxford University Press, 2003.

Stein, Eric Andrew. "Hygiene and Decolonization: The Rockefeller Foundation and Indonesian nationalism, 1933–1958." In *Science, Public Health and the State in Modern Asia*, edited by Liping Bu, Darwin H. Stapleton, and Ka-che Yip, 51–70. London: Routledge, 2012.

Tournès, Ludovic. "La fondation Rockefeller et la naissance de l'universalisme philanthropique américaine." *Critique international* 35 (2007): 173–197.

Weindling, Paul. "Modernizing Genetics: The Role of Foundations in International Population Studies." In *American Foundations in Europe: Grant-Giving Policies, Cultural Diplomacy and Trans-Atlantic Relations, 1920–1980*, edited by Giuliana Gemelli and Roy MacLeod, 167–179. Brussels: P.I.E. Peter Lang, 2003.

Archives

China Medical Board, Inc. Archives. Rockefeller Archive Center, Sleepy Hollow, New York, USA.

Lewis W. Hackett Papers, Rockefeller Archive Center, Sleepy Hollow, New York, USA.

Peking Union Medical College Archives, Chinese Academy of Medical Sciences and Peking Union Medical College, Beijing, PRC.

Rockefeller Foundation Archives. Record Groups 1.1, 1.2, 5.2. Rockefeller Archive Center, Sleepy Hollow, New York, USA.

CHAPTER 5

Making Coffee, Making Space

Coffee Shops as Sites of Cultural Encounter

Helena Grinshpun

1 Introduction: Why Coffee?

Ordinary substances of food and beverage have been widely discussed as an axis of cultural, political, economic, and ideological encounter in various historical and geographical contexts. As such, they have served to demarcate cultural boundaries and assert identities and have become part of an ongoing dialogue on culture. Among these substances, coffee occupies a place of honor: due to its unique historical record, coffee has accumulated multiple cultural connotations and interpretations, making it a valuable case for exploring cross-cultural dynamics. Two references, although taken from two entirely different contexts, exemplify an important point that should be made before approaching a subject as ordinary yet as complex as coffee.

Robert Liberles, in his volume on Jewry in early modern Germany quotes August Ludwig Schlözer, a German Enlightenment figure, who maintained that the introduction of tobacco, sugar, coffee, and tea in Europe represented an even more significant revolution than political revolutions, wars, and treaties between nations.[1] Comparing consumables with major events in world history may sound like a blasphemy of sorts—however, the German commentator was not alone in this dramatic perception. Elise Tipton, in her study on the early modern café in Japan quotes Murobushi Kōshin, a Japanese writer and critic, who spoke of liberation in the modern city—not only liberation of the townspeople from their low status in the feudal hierarchy, or liberation of the intellect from the Neo-Confucian orthodoxy, but also liberation for women, for relations between men and women, and for drinking. The café symbolized this modern liberated spirit and, as a symbol of the process of modernization, ranked in significance with the establishment of the Japanese Diet.[2] In fact,

1 Robert Liberles, *Jews Welcome Coffee: Tradition and Innovation in early Modern Germany* (Waltham: Brandeis University Press, 2012), ix.

2 Japan's National Diet is a legislative body established in 1889 as a result of adopting the Meiji Constitution.

 | DOI:10.1163/9789004435506_007

Murobushi went further, claiming that the café was even more significant than the Diet: whereas constitutional government represented the aspirations of the ruling elites and the "dying enlightenment" of the older generation, the café symbolized youth and the future.[3] Here, again, a mundane site is mentioned as a stage for far-reaching transformations.

Early modern Germany and early modern Japan are worlds apart. In fact, Germany was reluctant to welcome coffee, while Japan, as we shall see, embraced it. The reason behind these two responses was, however, the same; in both cases, coffee was perceived as a symbol of the advent of new times. This was true both for the beverage and the coffee house environment in which it was consumed. Coffee in itself did not make revolutions, but it symbolized revolutions, being, as it was, identified with change—and not just material change in the everyday life and social organization, but in more profound layers of value systems and beliefs.[4]

Along with other consumables whose intake has become an internalized habit, coffee represents simultaneously a powerful substance and a potent symbol. Coffee's material power is inherent in its being an addictive stimulant with vast economic significance as one of the world's most traded commodities. Coffee's symbolic power lies in its ability to cross national boundaries, initiate intercultural encounters, evoke fantasies, and forge rituals. Coffee is also one of the world's most travelled commodities; its peculiar historical trajectory and constant movement across continents has shaped its social and cultural characteristics. The encounters forged through these travels have been defined not only by rational economic considerations, but also by the highly subjective and case-sensitive mechanisms of cultural interpretation and imagination. These latter mechanisms are the focus of this investigation.

This essay explores how both the substance and the social place where coffee is taken—the coffee house—have carved various spaces of encounter in Japan's modern history, both in individual and collective terms. Coffee is a prism through which changes undergone by Japanese society can be traced, from the reforms of modernization in the Meiji era to the membership in the global village of recent decades. Moreover, as we shall observe, these changes and their effects may be traced to the level of individual life courses. The following sections first briefly outline the trajectory of coffee as a travelling commodity, and then trace the role of Japanese coffee and cafés in Japan's transformations, focusing on the manner in which they were integrated into Japan's

3 Elise Tipton, "The Café: Contested Space of Modernity in Interwar Japan," in *Being Modern in Japan*, ed. Elise Tipton and John Clark (Honolulu: University of Hawaii Press, 2000), 119.

4 Liberles, *Jews Welcome Coffee: Tradition and innovation in early modern Germany*, xiii.

collective and personal memory. The cafés' most recent incarnation—the coffee shop chain—is then discussed to show how these provide a site for everyday experiences of globalization. Lastly, a new vector in coffee's movement, namely, the export of Japanese coffee culture to the West is explored. The case of coffee demonstrates how an ordinary substance can generate meaningful encounters both reflecting and affecting the complex of elements that comprise "culture."

The major theoretical assumption that frames this investigation is that ordinary substances and everyday practices serve as points of "big" intercultural encounters. Japan's westernization, modernization, and globalization represent examples of such encounters in which cultures are translated into concrete practices that are appropriated, interpreted, and often modified to fit local circumstances. This perspective highlights the encounter between cultures as a process of creative interpretation rather than a power game between colonizer and colonized. Through the case of coffee and cafés, this study demonstrates the manner in which particular historical moments shaped the nature of Japan's encounters, from its exposure to Western civilization to the public intermingling of the sexes. In order to substantiate this view, this chapter integrates some interview data collected at earlier stages of research in Japan.

There are surprisingly few academic studies that examine the dramatic societal and cultural changes brought by the expansion of coffee culture in East Asia. The majority of such literature regarding coffee and coffee shops focuses primarily on the areas of coffee's mass consumption and production, namely, Europe and the Americas. There are a number of academic works that explore various historical aspects of coffee's incorporation into the Japanese scene, such as Hirofumi Wada's historical overview of Japanese coffee and cafés and Elise Tipton's 2000 study of café waitresses in the 1930s. A recent book by Merry White significantly fills the lacuna by providing an insightful perspective on Japanese coffee life and touching upon some fascinating coffee-related cultural trends.[5] However, no study has so far sufficiently addressed one of the most important aspects of coffee in Japan, namely, its role as a global cultural commodity whose incorporation into everyday routine in Japan reflects the complex relationship between global and local, foreign and native forces. Moreover, no comprehensive research has dealt so far with global coffee shop chains' contribution to this relationship.

Most certainly, coffee is not the only substance allowing for such a perspective. Japan has a long record of using food and drink in making contact

5 Merry White, *Coffee Life in Japan* (Berkeley: University of California Press, 2012).

with other civilizations—both as a ground for actual encounter, and as a metaphoric space of cultural borrowing and appropriation. In pre-modern and early modern Japan, food and drink often functioned as social lubricants. Laver discusses, for example, how butter, wine, and olive oil served to facilitate the forming and maintaining of the relationships between Dutch merchants and Japanese officials in the late Edo period (1603–1868).[6] During the Meiji period (1868–1912), formal dinners held by foreign diplomats and their Japanese hosts were a stage where the Japanese and the foreigners learned about each other's rules of public conduct and gender relations.[7] The act of partaking of meat by the Meiji Emperor, made public in 1872, can in itself be regarded as a symbolic encounter of the Japanese physique with Western civilization and its perceptions of health and nutrition. Coffee can be analyzed as a part of this complex landscape of cultural connections and intersections.

2 The Coffee Trajectory

The history of coffee goes as far back as the ninth century. For centuries prior to its discovery by Europeans, coffee was grown by Ethiopian tribes.[8] It is believed that as a beverage it was first consumed around the fourteenth century in Yemen. By the end of the fifteenth century, coffee was widely consumed in Mecca; it was taken at first as a medicinal substance but soon became a drink popular at social encounters. Coffee houses were established in which men came together to listen to music and play chess and backgammon.[9] In 1532 coffee drinking was recorded in Cairo, where it raised complaints of the pious believers as intoxicating and thus unlawful for Muslims. In the sixteenth and the seventeenth centuries coffee-drinking as a communal ritual gained a foothold in Turkey, where it was then discovered by the Europeans.

Associated with the Orient, in Europe coffee came to be perceived as new, exotic, and thus as a fashionable product. Along with other foreign products, such as tobacco and spices, coffee was consumed as a cultural symbol, an

6 Michael Laver, "Butter Diplomacy: Food and Drink as a Social Lubricant in Dutch East India Company Trade with Japan," *Education about Asia* 17, no. 1 (2012): 5–8.

7 Sally Hastings, "A Dinner Party is Not a Revolution: Space, Gender and Hierarchy in Meiji Japan," in *Manners and Mischief: Gender, Power, and Etiquette in Japan*, ed. Jan Bardsley and Laura Miller (Berkeley and Los Angeles: University of California Press, 2011), 95–113.

8 It is believed that in Ethiopia, coffee beans were chewed as a stimulant during religious worship or long journeys.

9 Ellis Markman, *The Coffee House: A Cultural History* (London: Weidenfeld & Nicolson, 2004), 14.

emissary from a fabled world.[10] By the end of the seventeenth century, coffee houses became an integral part of the urban landscape in Venice, London, Vienna, and Paris. The coffee houses offered their customers a mediated experience of exotic cultures, wherein the coffee ritual became a setting to enact the fantasy of the Orient. Soon enough, European coffee houses became the new social centers of the era. In their ability to facilitate public debate and provide a forum for leisure, socializing, conducting business, and exchanging information, coffee houses evolved into ideal public spaces of their time.[11]

This public space had its own audience, however, which largely excluded illiterate and female customers. Although the banning of women from early European coffeehouses was not a universal rule, it appears to have been common. Historians depict coffeehouses as a male-dominated domain where men could partake in conversation without associating with women; even if not formally exclusive, coffeehouses were not considered a place for a woman who wished to preserve respectability. While English coffeehouses positioned themselves as egalitarian environments open to all subjects regardless of class, gender, or merit, conversation revolved around topics such as politics, business, and cultural criticism, topics that were not supposed to concern women and thus their participation within coffeehouses was not welcomed.[12] As such, complaints were commonly vocalized by women, who argued that coffee made men impotent and contributed to the nation's failing birth rate.[13] Although women workers may have been physically within the male public sphere of the coffeehouse as servers or even proprietors, their position prevented them from participating equally in that public sphere.[14]

A different setting was forged by coffee in the European colonies. In the colonial English-speaking Atlantic World of the eighteenth century, coffee houses served to promote a sense of shared cultural habits and helped middle-class men throughout the Empire to imagine themselves as related through taste, lifestyle, and ideas. When Britain's attempt at pushing the limits of economic

10 Wolfgang Schivelbusch, *Tastes of Paradise: A Social History of Spices, Stimulants and Intoxicants* (New York: Pantheon, 1992), 6.

11 Jürgen Habermas, *The Structural Transformation of the Public Sphere*, trans. Thomas Burger (Boston: Beacon Press, 1989).

12 Brian Cowan, "What Was Masculine About the Public Sphere? Gender and the Coffeehouse Milieu in post-Restoration England," *History Workshop Journal* 51 (2001): 127–157.

13 According to "The Women's Petition Against Coffee," issued in 1674, coffee made men "as unfruitful as the sandy deserts, from where that unhappy berry is said to be brought." (retrieved from https://quod.lib.umich.edu/e/eebo/A66888.0001.001?rgn=main;view=fulltext accessed September 18, 2020).

14 Ibid.

domination through the Tea Act of 1773 turned tea into the flashpoint of rebellion in America, coffee was promoted by the revolution leaders, eventually taking over as America's national drink. The same coffee that fueled enlightenment in Europe and anti-colonial patriotism across the Atlantic, shaped the colonial geography of South America, where colonial coffee plantations relied heavily on slave laborers. More often than not, coffee cultivation involved large-scale displacement and exploitation of indigenous ethnic groups; harsh conditions led to uprisings and anti-colonial coups.

Having travelled across continents and civilizations, coffee can be regarded as a manifestation of movement and transition; coffee culture is a product of multiple encounters between East and West, the First and the Third World, the colonizer and the colonized, the center and the periphery. The coffee house became a site in which encounters acquire form and substance. The next section explores the coffee substance and the social space of the coffee shop as a site of Japan's encounter with Western civilization. It demonstrates how the historical circumstances of Japan's appropriation of coffee carved physical and metaphorical spaces of encounter, generating an ongoing dialogue on culture.

3 Spaces of Japan's Encounter: From Modernity to Banality

Incorporated into the European lifestyle as an attribute of the exotic Orient, coffee set its foot in East Asia as a symbol of Western civilization. Coffee was first brought to Japan by Dutch traders in the seventeenth century, but did not become a familiar commodity until the end of the nineteenth century, when, after more than two hundred years of seclusion, Japan was forcibly opened to Western trade. In contrast to Europe, where the Orient provided material for exotic fantasies, in Japan, it was the Occident that possessed appeal. Along with other items of Western civilization—clothing, furnishings, and food—coffee was part of the national project to mold the Japanese body into a modern body. While large-scale reforms in education, economy, and politics aimed at changing the mindset of the rapidly modernizing nation, substances such as coffee were mediums through which modernization was internalized in its most embodied form. Coffee houses, with their long-standing association with novelty and public culture, were the site of this internalization.

In 1888, the first Japanese coffee house, named Kahiichakan, opened in Tokyo. The man who founded it was Tei Ei Kei (1859–1895), in himself a personification of cultural encounters. Born to a merchant from Nagasaki, he was adopted by a Taiwanese secretary in Japan's foreign ministry, spoke several languages, and developed a taste for coffee in America, where he attended

Yale University. He then picked up the love for coffee shops in London, where he passed on his way back to Japan.[15] Tei Ei Kei envisioned Kahiichakan to become a place of cultural exchange where knowledge would be absorbed along with coffee, and invested heavily in equipping it with Western facilities and refined paraphernalia.[16] Having aspired to more than it could accomplish without a solid financial foundation, the coffee house went bankrupt five years after its opening. Tei Ei Kei moved to the U.S. and died, rather ironically, in Seattle, the cradle of contemporary global coffee culture. His grave is visited by Japanese coffee aficionados; a monument, erected in his memory at a spot where his coffee house once stood, demonstrates the power of coffee in Japan rather than it does the success of Tei Ei Kei's coffee house.[17]

Although Tei Ei Kei's endeavor had failed, his vision proved long-lasting. During the Meiji era, coffee shops gained popularity and became a symbol and a major site of Japan's modernity. The earliest forms of these establishments were modeled on the English coffee house or French salon. The coffee shops served as entry points for foreign products, and shaped new local fashions and trends that resonated with the wider international context. They offered customers coffee along with Western architecture and décor, Western seating, and Western food, served by waitresses dressed in Western clothing. Most concentrated in Tokyo's Ginza—a district designated by the Meiji government as a "model of modernization." Most coffee shops carried European-sounding names, such as Café Printemps, Café Lion, Café Paulista, and Ginza Palace, among others.

Rapid urbanization and modernization produced the need for public spaces where newly urbanized and modernized people could practice being urban and modern. The early Japanese coffee shops provided a space for both gathering and displaying new identities. The first decades of the twentieth century further strengthened the association between coffee and modernity. The already established link between modernity and material culture—along with a consensus that the West was a desirable model—set the scene for coffee shops' appeal. In the 1920s and 1930s, coffee shops represented an increasingly visible segment of urban life, and offered an accessible space to accommodate various public expressions of *modan seikatsu* ("modern life"). The coffee shops provided one of the few public settings for *moga* and *mobo* (modern girls and boys) to meet and mingle socially. The "modern girl" in particular is

---

15 Merry White, *Coffee Life in Japan* (Berkeley: University of California Press, 2012), 9.

16 Naoyuki Takai, *Nihon Kafe Kōbōki* [The Rise and Fall of Japanese Café] (Tokyo: Nihon Keizai Shinbun Shuppansha, 2009), 93.

17 White, *Coffee Life in Japan*, 8.

to be seen as one of the most predominant, even if contested, protagonists of those years.[18] A debated equivalent of the Western "flapper," a *moga* was modern, independent, provocative, and appealing—and she was to be found, along with other sites of new consumerist sociability, in a café.

The fact that the era's coffee shops became one of the most commonly mentioned sites of Japan's modernity is linked to the controversial figure of the *jokyū*—the café waitress. The young lower-class women hired as *jokyū* had come to the big city to find work, and as such they were part of the broader shift of urbanization that shaped the identity of modernizing Japan. Due to their active presence in the public space of the café, their independence, and their often provocative behavior, *jokyū* became the working-class embodiment of the *moga* and a powerful image around which the discourse on gender and modernity revolved.[19]

Through the presence of the *jokyū* and the *moga*, the cafés became sites of social encounter between men and women—an encounter previously limited to the private sphere or to specific public settings. The conservative rules of public conduct designated respectable women to the private domain. Hastings describes how in the formal dinners of early Meiji era the issue of women's participation became a ground for cultural confusion: while for Western diplomats the presence of wives and daughters represented an anticipated gesture of hospitality, their Japanese counterparts perceived it as a violation of an accepted order.[20] The cafés were among the first sites where free mingling of sexes was acceptable, even if at times criticized.

The cafés' role diversified along with their proliferation: a growing number no longer catered just to the elite, but served a wider clientele. Their persisting association with westernization, however, was one justification for increasing restrictions in the late 1930s, when the attractiveness of the café was criticized as a demoralizing aspect of modernity. Some of these places indeed had a subversive agenda, providing a place for the intelligentsia, students, artists, and labor activists to rail against Japan's building militarism.

The import of coffee stopped toward the 1940s—during the war, few coffee shops were able to offer their clients anything other than a coffee surrogate made from substitute ingredients. During those dark times, the few cafés that did not shut down served as refuge points for people to have the comfort of

18 Miriam Silverberg, *Erotic Grotesque Nonsense: The Mass Culture of Japanese Modern Times* (Berkeley: University of California Press, 2006), 51.

19 Ibid, 73–74.

20 Hastings, "A Dinner Party is Not a Revolution: Space, Gender and Hierarchy in Meiji Japan," 95–113.

others' presence.[21] The postwar era witnessed a proliferation of coffee shops. Japanese society as a whole had undergone numerous social, political, and economic transformations, in which the U.S. served as a frame of reference. One manifestation of the American cultural influence was jazz, which was introduced in the pre-war era but did not gain widespread popularity until the 1950s. This trend facilitated a propagation of so-called "jazz cafés," which became highly popular among the younger generation and aspiring intelligentsia. The "jazz cafés" provided the means of coming in contact with the world by offering jazz on vinyl records, which otherwise were nearly impossible to acquire.[22]

The coffee shops of the 1960s and 1970s hosted expressions of trends as diverse as artistic avant-garde, protests against the U.S.-Japan security treaty, feminism, and sexual revolution. Many of them became sites of political activism where Japan's civil society was being molded. The cafés continued to evolve in response to changes in urban life, offering their patrons a variety of spaces as diverse as their clientele. In the 1960s, coffee entered the sphere of home consumption, marking its domestication. One key development behind the transformation of coffee into a commonplace drink was the invention of canned coffee.

Almost a century after Tei Ei Kei opened his Kahiichakan, Miura Yoshitake (1901–1980) brought Japan's coffee culture to a major turning point—the invention of a coffee can. Miura graduated from Waseda University and managed a green tea store while pursuing his studies of coffee. In 1935, he opened a coffee salon in the cafeteria of the Shirokiya department store in Tokyo. His coffee, brewed in his unique flannel-drip style, soon became popular for its hearty aroma and rich flavor. He then opened a coffee shop in Ginza called Yoshitake, but gave up on it when the war worsened. Miura dreamt of getting people everywhere to enjoy his coffee, even in Europe. He partnered with a canning factory and spent several years developing Mira Coffee, a can of sweetened coffee that went on the market in 1965.[23] An advertising pamphlet from the time read: "In painting we take pride in Tessai Tomioka and in ceramics [Sakaida] Kakiemon. In coffee we can boast of [Miura] to the world."[24]

---

21 White, *Coffee Life in Japan*, 64.

22 Eckhart Derschmidt, "The Disappearance of the Jazu-Kissa," in *The Culture of Japan as Seen through its Leisure*, ed. Sepp Linhart and Sabine Fruhstuck (Albany: State University of New York Press, 1998), 303–312.

23 "Mira" is a derivative of "Miura."

24 Tomioka Tessai (1837–1924) was the pseudonym of a painter and calligrapher in imperial Japan. He is regarded as the last major artist in the Bunjinga tradition and one of the first major artists of the Nihonga style. Sakaida Kakiemon (1596–1666) was a Japanese potter

Due to financial difficulties, Mira Coffee went off the market three years afterward, but in 1969, Ueshima Coffee Corporation released canned coffee with milk, which has been Japan's staple ever since.[25] In 2014, to commemorate the fiftieth anniversary of the world's first canned coffee, Miura's hometown erected a memorial and created a certification system for making "Yoshitake coffee," to be sold at local cafés and restaurants.[26] Miura's figure was perhaps less dramatically cosmopolitan than Tei Ei Kei's; however, his undertaking was no less daring. In his endeavors, he followed the logic of modernization in its most explicit sense: Shirokiya department store had been part of urban legend as one of the milestones in Japan's path towards internationalization[27]; Ginza was assigned as a site of exercising modernity; finally, putting technological innovation in service of Japan's creativity was, at the time, at the core of the Japanese national agenda.[28]

The 1980s witnessed a coffee shop boom, as coffee shops competed among themselves, offering not only different styles of coffee, but also various gimmicks, atmospheres, and styles of décor—from simple neighborhood *kissaten* (local coffee shops) where coffee was served along with home-made curry, to classy cafés specializing in sophisticated methods of coffee preparation. Cafés became intertwined with local history. Many of them have accumulated "memories" over several decades, lending coffee its localized flavor. The 1990s brought new forms, new styles, and interpretations drawing from new circumstances of Japanese life.

Coffee and cafés were part of Japan's national agenda in its formative years, helping to assert its identity as a modern, urban, and civilized nation. Early modern cafés were sites of social encounter between men and women, both within the boundaries of the emerging urban middle class and between the middle-class clientele and the working-class *jokyū*. Later types of the café

---

who invented the style now named after him.; advertisement from *Yomiuri Shimbun*, October 2015 and available at https://www.asiaone.com/worlds-first-canned-coffee-celebrates-50th-anniversary-0, accessed September 28, 2020.

25 Ueshima Coffee is one of the largest coffee manufacturers in Japan.

26 Ibid.

27 Shirokiya was an alleged site for changing underwear customs among Japanese women. In a fire that broke out in the store in 1932, several kimono-clad saleswomen refused to jump from the roof into safety nets because they were ashamed to be seen from below, and as a result they died. It has been alleged that in the aftermath of the fire, department store management ordered saleswomen to wear underwear under their kimono, and the trend spread.

28 During the postwar period, the acquisition, effective adaptation, and improvement of technologies by Japanese industry served as the basis for Japan's rapid economic growth.

produced yet new types of encounter, such the exposure to jazz music and American culture. Throughout decades and encounters, coffee has come to be a part of people's lived experiences embedded in Japan's collective and individual memory.

Let us consider, then, some of these memories in the form of personal narratives. Mr. Y., from a small town deep in the mountains of Yamaguchi prefecture, covers his glass when I offer him a beer. He doesn't drink alcohol, he says, but loves coffee. He talks about the cafés of his youth: the Showa cafés, with their splendor (*gōka*) and old-fashioned but chic (*shibui*) atmosphere. They served simple dishes: for instance, curry, and Japanese-style spaghetti with ketchup. People would come for a breakfast ("morning set") or lunch (a simple *tanpin* plate, not the elaborate lunch sets of today) or just a coffee; for a meeting or a date, after work with friends or alone. "*Natsukashii*," he says, using a word that expresses soft nostalgia. Coffee's place in individual memory resonates with the common past—not the "big" past of major historical encounters, but rather the "small" past of personal events.

Mrs. S., a middle-aged tea ceremony (*chanoyu*) teacher from a village in Gifu prefecture, is also a coffee-lover. She nods seriously when I inquire about *chanoyu* but laughs at my question of whether she drinks the traditional green tea (*matcha*) at home. "Of course not," she says, only during classes or at cultural exchange (*kokusai kōryū*) events. But she makes and drinks coffee at her home every day. Mr. T, the owner of a small café in Tokyo, shrugs his shoulders when asked about coffee's image in Japan: the Japanese don't think of coffee as Japanese, neither do they see it as foreign. Having grown up with coffee as part of Japan's common culture, members of Japan's baby-boom generation like him see the beverage as just one part of Japanese life—a part more natural than that of *matcha*. For the contemporary Japanese, coffee became a marker of the everyday life much more than the ritualized *matcha*. What used to be an exotic commodity became a commonplace; *matcha*, on the contrary, became a symbol of an exclusive tradition.

A parallel with green tea is surprisingly useful in order to determine the particularities of coffee's incorporation into Japanese culture. Green tea in its mundane form, *ocha*, is a widely popular beverage consumed in Japan on an everyday basis. The powdered green tea, *matcha*, has been adopted as a marker of Japanese cultural legacy and moved to the highly traditionalized space of a ritual. *Matcha*'s representations have undergone some remarkable changes since *chanoyu* was developed in the sixteenth century. As the modernizing Japanese nation of the late nineteenth century turned to Western cultural fashions, *chanoyu* suffered from neglect, but was later redefined as an expression of Japan's moral universe. In the early twentieth century, the tea ceremony was recruited to foster the spirit of patriotism and national uniqueness essential for the efforts of military mobilization. In the postwar era, the tea ceremony became a powerful symbol of national heritage emphasizing the tranquil nature of Japanese aesthetics.[29] Today, *matcha* is perceived both within Japan and overseas as one of the most recognizable icons of Japanese culture. The tea ceremony molds the practitioner's body into a sentient experience of Japaneseness, crafting a cultural space associated with static tradition.[30] Coffee, on the contrary, has for centuries been crafting spaces of change and innovation, molding traditional bodies into their newer states, whether of Enlightenment, assimilation, or modernization. Despite tea's precedence over coffee, the two beverages represent two separate modes of cultural work, one referring to homogeneous manifestations of tradition, the other to dynamic processes of change.

Although the internalization of coffee has made its drinking a commonplace practice, the acknowledgement of the encounters embedded in its path still feeds cultural imagination. In fact, the cultural "baggage" of coffee plays a part in the way it is incorporated into Japan's everyday landscapes. The material culture of Japanese coffee—the coffee vocabulary, utensils, and the design of the coffee spaces—usually carries a distinct foreign stamp. There is a vast use of foreign terms and slogans in the coffee business, written either in English or katakana, the alphabet used for foreign loanwords. While a Chinese character compound (kanji) exists for the word "coffee," the use of its katakana version predominates. A Japanese coffee shop (*kissaten* or *kissa*) represents today a distinctive genre whose most common style has come to include a set of features, such as an emphasis on manually brewed coffee, a small pool of "regular" clients, and a relatively small store space. More often than not, however, the décor and general atmosphere of the *kissa* incorporate cultural images referring to "other," mainly Western cultural contexts. The musical background, decorative patterns featuring non-Japanese visual motifs and the formal outfit of the coffee master and the waiters create a microcosm that is symbolically remote from the actual location. The tableware is comprised of porcelain cups, mugs, saucers, silver teaspoons, milk jugs, sugar bowls and other attributes rather atypical of a traditional Japanese table setting. Over the course of decades, the *kissa* developed a special menu perceived to be appropriate for coffee, most of which is firmly associated with Western cuisine. Japanese cafés rarely serve Japanese dishes; although local tastes and cooking techniques are

29 Tim Cross, *The Ideologies of Japanese Tea: Subjectivity, Transience and National Identity* (Folkestone, UK: Global Oriental, 2009).

30 Kristin Surak, *Making Tea, Making Japan* (Stanford: Stanford University Press, 2013), 13.

incorporated into various café foods, their foreignness is nevertheless clearly marked—for example, by referring to rice as "*raisu*" in order to distinguish it from the same rice (*gohan*) served at local eateries.[31]

4 The Postmodern Encounter and the Globalization of Coffee

If modern encounters produced an elaborate coffee culture that nevertheless incorporates elements of coffee's foreign cultural baggage, what is the nature of the post-modern encounter accommodated by coffee in Japan? This section focuses on the globalized face of Japanese coffee as epitomized by global coffee shop chains. The chains entered the Japanese market in the 1990s, as speed and convenience became a crucial life factor. The first chain, Doutor, was founded by a Japanese entrepreneur inspired by Brazilian coffee culture; the second was the American Starbucks. Recently, the number of independent coffee shops has decreased, while the number of chains has seen a slow but steady rise. Starbucks, Tully's Coffee, Seattle's Best, and other global café chains have gained exceptional popularity in Japan, and created a new niche that enabled smaller chains, both local and regional, to enter the coffee shop market.[32] Today, the chains have become commonplace throughout Japan, although their popularity is still especially evident among the young urban middle class.

One of the main effects of the coffee chains has been the fact that they made coffee more visible. The ubiquitous chains expanded coffee consciousness to include those who would not normally drink coffee: mainly members of the younger generation who were born to affluence, an unprecedentedly broad consumer choice, and taste for novelty, which the *kissa* could not, or would not, address. The chains redefined coffee from an older men's drink taken at a *kissa* (often with a newspaper and cigarette) or an accessible but hardly refined canned coffee to a trendy beverage suiting diversified tastes. This was carried out through several means: the incorporation of a uniform visual language that has come to signify the global coffee culture; expanding the menu to include a wide variety of sweetened caffeinated beverages; and the general staging of an accessible and hip urban coffee experience.

---

31 White, *Coffee Life in Japan*, 123.

32 These include local chains such as Café Veloce, Hoshino Coffee, Ueshima Coffee, Becks, San Mark Café, Komeda Coffee, and foreign chains such as South Korea's Holly's Coffee and Italy's Segafredo Zanetti.

An important attribute of this experience is its association with movement and mobility. As shown above, coffee traveled extensively before reaching Japanese shores. The twentieth century witnessed coffee's increasing importance as one of the staples of international economy and trade. Global chains represent an integral part of this new landscape, crossing national borders and carrying commercialized artifacts of global culture; coffee has become one of these artifacts. Moreover, the notion of movement itself became part of today's coffee culture. Owing largely to its American interpretation, coffee came to be associated with an active, dynamic lifestyle. Coffee-on-the-go (with the Starbucks paper cup as its epitome) has become one of the most prominent icons of contemporary urban middle-class culture. Curiously, the concept of a take-away coffee was regarded a major obstacle for the chains' favorable reception in Japan, where drinking and eating on the move is considered improper. Successfully popularized as an accessible attribute of global lifestyle, the concept turned out to be one of the chains' major victories.

The chains treat coffee as a global cultural saga embedded in concrete images, tastes, and practices. The exotic names of the coffee beans and blends send the coffee drinker to faraway lands associated with coffee growing. The use of foreign words (mainly Anglo-Italian concoctions) in the chain's standardized coffee vocabulary creates a cosmopolitan air of global lingua franca. The cultural space forged by the chains resonates with coffee's "baggage." The standardized décor makes appeals to the enchantment of foreign cultures by extensively using images of remote lands, defined by Naomi Klein as the "Third World aura."[33] The motif of travel is addressed by frequent references to metaphoric journeys made possible by drinking the coffee whose beans are named for the remote lands where they are grown and cultivated. The fact that the format of the coffee experience offered by the chains is the same in Kyoto, New York, or Dubai, creates a sense of connectedness to the global tribe. The symbolic power of global chains is thus inherent in their ability to connect materially and figuratively between multiple locations on the globe, inserting the coffee-drinker into the network of global production, distribution, and consumption. As such, the chains provide an accessible site for mundane experiences of globalization. What is consumed here is not a particular site—the Third World that gave us the bean, Europe that gave us the coffee house culture, or America that popularized it—but the entire range of images that together create a colorful pastiche encompassing both the exotic and the familiar. While, a century ago, Japan's encounter with Western civilizations

---

33 Naomi Klein, *No Logo* (New York: Picador, 2000).

took place in the realm of borrowing and learning, today it occurs in the realm of consumption.

Interestingly, one manifestation of the coffee experience has been its gendered nature. When visual representations of Japanese coffee are examined, the dominance of male representation becomes evident. Especially in the sphere of advertisement, the main protagonists are men: local coffee brands often hire male celebrities, both foreign and Japanese, to be their spokesperson; some have even earned sharp criticism for their advertisement's sexist content that downplays the role of women.[34] This trend is particularly evident in advertisements of canned coffee—one of the most proliferating segments of the local coffee industry. Canned coffee, sold in vending machines and convenience stores and aimed mainly at those who need a quick caffeine "fix," signifies movement, work, and speed. Through coffee marketing, the association between men and mobility is reinforced, as contrasted with female representations of domesticity often using tea as a cultural marker. The chains, on the other hand, have been actively targeting female customers as their main audience and gearing their product to women's taste. Some items on the menu are marked as specifically women-oriented, such as the *filone* bread roll, marketed in a Starbucks leaflet as especially suitable for female customers due to its relatively small size fitting perfectly the female mouth; the wide selection of sweet milk-based beverages also appears to cater more to women than to men.

The chains have produced not only a women-friendly product, but also a women-friendly space. The ban on smoking has become one attribute of this space, which has a clearly gendered nature. Smoking is often mentioned as a cultural trope depicting Japanese corporate masculinity, and it has long been an emblematic element of the *kissa* landscape. While the local *kissa* remain a largely male domain, the chains' standardized (and smoke-free) space appears to be addressing the female demand for a neutral ground where a woman would feel comfortable. This characteristic was described by my interviewees as "easy to enter" (*hairiyasui*); for many of them, "easy to enter" more often than not meant "easy to enter alone."[35] The ability to go alone

34 Boss Coffee's brand images feature a recognizably Western man with a pipe and the company has hired American actor Tommy Lee Jones as its spokesmen; another popular coffee brand, Georgia, has been represented by Kyle McLachlan; advertisements for Roots coffee feature Brad Pitt.; On Georgia Coffee's controversial advertisement, see http://www.tanteifile.com/geinou/scoop_2014/03/02_01/ (Japanese), accessed June 30, 2020.

35 As part of research I conducted between 2007 and 2009 and in 2011, about thirty Japanese Starbucks' customers and baristas were interviewed to gather information on their subjective experience and interpretation of the global chains.

appeared to be especially valuable in contrast to the *kissa* that were described by female respondents as men's spaces, not very comfortable to enter, and unpredictable.[36]

This function of the chain-store café appears especially relevant for women belonging to the younger generation who are actively seeking new modes of self-expression and self-indulgence through consumption. With their growing economic power and reluctance to sacrifice high standards of living to marriage and childrearing, women have become Japan's major consumer force, and are increasingly targeted as such. The coffee shop space, which in the early twentieth century was accommodating expressions of women's newly acquired emancipation, in its postmodern incarnation comes to serve as a stage for new expressions of economic and social freedom.

Japan's participation in global consumption is not confined to these trends. As global coffee chains occupy an ever-growing niche in the Japanese coffee market, the *kissa* style is becoming increasingly popular outside Japan. Japanese-style coffee shops are opening in big cities of North America and Europe, branded as a distinct cultural and culinary experience. This trend fits into the so-called "Third Wave of Coffee" agenda, referring to a current movement that considers coffee to be a craft rather than a mass-produced commodity, and adheres to three main principles: artisanship, aesthetics, and traceability.[37]

Situated on a street dominated by specialized Japanese restaurants in New York's East Village, the "Hi-Collar" (*Haikara*) coffee shop promotes itself as "an attempt to introduce the slower, more meticulous and leisurely *kissaten* style of coffee shop to the hurried, harried world of New York City coffee."[38] The name Hi-Collar derives from the term *haikara*, which is defined as elite or Western-modern, referring to the starched high collar worn by Western-dressing young men of the late Meiji period.[39] The reference to Western culture does not end here; the slogan of the coffee shop is "Flirting with the West." One of the main attractions of the coffee shop is its "morning set" (*mōningu setto*)—a modern Japanese version of the Western breakfast consisting of toast, eggs, and coffee. The Japanese reading of a Western meal, re-introduced to the Western context as an attribute of Japan's highbrow coffee culture, "morning

36 Helena Grinshpun, "The City and the Chain: Conceptualizing Globalization and Consumption in Japan," *Japan Review* 24(2012), 185.

37 From Coffee Magazine, https://magazine.crema.co/third-wave-f6479681dcf9, accessed August 23, 2018.

38 http://hi-collar.com/, accessed January 31, 2017.

39 White, *Coffee Life in Japan*, 123.

set" represents an illustrative example of how coffee-related cultural trends and interpretations travel and transform.

Hi-Collar is not alone in its venture to disseminate Japan's coffee culture abroad. Recently, Ogawa Coffee, one of the oldest coffee-house chains in Kyoto, opened its first overseas store in downtown Boston. Making use not only of Japanese coffee brewing expertise, but also of distinctively Japanese design motifs (such as Japanese ceramic cups and sakura blossom latte art), Ogawa coffee house aspires, according to its website, to become an urban oasis of perfect taste and refined aesthetics.[40] Interestingly, in its attempt to build a distinct cultural image, Japanese coffee culture seems to draw from a pool of images evoking parallels with its tea tradition.

Indeed, as *kissaten* become distinguished as sites of Japanese coffee culture, the media (both domestic and foreign) praise the power of tradition in Japan's cultivation of a refined coffee experience. A 2013 issue of the magazine *Discover Japan*, for example, points to the symbolic connection between green tea and coffee as a means to rediscover the magic of Japan.[41] The references to tea—the acquired taste, the ceremonial nature of tea practice, and its long-standing cultural heritage—define coffee in terms of a novelty anchored in a long tradition, and fit into the nostalgic narrative of returning to the roots of the nation. Such references lend coffee yet another layer of authenticity—one borrowed from Japan's own past. *Kissaten* recreate the air of a tea ceremony through the ceremony of coffee, substituting one civilized stimulant with another and shifting the emphasis from Japan's own culture to a culture skillfully appropriated by Japan.

The export of Japanese coffee "back" to the Occident from where it arrived 150 years ago is undeniably a fascinating cultural development. What is more interesting, however, is the encounter between Japan and its cultural "other," emerging in this context. Japan's export of culinary trends can be seen as part of the recent decades' shift from technological "hardware" to cultural "software." Accompanying this shift is the growing interest in Japan's global cultural influence, both within and outside of Japan. Involved here is also a certain narcissistic discourse that celebrates the transnational dissemination of Japanese popular culture.[42] This discourse contains a measure of ambivalence,

---

40 http://www.ogawacoffeeusa.com/, accessed January 31, 2017.

41 Published by EiShuppansha publishing house with the aim to "re-discover the magic of Japan's things, people, and places" (from the magazine's official website); available at http://discoverjapan-web.com/, accessed November 30,2019.

42 Koichi Iwabuchi, "Soft Nationalism and Narcissism: Japanese popular culture goes global," *Asian Studies Review* 26, no. 4 (2002): 447–469.

determined by the difficulty in apprehending precisely what is "Japanese" about Japanese popular culture and by the increasingly de-centered nature of global soft power.[43] Coffee is the quintessence of this ambivalence, representing a cultural commodity that is "not precisely Japanese" and is largely de-centered, due to its association with a wide range of locations related to coffee production and consumption. The representation of Japan's coffee culture (both within Japan and abroad) as informed by its long-standing tea tradition grants coffee stability and cultural clarity, turning the two cultured substances—coffee and tea—into powerful allies.

5 Conclusion: Coffee Encounters from Perry to Starbucks

How do specific times and places define the nature of intercultural encounters? In order to answer this question, we could look at big macro-scale encounters, such as that between Commodore Perry's black ships and Japan; this essay chose, however, to look at a rather small-scale encounter that nevertheless affected the complex of elements that we call "Japanese culture." In a manner similar to other substances such as butter, meat, or wheat, coffee helped to mold the Japanese body into a modern body; but, more importantly, it helped to carve, physically and metaphorically, new spaces of Japanese modernity. Japan has long since departed from the need to emulate the West and moved toward fulfilling new projects for which the West no longer serves as a model. In fact, Japan has often resorted to its own tradition as a hegemonic model shaping the discourse on culture. The ceremonial order created around tea represents one component of this discourse. Curiously enough, coffee's reputation as a sophisticated cultural commodity resonates with the established images of Japanese tradition, of which perfection and refinement have been an acknowledged part.

This is not to say that coffee was "Japanized." Japan's tendency to borrow and reproduce various elements of non-native culture and lifestyle has been often labeled as "Japanization," referring to a process of refining foreign content with Japanese aesthetical sensibilities. It assumes a one-directional (and one-dimensional) action that ends as soon as the Japanese modification is applied to a foreign substance. The story of coffee's appropriation in Japan undermines this rather simplistic perspective by demonstrating the complexity and multi-directional nature of the process. Coffee culture entered Japan as

43 Ibid, 448.

an attribute of Western civilization; its various manifestations were localized as sites of socializing, emancipation, cultural learning, political activism, or just the flow of everyday life.

The story of coffee also highlights the nature of Japan's modernization—or, rather, its peculiar path to modernity—in which coffee played a part. To Eisenstadt, modernity is a reaction to particular historical changes, and Japan's modernity can be defined in terms of a dynamic dialogue between traditionality and innovation, between the search for authenticity and the desire to modernize.[44] Indeed, while Japan's interpretation of modernity assumed no rigid division between the Japanese and Western modes, it nevertheless retained their symbolic distinction. Despite its domestication, coffee retained its foreign "odor" that still informs its marketing and the design of coffee spaces. With the advent of globalization, coffee came to serve as a venue for Japan's participation in a global lifestyle whose images were diffused by global agents of consumption and popularized by global media. Moreover, Japan's export of its coffee format overseas may be regarded in the context of its growing influence as the world's post-modern "soft power."

Encounters often imply power relations. The encounters fostered by coffee have been shifting the focus of power between Japan and its "other," creating a landscape in which culture moves in multiple directions and in which particular historical moments shape the nature of particular encounters. The encounters discussed in this essay were not limited to those between East and West, the global and the local: in the course of 150 years, coffee and cafés provided a space for much wider range of contacts. In this process, new hybrid forms were often produced, varying from the jazz café and manga *kissa* to the *matcha* latte. Manga *kissa* (Japanese comics cafés) are places where people pay for the time they stay to read manga. A *matcha* latte is a beverage made from powdered green tea prepared with steamed milk in a manner similar to the café latte, which became extremely popular with the proliferation of coffee chains. Having departed from both the imported Western and traditional Japanese formats, such forms indicate the multiplicity of vectors and cultural variations emerging when one culture meets another.

This landscape is not without tension, however. Most certainly, foreign-inspired trends often push aside locally conceived indigenous forms, causing loss of local content and authenticity. This is especially true for global actors capable of altering, due to their global reach and ubiquity, the very fabric of

44 Shmuel Eisenstadt, *Japanese Civilization: A Comparative View* (Chicago: University of Chicago Press, 1996).

the local landscape. While the proliferation of global coffee chains in Japan has caused a gradual decline in the number of independent *kissaten*, it simultaneously (and rather paradoxically) reinforces the *kissa* style by underpinning its sense of genuineness. Recently, local coffee makers increasingly define themselves through the contrast with the chains—as genuine, real, relating to real people and not the faceless consumer crowd. This way, coffee chains may be contributing to the further indigenization of Japanese coffee. This indigenization often takes place on a micro rather than macro level—while a part of collective memory, coffee also nurtures individual projects, visions, and interpretations that become no less significant for the shaping of Japan's coffee culture.

Coffee has mutated considerably as it crossed national and cultural boundaries, shifting from a medicinal substance to an exotic artifact and then to a mundane beverage without which life would be nearly unimaginable. The taste of coffee has also changed drastically on its path between the coffee stalls of Constantinople and Japanese cafés in New York City. However, the role of coffee as a site for encounter continues to trigger both imagination and economy, creating new spaces of culture.

Bibliography

Cowan, Brian. "What Was Masculine About the Public Sphere? Gender and the Coffeehouse Milieu in post-Restoration England." *History Workshop Journal* 51, no. 1 (2001): 127–157.

Cross, Tim. *The Ideologies of Japanese Tea*: Subjectivity, Transience and National Identity. Folkestone, Kent, UK: Global Oriental, 2009.

Derschmidt, Eckhart. "The Disappearance of the Jazu-Kissa." In *The Culture of Japan as Seen through its Leisure*, edited by Sepp Linhart and Sabine Fruhstuck, 303–312. Albany: State University of New York Press, 1998.

Discover Japan: An Insider's Guide (official website), accessed November 20, 2019, http://discoverjapan-web.com/.

Ellis, Markman. *The Coffee House: A Cultural History*. London: Weidenfeld & Nicolson, 2004.

Grinshpun, Helena. "The City and the Chain: Conceptualizing Globalization and Consumption in Japan." *Japan Review* 24 (2012): 169–195.

Habermas, Jurgen. 1989. *The Structural Transformation of the Public Sphere*. Translated by Thomas Burger. Cambridge, MA: MIT Press.

Hastings, Sally. "A Dinner Party is not a Revolution: Space, Gender and Hierarchy in Meiji Japan". In *Manners and Mischief: Gender, Power, and Etiquette in Japan*, edited by Jan Bardsley and Laura Miller, 95–113. Berkeley and Los Angeles: University of California Press, 2011.

Hi-Collar Café (official website), accessed January 31, 2017, http://hi-collar.com.

Iwabuchi, Koichi. "Soft Nationalism and Narcissism: Japanese popular culture goes global." *Asian Studies Review* 26, no. 4 (2002): 447–469.

Klein, Naomi. *No Logo*. New York: Picador, 2000.

Laver, Michael. "Butter Diplomacy: Food and Drink as a Social Lubricant in Dutch East India Company Trade with Japan." *Education about Asia* 17, no. 1 (2012): 5–8.

Liberles, Robert. *Jews Welcome Coffee: Tradition and Innovation in Early Modern Germany*. Waltham: Brandeis University Press, 2012.

Ogawa Coffee USA (official website), accessed January 31, 2017, www.ogawacoffeeusa.com.

Schivelbusch, Wolfgang. *Tastes of Paradise: A Social History of Spices, Stimulants and Intoxicants*. New York: Pantheon, 1992.

Silverberg, Miriam. *Erotic Grotesque Nonsense: The Mass Culture of Japanese Modern Times*. Berkeley: University of California Press, 2006.

Surak, Kristin. *Making Tea, Making Japan*. Stanford: Stanford University Press, 2013.

Takai, Naoyuki. *Nihon Kafe Kōbōki* (The Rise and Fall of Japanese Café), Tokyo: Nihon Keizai Shinbun Shuppansha, 2009.

"The Advertisement of Georgia Canned Coffee is Chauvinistic!: The Feminists' Criticism" (Japanese), Tantei File portal, accessed June 30, 2020, http://www.tantei-file.com/geinou/scoop_2014/03/02_01/.

The Women's Petition against Coffee (full text), accessed September 18, 2020, https://quod.lib.umich.edu/e/eebo/A66888.0001.001?rgn=main;view=fulltext.

Tipton, Elise. "The Café: Contested Space of Modernity in Interwar Japan." In *Being Modern in Japan*, edited by Elise Tipton and John Clark, 119–135. Honolulu: University of Hawaii Press, 2000.

White, Merry. *Coffee Life in Japan*. Berkeley: University of California Press, 2012.

Yomiuri Shimbun. "World's First Canned Coffee Celebrates 50th Anniversary," October 2015, https://www.asiaone.com/worlds-first-canned-coffee-celebrates-50th-anniversary-0.

PART 2

And Beyond

CHAPTER 6

Puentes de la Communidad

Building Bridges in an Early Childhood Center

Donna Heckman Stapleton

Globalization and expanded transportation have made immigration of people more prevalent, and American public schools, as educators of the people, are consistently facing more diversity and the impact of other cultures.[1] This chapter is a case study regarding the consequences of migration and family engagement with a public school in the United States, and an effective response to those consequences. The response, a program titled *Puentes de la Communidad* (Community Bridges) avoided the "deficit models" that have shaped many American education responses to communities of immigrants who have crossed cultural borders.[2] Accordingly, this chapter describes a successful program of crossing cultural and social borders in the service of early childhood education, and parental engagement in the process. It argues that border-crossing has been done, and can be done, wisely and respectfully in order to create effective, efficient, and positive outcomes for institutions and their diverse constituents. It is critical to understand and become more culturally competent and utilize strategies to reach across boundaries and barriers in order to have our institutions benefit from the diversity and the skills that are often hidden by estrangement and communication barriers.

In the early childhood program that I will describe, the staff rejected deficit models which have been used to describe the literacy inabilities of minority youth and parents. This program used a strength-based model for assessment and processing. It approached the plan and the program by looking at the skills, commitments, and assets of the minority community/constituents, in order to privilege their voices and concerns. The program goal was to tap the skills and commitment of the minority parents (largely Hispanic/Latinx) and consequently empower them as they engaged with challenges of public

1 Harry I. Chernotsky and Heidi H. Hobbs, *Crossing Borders: International Studies for the 21st Century* (Los Angeles: CQ Press, 2013), 15.

2 Valerie Kinloch, *Crossing Boundaries: Teaching and Learning with Urban Youth* (New York: Teachers College Press, 2012), 6.

 | DOI:10.1163/9789004435506_008

education in a new culture that emphasizes literacy, verbal interaction, and oral communication.

Typically, when minority children attend English-speaking schools they are more able interpreters and consequently they often take on more power within their families while parents become more dependent and less assertive. American schools expect and desire parental communication and assertiveness.

Communication is the one central skill needed to be successful in any culture, and more so in a democratic American environment.

> We expect schools in a democratic society to be defined by a spirit of cooperation, inclusion, and full participation, places that honor diversity while building unity.[3]
>
> ...schools would aim for ... a commitment to free inquiry, questioning, and participation; a push for access and equity and simple fairness; a curriculum that encourages independent thought and judgment; a standard of full recognition of the humanity of each individual.[4]

Increasingly, schools are challenged to recognize these human rights, and

> This means teaching toward freedom and democracy, and it's based on a common faith in the incalculable value of every human being; it assumes that the fullest development of all is the condition for the full development of each, and, conversely, that the fullest development of each is the condition for the full development of all.[5]

This chapter is the story of a novel public school venture created from 2003 to 2010 to work with the increasingly multicultural constituency of an urban-suburban New York area (USA) school. I report on this venture as a participant-observer, and will discuss the premises held by the constituents, the context of the school, the concerns observed (problem to be solved), the boundaries needing to be crossed, the issues considered, the program goals and facets, the personnel engaged in the program development and delivery, the institutional response to the novel program, and the outcomes. I will highlight the complexity of crossing borders, the risks of reaching out to empower the less powerful, and the efforts on the part of the service providers to give up power in favor

3 Kinloch, *Crossing Boundaries*, x.
4 Kinloch, *Crossing Boundaries*, ix.
5 Kinloch, *Crossing Boundaries*, x.

of those on the other side of the borders. Although each individual brought different expectations to the project, the effort, commitment, vision, and personal discipline required were extraordinary.

Overall, this is a story about connecting immigrant parents with their children's school through a multi-pronged set of opportunities developed by a school staff that drew on its own border-crossing experiences and its cumulative knowledge of the immigrants, including the use of scholarly concepts and data, to create a successful school-community program. These elements included extensive planning, personal commitments, reflections, and critique of personal interactions with parents, and multi-faceted partnering of the school and the community. While this case study does not claim to provide a blueprint for all cases of societal border-crossing, it does illuminate several elements that are likely to undergird success.

1 Setting

The New York urban-suburban school district's population has been diverse for many years. This population is composed of a wide range of socioeconomic groups whose members live in housing ranging from five-thousand-square-foot homes that shelter world business and political leaders, to 450-square-foot apartments that shelter first-generation immigrants, many from Mexico, who often work in the service sector of the economy. The suburb has a population that varies from multigenerational residents to very transient residents due to emigration trends and national and international trade and diplomacy tasks focused in the New York metropolitan area.

This chapter focuses on the public Early Childhood Center, housed in an attractive, stone elementary school building constructed in the 1930s and part of the public school system serving approximately eleven thousand students. In the Center, during the period under discussion, support staff included two social workers, a school psychologist, three speech therapists, a reading specialist, two English-as-a-Second-Language (ESL) teachers, two registered nurses, several teaching assistants and paraprofessionals, three administrative assistants, an assistant principal, and a principal, who served approximately 650 children and their parents. Many of the staff in the Center were monolingual but about thirty percent were bilingual, with their secondary or primary language being Spanish (from their childhoods in the Caribbean Islands, Spain, South and Central America and Mexico). As a school staff we daily experienced the reality noted by organizational-culture observer Michael Shaw that "people carry into the organization the accumulated social and ethnic cultures of virtually every social and ethnic group to which they belong or to which they belonged in the past."[6] Several of the staff had worked in non-public missionary settings outside of the United States and in social service ventures within the United States prior to their employment in the school.

As a monolingual social worker I contributed to the planning and implementation of *Puentes*. I brought to the program two years of inner-city missionary work, five years of assisting clients with mental health and identity issues, twenty years in school social work in multi-ethnic settings, a graduate degree in the science of social administration, post-graduate education in school administration, undergraduate and graduate teaching in social work and social science, and global travel experience, including rural and urban Mexico. Throughout my career I was consistently committed to empowering minorities and assisting clients with cross-cultural, cross-border, and personal transitions.

As a participant-observer of the venture that was developed at the Early Childhood Center, I will, in this chapter, reflect on and analyze how the program created to address the multicultural and multilingual population of the Center was developed and became so successful in addressing needs, bridging the gap in educational awareness, and overcoming evident barriers. As a monolingual English-speaking social worker addressing the children and parents of the Latinx community and the other ethnic and cultural families coming to the school, it was apparent that I, along with other members of the school staff, needed to be aware of and sensitive to cultural diversity. In order to overcome obstacles in communication, address boundaries between the school and family expectations, and improve problem-solving, we, as a school, needed to respond to and empower minority parents. In order to have minority parents more engaged in the education of their children, I was often in conversation with the bilingual English-as-a-second-language (ESL) teacher, bilingual social workers, and the psychologist about concerns and problems that occurred, and ultimately we began envisioning a parent outreach program.

2 Vision

As a social worker I was relying upon my skills in problem assessment and program development, group work management, and sixteen years of working

6 Michael Shaw, *Finding the Rainbow: Organisational Culture—The Key to Corporate Performance* (Johannesburg, South Africa: Ravan Press, 1997), 8.

in schools with interdisciplinary teams and program administrators. I was, at the time of the new program's development, keenly aware of points of vulnerability and potentially-defeating behaviors. Now, having been removed from the school by several years of retirement I can see the complexity of the program production and its reliance on the character and commitment to the many professional goals the staff of the *Puentes* program possessed. I see ever more clearly that such a program required all the participating staff members' understanding of both the observable and subtle aspects of crossing borders, their willingness to subjugate their own egos and empower other's egos, and their willingness to share power and shift some power without alarming the larger institution's and community's stability.

My graduate education at Case Western Reserve University's School of Applied Social Science had focused on the ecological approach to assessing problems, creating policies, and creating programs.[7] I specialized in understanding medical and educational problems and providing social work interventions in "host settings" (settings where the primary institutional missions were not social service). I had an affinity with people, and understood other cultures and their demands and expectations. I enjoyed interdisciplinary teamwork. Working as a school social worker in such a diverse settings was exciting and challenging. Specifically, serving a diversity of parents and students in this inner-ring suburban setting led to new insights and skill development daily.

It has long been established that parental engagement in schools is directly related to student achievement and success in the schools. My designated role in the schools was to link parents with the schools and link schools to parents. In my experience as a school social worker in four different school districts in Ohio and New York, where I worked in thirty-three different schools, *Puentes de la Communidad* was the most outstandingly successful venture I have observed. I had worked in primary, secondary, and post-high-school settings, and had been engaging and empowering parents from a range of socioeconomic, ethnic, racial, and cultural groups. I had developed programs to address and ameliorate many school-related problems, but this larger multidisciplinary and multi-cultural group of school personnel was the most complex work group in my experience. It heightened my sensitivity to the many components of having a group of peers facilitate cultural and educational boundary crossings.

---

7 E.g., John T. Pardeck, *Social Work Practice: an Ecological Approach* (Westport, CT: ABC-CLIO, 1996).

3 The Early Childhood Center

It is clear that parents are the first teachers of children, and that how they view education and the manner in which they teach children is formative.[8] The Early Childhood Center in this school district was a "magnet" program designed to attract and engage parents and children from throughout the district.[9] The Center was populated by children whose parents were socioeconomically, racially, and culturally diverse, and who had many strengths and made special efforts to have their children enrolled in the program. The parents had entered their children in a lottery to gain a space in the school that served students from the entire community and not just those from its own neighborhood.

The parents, who had come from different parts of the world, were engaged, motivated, and intelligent. We were aware of their assets, resources, strengths, and commitments to their children. Michael Shaw writes that "the causes of [organizational] culture are many and varied and they stem primarily from the behavior and activities of the organization's founders and its leadership."[10] We were privileged to have as head of the entire city school system a superintendent who had spent a career teaching in the school district and had great pride in the schools' achievements and a strong commitment to the diversity of the community.

At the Early Childhood Center we learned that many of the Hispanic parents felt culturally disconnected, often by having come from rural areas in the Mexican state of Jalisco only a few months earlier. Some were saddened by their own limited education, with most having had only eight years of schooling. Having seen our Latinx and other non-English-speaking parents' eagerness to have their children attend the magnet school and their ability to overcome the bureaucratic obstacles to such attendance, it was easy to "… reject deficit models that have traditionally defined the literacy abilities of students [and parents] of color."[11] Our ESL teachers and our bilingual school psychologist and bilingual school social worker had observed the parental strengths, concerns,

---

8 "Parents are a Child's First Teacher," accessed February 18, 2017, at www.urbanchildinstitute.org.

9 Magnet schools encourage diversity. "Student interest in a theme is the only eligibility criteria," and "What are Magnet Schools?," accessed February 18, 2017, at www.magnet.edu.

10 Shaw, *Finding the Rainbow*, x, text changed to conform to American spelling.

11 Kinloch, *Crossing Boundaries*, 6. The author further states: "In this rejection, *Crossing Boundaries* reflects [a] … commitment to privileging the voices of students who too often have been marginalized in public debates on educational improvement and academic achievement."

and motivations, and with their understanding of second language acquisition, had worked to build the Spanish-speaking parents' self-confidence as educators. They wanted to encourage the idea that one researcher has summarized as "the bits of advice, the *consejos* [expertise] parents should be able to offer children in their everyday interactions with them."[12] They had worked with individual Spanish-speaking parents to expand their engagement with school activities, and had reinforced the idea that the parents were indeed their children's first and most important teachers. The Early Childhood Center's bilingual staff and teachers became crucial actors in planning a program to bridge the gaps experienced by Spanish-speaking parents and their children. They understood the impact of language barriers and wanted to develop a means to empower parents.

Although all of us were school district employees, each of the support and pupil personnel staff and teachers who grew interested in addressing the minority parents programmatically had different roles, skills, identities, and professional mandates. We had our own boundaries to cross as we attempted to create a programmatic response. As individuals we had varying cultural and professional identities (Germanic, Hispanic, White, Asian, African-American; mental health specialists, speech and language facilitators, general education teachers, parents, etc.), and some of the staff were first- and second-generation immigrants. Staff had some work to do to overcome strong identity boundaries and barriers, so that we could develop a program that would acknowledge experiences of being a minority, recognize feelings and patterns of behavior when language and jargon were not understood, and observe differences in cultural responses to various situations so that we could consistently engage all who were to participate. We, as committed staff who saw barriers to parental engagement, had to do our own "forming, storming, and norming" before performing.[13] We believed that our diversity could lead to a more comprehensive understanding of the challenges we faced, and create a more balanced and effective program.[14]

---

12 Lily Wong Fillmore, "When Learning a Second Language Means Losing the First," *Early Childhood Research Quarterly* 6 (1991): 343. Thanks to Dr. Laura Raynolds for recommending this research.

13 These are well-recognized phases of group work and group process across all institutions. See David B. Egolf and Sondra L. Chester, *Forming, Storming, Norming, Performing: Successful Communication in Groups and Teams*, 3rd ed. (Bloomington, IN: iUniverse, 2013).

14 According to one guide, "diverse workforces are … rich seedbeds for new [organizational] ideas": *Managing Diversity: Expert Solutions to Everyday Challenges* (Boston, MA: Harvard Business Press, 2009), 5.

We had several meetings to share the things we had heard from the Spanish-speaking parents, our own experiences within groups, our own learning styles, our own personal experiences as students and parents, and to discuss things that we had hoped would have been offered to us as learners and parents. We did some significant introspection and group work before developing the specifics of the program and engaging parents, because, while such diversity within the staff could provoke conflicts, we regarded them as cues and assets in developing the program.[15] The staff's introspection foreshadowed parents' needs.

Most of the staff who volunteered to develop this program had already been working together on child-centered team assessments and the design of individualized interventions. The school social workers and the school psychologist had carefully developed child-centered teamwork, insisting that each discipline had merit and should be able to honestly contribute insight into the strengths and needs of students and families. Specifically, educational planning was adjusted and modified to meet the needs of students who were outside of the norms: these included underachieving students, handicapped students, and students who presented management challenges in the regular classrooms.[16]

Important to the context of program planning was the Early Childhood Center's long-standing adoption of the Reggio Emilia philosophy of early childhood education which had been developed in northern Italy after World War II. Emphasizing learning by kinesthetic activities and in natural settings, it had taken root at the Early Childhood Center in the 1990s, and was firmly in place when I arrived in 1997. In a school utilizing the Reggio Emilia philosophy, social workers are important figures, observing student-teacher interactions, participating actively in classroom discussions, and providing social services in a consultative manner. In a recent article Lella Gandini has commented that

> Waldorf, [and] Montessori [philosophies] … have many points in common [with Reggio Emilia] … they are built on coherent visions of how to improve human society by helping children realize their full potential as intelligent, creative, whole persons. Children are viewed as active authors of their own development … [while] partnering with parents is highly valued in all three approaches, and children are evaluated by means other than traditional tests and grades.[17]

15 *Managing Diversity*, 7–18.

16 *Managing Diversity*, 31–33.

17 Carolyn Pope Edwards, "Three Approaches from Europe: Waldorf, Montessori, and Reggio Emilia," *Early Childhood Research and Practice* 4:1 (2002), unpaginated online

The Reggio Emilia approach, as practiced at the Early Childhood Center, strongly reflected its adaptability for children with disabilities and language deficits. The children's own voices were privileged, as were the children's interconnections with their environments outside of school—including parents, siblings, and native culture. And, although the Reggio Emilia approach was designed originally for early childhood education, it had been expanded over time into primary education settings, and was a good fit for our Early Childhood Center that served three-year-olds through second-graders in the very diverse school district. As a social worker regularly visiting classrooms, I was impressed by the teachers' encouragement of student exploration and problem-solving, as well as the learning-by-doing, that are hallmarks of the Reggio Emilia approach to education. Developing an outreach to immigrant families was not only clearly congruent with Reggio Emilia's educational philosophy, but also its home and school connection component.

The staff at the Center was accustomed to presenting worrisome and difficult teaching-learning situations to the child-centered pupil services team, the school social workers, the school psychologist, the school nurse, the reading specialists, the speech and language therapists, and the administrative staff. Consequently, much communication work had been done to give credit and respect to each person's professional training, expertise, and experience. The child-centered pupil services team provided some direct service to families and students but typically worked collaboratively with teaching staff to facilitate home–school communication, adjust classroom management techniques, provide encouragement to students, and assess needs for remedial and special education services.[18]

At the beginning, there had been some role conflicts and competition between teachers and support personnel about direct communication with parents, some disputes between social workers and psychologists about assessment of students' learning difficulties and behaviors, and some professional perspective issues between some of the monolingual speech and language therapists and ESL instructors about the critical impediments to language development and mastery. The hours of work and leadership of the "child-centered" team discussions and conscious "team-building" efforts had resolved some of those identity and cultural issues, and laid a foundation for

journal; Lella Gandini, "Values and Principles of the Reggio Emilia Approach," accessed September 15, 2016, at www.learningmaterialswork.com/wp-content/uploads/2016/06/ValuesandPrinciples.pdf.

18 Special education services are designed to address students with physical, intellectual, and emotional disabilities that cannot be attributed to social and cultural histories.

the various professionals to work more cooperatively and analytically. We learned to understand each others' language, perspectives, and values and to trust each other and value each other's contributions to the school's central mission and the team's goal attainment: development of more engaged and effective students. The child-centered team had practiced crossing boundaries and professional divides, and recognized the feelings and identity problems that could develop.

The metropolitan-suburban school district discussed here, located in a culturally-diverse area of the United States, recognized the political and social power of diverse groups and was accustomed to having parents participate actively and assertively in the school. It had a strong Parent-Teacher Association (PTA) and had actively-contested elections of committed school board members who managed the federal, state, and local resources, oversaw public education mandates, and maintained overall educational goals with flexibility to address local concerns. The district's parents, staff, and community took pride in the schools' successes, and parents were routinely seen within the schools as volunteers and advocates, and were often hired as part-time "paraprofessionals" who supervised lunchtimes, playground activities, and who did some record-keeping. Many of the professional staff also chose to live in the school district and had children who were enrolled in its schools, giving them two identity groups.

4 From Vision to Program Development

As our programming team of volunteer staff (generally about twelve people) considered planning a special program to engage immigrant parents, tap their strengths and skills, and expand their involvement in the educational process of their children, bilingual parents were recruited. These parents, who had been engaged with the bilingual social worker and who had expressed concerns about their children, were invited to join the planning group and provide assistance with the conceptualizing and delivery of the program. We engaged those parents' cultural expertise and urged their active participation in the program implementation. In this we were following Jorge Duany's recommendation that "scholars should use qualitative techniques such as participant observation and intensive interviewing to document migrants' cultural repertoires, identities, and interactions."[19] The team developed a questionnaire

19 Jorge Duany, *Blurred Borders: Transnational Migration Between the Hispanic Caribbean and the United States* (Chapel Hill: University of North Carolina Press, 2011), 9. Our team

about topics of potential interest to parents and sent it to all of the Center's parents.[20] We received a substantial response and used that to develop topics and materials for the program.

Soon there was consensus that the problem we wanted to address was the hesitancy of non-English-speaking parents to vocalize concerns about their children's performance in school, and reports by Hispanic parents that they could not assist in their children's educational process due to their own limited schooling and minimal English fluency. Noting similar situations, Duany has noted that some scholars have "suggested that transnationalism, not assimilation, better explains the cultural dilemmas of today's immigrants."[21] Our Hispanic parents often felt ill-equipped to give advice to their children when they were in this new nation with both language and cultural differences. They also were committed to preserving their identities as Spanish speakers who regularly visited their countries of origin. We did not believe that a major goal of the Early Childhood Center should be to expect a language shift in the Mexican-American households—a shift that could have negative consequences.[22]

There was also a consensus that the policy of having a democratic, egalitarian approach was critical to the program. This fit with the amicable diversity of the community setting, the Reggio Emilia approach to education, and the ecological approach to intervention which was the core philosophy of most of the pupil personnel and support staff. Belief in the empowerment of immigrants and underserved populations was strongly held by most of the staff who volunteered to plan and deliver this outreach program. The individual team members had had several experiences of crossing boundaries and engaging with "foreign" languages, ideas, and communication styles, and our goal was to empower and facilitate the development of skills in English-as-second-language families, so that school performance, parental engagement and confidence, and therefore student performance, would improve overall.[23] We were willing to risk new strategies and invest in outreach to the thirty percent of the school population who needed to bridge the cultural gap to become more

---

was composed of Master's and Ph.D.-holding personnel who continued to take graduate-level coursework, attend academic conferences, and develop intervention programs, derived in part from knowledge of current social science research. We were committed to data-driven solutions to problems.

20 Our questions were similar to those reported in: Fillmore, "When Learning a Second Language Means Losing the First," 326.

21 Duany, *Blurred Borders*, 28.

22 Wong, "When Learning a Second Language Means Losing the First," 332–333.

23 For parallel considerations in a business environment see: *Managing Diversity*, 36–39.

successful in the US public education system. We recognized the importance of dialogue between immigrant parents and school staff. We accepted the dangers of misunderstandings and mistakes, reckoning that the benefits of dialogue far outweighed the inevitable errors in communication, which needed to be reconciled.[24]

The bilingual staff and ESL instructor, who were already sensitive to cultural differences, quickly gathered their observations and engaged their expertise.[25] They understood that the immigrant families had already given up a lot in coming to the United States,[26] and had already made major personal and cultural adjustments.[27] They knew that children learning English in school often took on more authority within the family as they routinely provided translation in conferences and community engagements,[28] and that "Mexican immigrant families, where parents are typically laborers with low levels of formal schooling ... transmitted to their children an emphasis on schooling and an ethic of hard work, though this [was] expressed in more general life terms rather than specifically with regard to academic achievement."[29] And, although there is increasing mobility in the world, "national identities remain salient in many localities."[30]

Our immigrant families continued to have frequent contact with their communities of origin, and many often returned to Mexico during the school year for annual holiday family gatherings. The Center's bilingual staff understood that Mexican cultural norms and mores remained significant for our immigrant families. Specifically, they observed that the parents' deference to our governmentally-funded schools, their hesitancy to speak up at school conferences, their deference to teacher authority and power, and their intentional agreement with teacher perspectives, sometimes created obstacles to problem-solving. As planners, we understood that the Latinx norms that parents held generally made them less assertive with bureaucracies, and less willing to risk alternative perspectives and defend their children's perspectives, than many

24 Kinloch, *Crossing Boundaries*, xi.

25 They were familiar with Paulo Freire's work, first published in Portuguese in 1968, and in English as *Pedagogy of the Oppressed* (New York: Herder and Herder, 1970).

26 Vivian S. Louie, *Compelled to Excel: Immigration, Education and Opportunity among Chinese Americans* (Stanford, CA: Stanford University Press, 2004), 124.

27 Louie, *Compelled to Excel*, 62–63.

28 Wong, "When Learning a Second Language Means Losing the First," 343.

29 Louie, *Compelled to Excel*, 186.

30 Andreas Wimmer and Nina Glick Schiller, "Methodological Nationalism and Beyond: Nation-state Building, Migration and the Social Sciences," *Global Networks* 2 (2002): 326.

English-speaking parents. For the success of our future program, we had to develop visions of how to empower the Spanish-speaking parents, build trust and comfort, and reinforce their skills that related to school performance.

We had to recognize that accomplishing our visions required re-examining our school's organizational culture and our perceptions of the immigrant culture.[31] The *Puentes de la Communidad* program that began to emerge in 2003 was designed to bridge cultural gaps and bring the Latinx parents to understand the Early Childhood Center, and even New York norms of open expression, debate, dialogue and more egalitarian collaboration.[32] In the broadest sense we supported the idea that "for a democracy to survive and flourish, those who have been silenced need to find their voices."[33] *Puentes de la Communidad* needed to provide ample time and space for Latinx parents to come into the school building, engage in a language and literacy activity led by staff, be encouraged to share personal emotional, social, and educational reactions to the language and literacy tasks, and have a sense of school hospitality. Nearly all the volunteer staff had heard immigrant parent tell stories of brief academic instruction in schools which were hierarchical and where students' and parents' skills and interests were commonly minimized. Nearly all the parents had reported that previous encounters with schools in their countries of origin had been proscribed, negative, and stressful. Many parents reported that their parents were never invited to their school unless there was a serious problem and complaint. However, the bilingual staff at our school had found that parents responded very positively to staff outreach and to their intentional advocacy.

5 Concrete Program Planning

We were committed, in developing the *Puentes* program, to having evenings of relaxation, good humor, smiles, positive feedback, and programming not constricted by assumptions. The volunteer staff was rigorously committed to listening, observing, and validating parent communication, so that anxiety, fear, and negative encounters would not occur.

---

31 Shaw, *Finding the Rainbow*, 9.

32 Victoria Rashbaum, 2009–2010 annual report, 14 May 2010, courtesy of Victoria Rashbaum, bilingual school social worker.

33 Kinloch, *Crossing Boundaries*, 11, quoting L. Darling Hammond, "Education for Democracy," in *A Light in Dark Times*, eds. W.C. Ayers and J.L. Miller, eds. (New York: Teachers College Press, 1998), 91.

Since confidence, success, and positive feedback about performance are directly related to engagement and risk-taking and therefore to furthering one's intellectual and social engagement in an activity, it seemed critical that we provide such experiences to the immigrant and ESL parents. Management theory recognizes that "negotiation styles vary widely across cultures."[34] We worked at minimizing cross-cultural misunderstandings by approaching immigrant families within their own frameworks of family and culture, while at the same time expanding their knowledge of the norms and expectations of a typical American school. With these observations, beliefs, and goals, we designed a program to target the needs of the parents' who spoke English as a second language.

The bilingual personnel began collecting an array of pre-school and early childhood-age books that had been published in both English and Spanish, for example, *Where the Wild Things Are/Donde Viven Los Monstruros, The Parrot Tico Tango/El Loro Tico Tango, New Shoes for Silvia/Zapatos Nuevos para Silvia, The Kissing Hand/Un Beso En Mi Mano*. These books were full of pictures, a range of family members, and situations: they were literacy building blocks. The bilingual ESL teacher, social worker, and psychologist convened all of the staff who had shown interest in planning and facilitating this outreach program. The books were read by the entire volunteer school staff, reviewed and discussed to determine our own social, emotional, and educational reactions and experiences with the storylines, language, and interpretation, the assumptions we held, and the memories they provoked. This preparation by the staff was done to pre-test the activity impact, and to help ourselves have some personal responses and comments that might be shared during the planned program with the parents. We were surprised to discover our own wide range of experiences and reactions: many of the staff, both monolingual and bilingual, had negative memories of their own educations; many of the staff had not had parents who read books to them; and there was much diversity in staff identification with the characters in the books. This range of individual staff identities made us better able to understand the immigrant families' responses and behavior.

The books that were chosen were specifically identified as being of interest to both children and adults. We tried to make sure that there was "a wide variety of books in Spanish that reflect[ed] Mexican-American culture, morality, and religious beliefs."[35] For example, open-ended questions were used

34 *Managing Diversity*, 67, 69.

35 Laura Raynolds, "Puentes: Educators and Parents Building Bridges Together," unpublished paper, 2010, courtesy of Laura Raynolds, English-as-a-second language (ESL) teacher.

and modeled during the *Puentes* sessions. Those questions affirmed diverse responses and led to more verbal expression and dialogue. We encouraged parents not to mimic school dialogue or to focus on formal language, but to use the Spanish- and English-language books they had (or that we encouraged them to acquire from the public library) to share their own stories and life lessons with their children in Spanish. We emphasized the casual, family-oriented aspects of taking "picture walks" and looking at books with their children, while at the same time validating language skills as keys to education.[36] We knew the parents could facilitate more language concept-development and skills using that process.

Those of us who believed in this novel program and wanted it to be successful began thinking about the impact and engagement that monolingual English-speaking staff could offer and provide. I specifically argued that parents who were English-dominant needed to be invited to participate in *Puentes* to maintain the policy of being democratic, egalitarian and increasing the empowerment of the immigrant parents without threatening the English-dominant parents or stigmatizing the immigrant parents who would engage in the evening program. I argued that it was important to give both the English-dominant parents and the immigrant, Spanish-dominant parents opportunities to mingle and have common experiences.

When boundaries and borders are crossed there is a correlated shift in power, with power diminishment, power sharing, and new empowerment. We wanted to have all parents within the school and all in the community welcomed and invested in the success of the *Puentes* program. We wanted to avoid what has been called a "pretend-to-be-democracy."[37] Our plans were rooted in a belief, like that of urban educator Valerie Kinloch, that "establishing explicit connections with engaging and learning … provides a framework for teaching and learning that opens up expansive possibilities for students to participate in collaborative meaning-making, text-making, and community-building processes."[38]

Those of us who were effectively monolingual had already intentionally worked with bilingual families in our regular roles—using our minimal

---

36 A "picture walk" allows recognition of words' similarities and differences. It occurs when the leader asks the learner to look at a book's pictures and the words on a page to consider what is going on prior to actual reading of the text. See "Pre-Reading Strategies," accessed 23 July 2017, at www.bankstreet.edu/literacy-guide/reading-strategies/pre-reading-strategies.

37 Kinloch, *Crossing Boundaries*, 56, quoting one of her students.

38 Kinloch, *Crossing Boundaries*, 58–59.

Spanish and their emerging English skills. Clearly, we could provide physical hospitality and encourage and host English-speaking parents who were also interested in expanding their educational engagement with their children. (American parents have been told repeatedly that their engagement with the school has a direct positive relationship to their children's school success.) And, I argued that we needed to be visibly supporting English-speaking parents, as well as immigrant parents, if our goal was to help parents cross social and cultural boundaries and become more integrated into all the school activities and processes.

We called the conceptualized program *Puentes de la Communidad*, translated in English as "Community Bridges" because it was intended to assist parents and staff to traverse language, social, political, professional, socioeconomic, and cultural boundaries, barriers, and identities, and create a more cohesive school community. After some months of conceptual planning, concrete plans and activities for the program began to occur. The staff agreed that program activities needed to be fun and exciting for parents, and primarily experiential with cross-cultural dialogue. For example, we agreed that we would invite and engage both English and non-English-speaking parents. The program was aimed primarily at empowering the large Mexican-American constituency, and facilitating all student learning, but we wanted European, African, and Asian immigrants, as well as English-speaking parents to attend the *Puentes* meetings, look at the same children's book, take picture walks, and share reflections so that they could feel more confident with their language and literacy skills.

The *Puentes* sessions would be presented in a small-group format with a group leader, working with five to ten parents who would be encouraged to take a picture walk through the selected book to look at illustrations and text with clues regarding the story, count similar objects, and find words and items they identified/recognized—for example, colors, animals, fruit, furniture, facial expressions, types of buildings,—and then later in the evening, with staff assistance, read the book for the event. Parents would be encouraged to talk in their preferred language about the thoughts and feelings that the book provoked, so that they could share their knowledge, experiences, and memories. To provoke opinions and verbal expression, staff specifically formulated open-ended questions, such as, "Who is in the picture?; Where are the people?; What does this remind you of?; Do you know what is going to happen?"[39]

39 Victoria Rashbaum, planning notes, 2003, courtesy of Victoria Rashbaum, bilingual school social worker.

In the *Puentes* program entitled "Increasing Your Child's Vocabulary While Enjoying Books Together," where *New Shoes for Silvia* was shared, there was discussion about disappointment, patience, difficulty with waiting, creativity, and resiliency. These were concepts that were included in their children's Reggio Emilia classrooms, and for which parent-child discussions could occur in their original language.

When *The Parrot Tico Tango* was shared similar questions were asked and parent reactions were sought. There was also an opportunity to discuss phonemic awareness, and the sounds that are made in various languages. When looking at *The Kissing Hand*, in the session entitled "Using Books to Help Children Express Their Feelings," the same open-ended questions were used in the parents' groups and their feelings, ideas, stories, and reactions to parent-child separation became obvious, and we encouraged parents to use the same open-ended questions in Spanish to elicit and respond to their children's feelings and concerns.

In each parent session, parents were asked to reflect on how much they already knew from taking the picture walk and scanning for words they recognized. When the books were actually read, parents were already able to feel connected to the books, see all that they could offer their children, and consider all that they could inquire about and elicit from their children. Because singing, which draws on memory, rhythm, and sound differentiation, has been shown to facilitate all sorts of language development, during the *Puentes* programs songs and rhymes, such as "Row, Row, Row Your Boat," "The Itsy Bitsy Spider," "Humpty Dumpty Sat on a Wall," "The Wheels on the Bus Go Round and Round," and the "ABC Song," as well as Spanish songs, were used to demonstrate the dynamics of language and literacy skills.

When "Teaching Language Through Everyday Activities at Home" was the topic, approximately 150 fathers and mothers, as well as extended family members, attended the session and used the cardboard-replica washers, dryers, laundry realia, and sports equipment that were provided.[40] The open-ended questions (mentioned above) elicited a large range of vocabulary and concepts that could be appropriately used during routine household tasks and play: colors, ownership, use, style, size, motion—all nouns, verbs, adjectives, and adverbs that were within family members' Spanish-language repertoires and could easily be verbalized with their children. Parental use of Spanish, as they talked to their children, was encouraged because it expanded language concepts and literacy skills, which could then be transferred into English within

40 Rashbaum, 2009–2010 annual report.

the school and community setting. We were creating what Kinloch has been termed "culturally relevant instruction."[41]

In the broadest sense, our work was in accord with Virginia Satir's observation that, "once a being has arrived on this earth, communication is the largest single factor determining what kinds of relationships he makes with others and what happens to him in the world about him."[42] We believed that elements of communication, body, values, sensory organs, expressive language, receptive language, and expectations of the moment all affect the brain, which Satir has called "the storehouse of knowledge."[43] And we anticipated that all of these features could be expanded and optimally engaged if they were not diminished by erroneous assumptions of ignorance and inadequate expressive language.

The "Puentes Committee" decided on the dates, times, and spaces needed for the program. We decided that evening meetings once a month would allow teaching and school staff to volunteer their time, beyond the contracted working hours, and would allow both professional and service-sector parents in the community, who worked during the daytime and had no flexibility in their hours of work commitment, to meet together to share experiences and learning.

The committee approached the school administration about having access to the school during evening hours when the Center was typically empty and locked, and permits were granted to have it opened and safely equipped with technical equipment, seating, lighting, and custodial support. Four areas of the Center were chosen for use. The gymnasium, which was immediately in the front and center of the building entrance, was used as the gathering site for all who attended. It was familiar to all the Center's parents, and was able to house the entire gathering: there, many songs such as *Yo Tenia 10 Perritos* (*I Had Ten Puppies*) were sung while snacks and beverages were offered and the evening activity was introduced to all present. Another area was used for English-dominant parent activities; and a third area, the library, with all of its resources and its colorful fairytale characters visible on the murals was used for the bilingual parent activities. Childcare, provided without cost for families, was located in the fourth area, the gross-motor activity room and the auditorium, where games were played and films could be shown. Providing for childcare was critical to the success of this outreach because we recognized that immigrant families always came to the Center with their entire family constellation.

41 Kinloch, *Crossing Boundaries*, 123.

42 Virginia Satir, *Peoplemaking* (Palo Alto, CA: Science and Behavior Books, 1972), 30.

43 Satir, *Peoplemaking*, 31.

The volunteer personnel offered to take specific responsibilities. In addition to facilitating the English-dominant group, the monolingual English speakers, volunteered to manage and develop physical materials for the program. Specifically, I designed and built a ten-foot-long cardboard model of a bridge (*puente*) with stones of many shapes and colors to symbolize the program and allow the first session's participants to attach notes with expressions of all sorts, but especially individual hopes, dreams, concerns, and expectations for their children.[44] The bridge with the widely-varying parental notes was then displayed throughout the many *Puentes* events. I also routinely designed table decorations (multicolored flower arrangements, ribbons, and streamers) which would be welcoming and evocative of both the school district's diversity and the immigrant cultures. The reading specialist and others designed and built a range of cardboard props for activities: for example, a giant red shoe, a clothes washer and dryer, a brown paper package, and other items which were used in various sessions.

The bilingual staff designed invitations to *Puentes*/Bridges which were printed in Spanish on one side of the sheet and English on the other side of the sheet and given to each student in the school. The invitations announced that the sessions and activities were designed to build parent-child communication and would be facilitated by the monolingual social worker and the bilingual social worker who were visible and who had done previous parent workshops. The invitations' welcoming style reinforced the Reggio Emilia mantra that "children and adults thrive when there is a strong sense of belonging and optimism for the future."[45] In designing the invitations we immediately confronted the language barrier: the Spanish word for parent is translated as "padre" and is suggestive only of the father, and we therefore redesigned the invitations to address both *padres y madres* (fathers and mothers). Our immigrant families used few "babysitters," and had little or no extended family who could volunteer to provide childcare during evening events. In fact, most of our upper-class English-speaking families also hired few babysitters and had no extended family nearby. Childcare was a necessity for the success of *Puentes* and, therefore, in the invitation we assured parents that it would be provided

44 The parents' questions were similar to those asked by researcher Wong, "Were they worried about their children losing the language of the home? Whose responsibility did they think it was to help them retain it? What did they want us to tell policy-makers and educators about their concerns as parents?" in Wong, "When Learning a Second Language Means Losing the First," 326.

45 "About NAREA: Our History. Our Philosophy. Our Impact," accessed September 15, 2016, at www.reggioalliance.org/narea.

at the Center during the discussion time and children within the family would be given adequate supervision.

Responses to the *Puentes* invitations began to come back and we saw in the responses that there was significant interest. The committee prepared for the programmed events during the school days, and was prepared to greet each family as it arrived. The families were gathered together for singing and food, then directed to the areas within the school with which they self-identified.

Some immigrant families (with primary languages from Africa, Europe, and Asia) chose to participate in the English-dominant sessions. Families from Mexico and Central America typically chose the Spanish-dominant group even though they came from a wide range of Spanish-speaking countries, with some language variations and significant cultural differences. Children went to an area to make crafts, play games, or watch a film under the supervision of several monolingual and some bilingual staff.

In the *Puentes* program we wanted to bring about interaction and interdependence and increasing communication and cooperation between school staff and parents, between professionals and non-professionals, between parents with strong English-language skills and parents with minimal and marginal English language skills, between parents and children regarding school assignments, activities, and academic skill development, and between dominant and minority cultures with very different school programming and experiences.

As Laura Raynolds, an ESL staff member deeply involved in *Puentes's* development concluded, "If Mexican-American parents appropriate school-mandated home reading for their own purposes and in ways that feel comfortable and appropriate, rich language that promotes the higher-order thinking skills in children will naturally and spontaneously accompany the parents' reading."[46] In contrast, the loss of the language of origin can have a disastrous effect on academic ability.[47]

6 Outcomes and Reflections

Our *Puentes* team, volunteering time in the late afternoons and evenings, was in fact a conglomeration of what Dennis Young has described as social entrepreneurs "engaged in breaking new ground in [their] administrative

46 Raynolds, "Puentes: Educators and Parents Building Bridges Together."

47 Wong Fillmore, "When Learning a Second Language Means Losing the First," 325, 344–45.

or organizational role rather than engaging simply in customary managerial practices or ordinary decision-making."[48] We were intentional "change agents" who were bringing new immigrants into the schools for a provocative and engaging set of amiable, amicable, and reassuring skill-building events. *Puentes* was a venture to empower non-English-speaking parents and to validate their language and ability to be effective parents in a largely English-speaking society. We attempted to foster what Kinloch has described as "creative pedagogies [with] … collaborative meaning-making, text-making, and community-building processes."[49]

The volunteer parents and teachers enjoyed these cross-cultural sessions and continued to volunteer for several years. The *Puentes* team observed them smiling and laughing, experiencing joy, expressing personal satisfaction, and having more candid parent-teacher discussions. Fathers, mothers and grandparents attended *Puentes* sessions monthly, and within several months bilingual parents became group discussion leaders. The conscious creative attempt to keep the events fun and relaxing continued: for example, fruit snacks were arranged to look like the fruits in the book illustrations.

Puentes events were photographed and the photographs were placed in the galleries in the Center's hallways for the entire school to appreciate, following the Reggio Emilia philosophy of showing learning activities and outcomes. The program continued to give books and folders with literature about suggested activities at home to individual families. Parents were encouraged to use the community's free public library with its extensive Spanish and English resources.

We developed a cohort of committed and engaged "alumni" parents and committed retired teachers who engaged intimately with *Puentes* session planning. Non-English-speaking parents who attended *Puentes* programs for multiple years developed English competency and eventually asked for English versions of the books that could then be read at home. They had become bilingual while retaining their language of origin.

Breaking free of traditional boundaries of disciplines, the *Puentes* team had become, in part, community organizers, as well as educators. We were "in

48 Rachel Mosher-Williams, "Introduction," in *Research on Social Entrepreneurship: Understanding and Contributing to an Emerging Field,* ed. Rachel Mosher-Williams. ARNOVA Occasional Paper Series, v. 1, no. 3 (Washington: Aspen Institute, 2006), 15, quoting Dennis R. Young, "Entrepreneurship and the Behavior of Nonprofit Organizations," in *The Economics of Nonprofit Institutions: Studies in Structure and Policy,* ed. S. Rose-Ackerman (New York: Oxford University Press, 1986).

49 Kinloch, *Crossing Boundaries,* 58–59.

community," engaging in demonstration, modeling and the practice of literacy-building strategies, not outsiders instructing and prescribing tasks that parents were required to perform.

7 Postlogue

While replication of the *Puentes de la Communidad* program would be desirable, one may caution that *Puentes* developed in a unique setting with many variables already in place providing its foundation. The staff's experiences in direct engagement with those with identities different from their own clearly facilitated its crossing of boundaries to work with minority immigrant parents who had diverse identities and needs. This program was extremely successful and was celebrated by its participants.

Fundamental to the success of *Puentes de la Communidad* were the individual experiences of the boundary-crossing personnel who already were in place; the Reggio Emilia philosophy of the Center; the community's long history with and commitment to diversity; the creative interdisciplinary teamwork that existed within the Center; and the weekly work of the child-centered study and evaluation team. Those factors facilitated the development of this creative, experiential program. One should also consider that in crossing borders, individuals, groups and institutions do their own cost-benefit analysis. We who volunteered to implement the program universally wanted to create a setting and framework where costs were minimized (there was no negative criticism, no shame, no role conflict, and no disabling cultural conflicts), and where benefits (expanded skills, pride of parenting, sense of welcome), and some tangibles (such as food, laughter, camaraderie, and books), were shared and given to participants.

Funding and institutional support were ever-present challenges for *Puentes*, and dependency upon non-fiscal off-budget personnel was ever more problematic as *Puentes* staff members faced personal changes. Health issues, leaves of absence, and retirements had significant impacts on the delivery of the program. Momentum was diminished as those personal changes produced personnel losses: the loss of the initiating bilingual social worker and the ESL teacher meant that fewer program sessions were produced and the absence of their specific and unique personal skills and commitments was felt when new session topics were not developed and programs were repeated. By 2015 much of the energy for the program was gone, and *Puentes* sessions were very sparse. Remaining enthusiasts looked to other institutional programs that would present *Puentes*-like activities.

Funds to pay for honorariums and to purchase supplies were required, but the costs of the program, both tangible and intangible (e.g., volunteer hours and provision of food and supplies) were always variables and sources of concern. Funding was very "soft." Some money came from the "Reading Is Fundamental" funded program; some money came from specific community grants which were obtained by the ESL teacher and the bilingual social worker; and some money came from specific grants requested from the ESL program director within the school district. With resources so limited and dependent, transfer of the program to more institutionalized groups, such as the Center's Parent-Teacher Association, was difficult.

The positive responses of administration and powerful community support organizations are important. Administratively, the Center's assistant principal was supportive of *Puentes* and invested time and energy in the program. However, the Center's principal, the district director of the ESL program, and the new school district superintendent, who came after the retirement of the supportive long-time superintendent, displayed no direct program support. The teachers' union leadership did not engage *Puentes* staff about the precedent of such voluntary time commitments and could present a counterforce in the future production or replication of the *Puentes* program.

American scholars of the intersection of public education and immigration have struggled with the impact of schools and educational processes. As Chernotsky and Hobbs have noted, "For many years, the perceived purpose of many societies was to create a common culture such that immigrants to a new place would restructure their identity or 'melt' into a common pot. The emphasis on assimilation submerged cultural differences into a broader, dominant culture."[50] One may return to Mai Ngai's previously quoted comment that "immigration poses challenges for several normative principles of democratic society. Liberalism's assumptions of universal equality and inclusion are qualified by the question of community definition, the drawing and maintaining of boundaries that simultaneously include and exclude."[51] Valerie Kinloch similarly argues that people always "view school as either an empowering place or as an institution equipped with alienating structures that are not named for what they are."[52] And finally, Vivian Louie states that for immigrants there is the hope "that education opens new vistas of opportunity in that it is a highly transportable good that never

50 Chernotsky and Hobbs, *Crossing Borders*, 180.

51 Ngai, "Brokering Inclusion," 135.

52 Kinloch, *Crossing Boundaries*, 111.

declines in value, and, equally important that it can never be forcibly taken away."[53]

The *Puentes* experience certainly validates the idea that we should approach teaching "as a reciprocal act, where teachers teach students, and students teach teachers in ways that are facilitative. We can no longer approach teaching as a one-sided act or activity where 'the teacher issues communiqués and makes deposits and students receive such deposits."[54] It has been said that "the success in institutions—schools, workplaces, and so on—is predicated upon acquisition of the culture of those who appear in power ... the culture of the school is based on the culture of the upper and middle classes—of those in power."[55] With increasing globalization and migration we must learn about other cultures, acquire skills, and find strengths that cross the usual boundaries of power. *Puentes de la Communidad* gave voice, attention and visibility to the commitment of non-English-speaking parents. Those parents who attended *Puentes* were students who taught us, the presumed teachers.

One might ask, why was this Early Childhood Center able to turn its vision into appropriate actions and into a successful program? In this case it had to do with the community's positive history of diversity, the original commitment of the Center to Reggio Emilia's student-centered approach, to a professional staff steeped in bilingual and multicultural encounters, to Latinx and other immigrant parents' commitment to educational attainment for their children, and, underlying all, a program vision that sustained all stakeholders through the long period of planning and execution.[56]

Bibliography

"About NAREA: Our History, Our Philosophy, Our Impact." Accessed September 15, 2016. www.reggioalliance.org/narea.

Chernotsky, Harry I. and Heidi H. Hobbs. *Crossing Borders: International Studies for the 21st Century*. Los Angeles: CQ Press, 2013.

53 Louie, *Compelled to Excel*, 54.

54 Kinloch, *Crossing Boundaries*, 122.

55 Kinloch, *Crossing Boundaries*, 93, quoting Lisa Delpit, *Other People's Children: Cultural Conflict in the Classroom* (New York: Norton, 2006), 25.

56 Shaw, in *Finding the Rainbow*, 4, suggests that successful organizations in multi-cultural environments evince "a specific identity, an attitude, a set of values and beliefs, a competency, [and] a personality" that others often do not develop.

Duany, Jorge. *Blurred Borders: Transnational Migration between the Hispanic Caribbean and the United States.* Chapel Hill: University of North Carolina Press, 2011.

Edwards, Carolyn Pope. "Three Approaches from Europe: Waldorf, Montessori, and Reggio Emilia." *Early Childhood Research and Practice* 4 (2002): 1, n.p.

Fillmore, Lily Wong. "When Learning a Second Language Means Losing the First." *Early Childhood Research Quarterly* 6 (1991): 323–346.

Freire, Paulo. *Pedagogy of the Oppressed.* New York: Herder and Herder, 1970.

Gandini, Lelia "Values and principles of the Reggio Emilia approach." Accessed September 15, 2016. www.learningmaterialswork.com/wp-content/uploads/2016/06/ValuesandPrinciples.pdf.

Kinloch, Valerie. *Crossing Boundaries: Teaching and Learning with Urban Youth.* New York: Teachers College Press, 2012.

Louie, Vivian S. *Compelled to excel: Immigration, Education and Opportunity among Chinese Americans*. Stanford, CA: Stanford University Press, 2004.

Managing Diversity: Expert Solutions to Everyday Challenges. Boston: Harvard Business Press, 2009.

Moser-Williams, Rachel. "Introduction." In *Research on Social Entrepreneurship: Understanding and Contributing to an Emerging Field,* edited by Rachel Moser-Williams, 7–11. ARNOVA Occasional Paper Series, 1:3. Washington: Aspen Institute, 2006.

Ngai, Mae M. "Brokering Inclusion: Education, Language, and the Immigrant Middle Class." In *Citizenship, Borders and Human Needs*, edited by Rogers M. Smith, 135–156. Philadelphia: University of Pennsylvania Press, 2011.

Pardeck, John T. *Social Work Practice: an Ecological Approach*. Westport, CT: ABC-CLIO, 1996.

"Parents Are a Child's First Teacher." Accessed February 18, 2017. www.urbanchildinstitute.org.

"Pre-reading strategies." Accessed July 23, 2017. www.bankstreet.edu/literacy-guide/reading-strategies/pre-reading-strategies.

Rashbaum, Victoria. Unpublished planning notes, courtesy of the author, 2003.

Rashbaum, Victoria. "2009–2010 Annual Report." Unpublished report, courtesy of the author, 2010.

Raynolds, Laura. c. 2010. *"Puentes: educators and parents building bridges together."* Unpublished paper, courtesy of the author.

Satir, Virginia. *Peoplemaking*. Palo Alto, CA: Science and Behavior Books, 1972.

Shaw, Michael. *Finding the Rainbow: Organisational Culture—the Key to Corporate Performance*. Johannesburg, South Africa: Ravan Press, 1997.

"Student Interest in a Theme Is the Only Eligibility Criteria." Accessed February 18, 2017. www. magnet.edu.

"What are Magnet Schools?" Accessed February 18, 2017. www.magnet.edu.

Wimmer, Andreas and Nina Glick Schiller. "Methodological Nationalism and beyond: Nation-State Building, Migration and the Social Sciences." *Global Networks* 2 (2002): 301–334.

CHAPTER 7

In Their Own Words

Russian Literary Translators as Actors on Cultural Borders

Elena Baibikov

> Without translation, I would be limited to the borders of my own country. The translator is my most important ally. He introduces me to the world.
>
> ITALO CALVINO, "The Fantasy World of Italo Calvino"[1]

Cultures may come in contact in various ways. It might take the form of a direct contact between populations or occur as an indirect but also highly individualized contact through the mediation of cultural goods, such as movies, books or works of art. Those who serve as mediators of cultural experiences and goods, for example interpreters and literary translators, appear to be significant actors at the cultural borders, creating opportunities for cross-cultural encounters.[2]

1 Frank MacShane, "The Fantasy World of Italo Calvino," *New York Times Magazine* (July 10, 1983): 23–50.

2 For a more detailed account on the nature of cross-cultural contacts see Itamar Even-Zohar, "Laws of Cultural Interference," in *Papers in Culture Research,* ed. Itamar Even-Zohar (Tel Aviv: The Culture Research Laboratory, 2010), 52–69. The notion of translation as cultural mediation gained recognition in the 1990's and since then it has been broadly discussed in numerous publications such as David Katan, *Translating Cultures: An Introduction for Translators, Interpreters and Mediators* (Manchester: St Jerome, 2004 2nd edition); Susanne Bassnett, "The Translator as Cross-Cultural Mediator," in *The Oxford Handbook of Translation Studies,* ed. Kristen Malmkjær and Kevin Windle, K. (Oxford University Press Canada, 2011), 97–107; Paola Attolino et al.'s (*Re*)*visiting Translation* (New York: Peter Lang, 2015) and many others. Eventually, this view on translation (and translators) could be found somewhat problematic, but to me it seems to be rather a problem of terminology. Cultural mediators possess an 'agency' of acting independently and making their own choices, they aren't necessarily advocates of mediated culture and their views of it could be critical. But whatever their views are, through their 'agency' they create contexts of cross-cultural contact; therefore, they are 'mediators' in the sense that they activate interaction between cultures.

 | DOI:10.1163/9789004435506_009

The term "cultural border," being physical in origin, often connotes the border/boundary of a state or a nation; it is assumed that if two national communities or "societies, identified with two distinct cultures come in contact, a cultural border is expected to form between them."[3] That is, an essentialist view of culture presumes a high degree of homogeneity within cultural areas with fixed borders.

The implied equation between a territory and a culture has prevailed in anthropological discourse[4]; in translation studies too it was common to most academic approaches to believe that "there is a border between two cultures well before any translator enters the scene."[5] Following a "cultural turn," an influential paradigm shift in the study of translation in 1980s, translators have come to be conceptualized as agents of a communicative process and cultural change, acting at so called cultural borders—borders that, just like physical ones, might be crossed or bridged.[6] And indeed, depending on a given research objective, translators were and still are referred to by most researchers as individuals who cross, eliminate, bridge, violate, or even create boundaries.[7]

3 Heewon Chang, "Re-examining the Rhetoric of the 'Cultural Border'," *Electronic Magazine of Multicultural Education* 1, no. 1 (1999).

4 Ibid.

5 Anthony Pym, "Alternatives to Borders in Translation Theory," in *Translation Translation*, ed. Susan Petrilli (Amsterdam/New York: Rodopi, 2003), 452.

6 See Christina Schäffner, "Action (Theory of "Translatorial Action")" in *Encyclopedia of Translation Studies*, ed. Mona Baker (London: Routledge, 1998), 3–5. See also Jeremy Munday, "Issues in Translation Studies," *The Routledge Companion to Translation Studies*, ed. Jeremy Munday (London: Routledge, 2009), 1–19; Myriam Salama-Carr, "Translators and the Dissemination of Knowledge," in *Translators through History*, eds. Jean Delisle and Judith Woodsworth (Amsterdam: John Benjamins & Unesco Publishing, 1996), 101–127; Helle V. Dam, "The Translator Approach in Translation Studies: Reflections Based on a Study of Translators' Weblogs," in *Haasteena näkökulma, Perspektivet som utmaning* [Point of view as challenge], *Perspektivität als Herausforderung. VAKKI-symposiumi XXXIII 7.–8.2.2013*, eds. Maria Eronen and Marinella Rodi-Risberg (Vaasa, Finland: VAKKI Publications 2, 2013), 16–35; Daniele Monticelli and Anne Lange, "Translation and Totalitarianism: the Case of Soviet Estonia," *The Translator* 20, no. 1 (2014): 95–111.

7 See, e.g., Jean-François Joly, "Preface," in *Translators through History*, eds. Jean Delisle and Judith Woodsworth (Amsterdam: John Benjamins, 1995), ix–xii. See also Douglas Robinson, *Becoming a Translator: an Introduction to the Theory and Practice of Translation*, 2nd ed. (New York: Routledge, 2003); Paula G. Rubel and Abraham Rosman, "Introduction: Translation and Anthropology," in *Translating Cultures: Perspectives on Translation and Anthropology*, eds. Paula G. Rubel and Abraham Rosman (New York: Berg, 2003), 1–22; Diana Roig-Sanz and Reine Meylaerts, "General Introduction. Literary Translation and Cultural Mediators. Toward an Agent and Process-Oriented Approach," in *Literary Translation and Cultural Mediators in 'Peripheral' Cultures. Customs Officers or Smugglers?*, eds. Diana Roig-Sanz et al., (Palgrave Macmillan), 1–37.

However, little research has explored what translators themselves say about this aspect of their work and how they conceptualize their professional action.[8]

In what follows, the focus of this chapter will be on literary translators, who in their intercultural encounters act as 'cultural mediators' and by this I mean communicative agents—persons who create contexts where cross-cultural contacts are highlighted or actually take place. Through the case study based on a survey of translators, the role of the individual in creating such contexts that allow the contesting of cultural borders is explored.

This study will also assess the way translators understand and conceptualize their professional action within the paradigmatic context of borders between cultures. The differences between the representations of conceptual and operational levels of translation will be examined.

1 Background of the Present Study, Its Objectives and Methodology

Recent developments and shifts in translation studies have brought to attention the relevance of translators as social and cultural agents and as a professional group.[9] Being a practicing translator myself I find this new research trend that was named *translator approach* (or translator studies)[10] to be a very promising perspective, descriptive in nature, for the understanding of intercultural communication and culture change.

8 However, recently there is a growing number of studies that, by employing the descriptive '*translator approach*,' address such issues as translators' status and working conditions, public and self-image, identity, power relations, etc. For example, see the following: Rakefet Sela-Sheffy and Miriam Shlesinger, "Strategies of Image-Making and Status Advancement of Translators and Interpreters as a Marginal Occupational Group: A Research Project in Progress," in *Beyond Descriptive Translation Studies: Investigations in Homage to Gideon Toury*, eds. Anthony Pym, Miriam Shlesinger and Daniel Simeoni (Amsterdam: John Benjamins, 2008), 79–90; Elena Baibikov, "Revised Translations, Revised Identities: (Auto) biographical Contextualization of Translation," in *Identity and Status in the Translational Professions*, eds. Rakefet Sela-Sheffy and Miriam Shlesinger (Amsterdam: John Benjamins, 2011), 173–188; Dam, "The Translator Approach in Translation Studies"; Rakefet Sela-Sheffy, "Translators' Identity Work: Introducing Micro-sociological Theory of Identity to the Discussion of Translators' Habitus," in *Remapping Habitus in Translation Studies*, eds. Gisella M. Vorderobermeier (Amsterdam: Rodopi, 2014), 43–55; Monticelli and Lange, "Translation and Totalitarianism."

9 See Dam, "The Translator Approach in Translation Studies"; Sela-Sheffy and Shlesinger, "Strategies of Image-Making and Status Advancement of Translators and Interpreters as a Marginal Occupational Group."

10 Andre Chesterman, "The Name and Nature of Translator Studies," *Hermes* 42 (2009): 13–22.

Culture change that happens, often as a result of intercultural communication and, more observably, in individual cultures, is possible because of the dynamic nature of culture. In her article dealing with the rhetoric of the "cultural border," anthropologist Heewon Chang shows that an essentialist view of societal culture—with its assumptions of culture as a "bounded, separate and homogenous system, expected to be shared by every member of society"—is not tenable when faced with modern multiculturalism.[11] Instead, Chang introduces the constructivist view of individual cultures where the clarity of "demarcation lines" are blurred.

The translator approach and Chang's assessment and re-examination of the essentialist view of culture provide a conceptual framework for this case study on how literary translators understand their roles and positions in intercultural context. I have adopted the cognitive metaphor theory of American cognitive linguist George Lakoff as an analytical framework.[12] By switching the focus from societal culture to cultures of individuals and looking closely at translators and their professional action as a locus of intercultural communication I will call into question the essentialist concept of "cultural border." Then, drawing on the professional self-representations of literary translators analyzed within the framework of the cognitive theory of metaphor, I will propose an alternative notion of cultural borders that highlights the creative potential of translators as communicative agents.

2 Data

The translation industry has many fields and specializations. Translators actively operate within two or more cultures, communicating information and ideas in different cultural contexts. Their professional competence involves complexities of competence: at a minimum not only linguistic and textual, but also cultural and social competencies.[13] I choose in this chapter to focus on top literary translators because they are typically conceptualized—by others and by themselves—as cultural mediators, transmitters of cultural values from

11 Chang, "Re-examining the Rhetoric of the 'Cultural Border'."

12 George Lakoff, "The Contemporary Theory of Metaphor," in Metaphor and *Thought*, 2nd ed., ed. Andrew Ortony (Cambridge: Cambridge University Press, 1993), 202–251.

13 Christina Schäffner, "Translation and Intercultural Communication: Similarities and Differences," *Studies in Communication Sciences* 3, no. 2 (2003): 93.

culture to culture, and artisans of communication.[14] As such they appear as highly relevant subjects for this study.

This study relies upon written interviews of a sample of renowned literary translators with a strong professional profile, selected from the Moscow-based *Guild of Literary Translators* as a main source of respondents. The Guild was founded in 2005. It is a non-profit professional organization, described by its founders as a "creative, professional association of translators of fiction, of both prose and poetry," with the main purposes of the "preservation and development of the artistic translation in Russia and the creation of such conditions under which the artistic translation would be the translator's direct labor."[15] The organization conducts seminars and meetings, provides grant support for the organization's members, and offers an award for the year's best literary translation into Russian in three categories: prose, poetry, and children's literature. The Guild functions as a founding partner of the Institute of Translation that awards an annual prize for best literary translation from Russian and organizes international congresses of literary translators (who translate both from and into Russian) in Moscow.

In February 2015, I contacted the secretary of the organization and received a list with email addresses of one hundred twenty-three of the Guild's current members. During the period from February to July 2015, I sent the questionnaire via email to the members and by August 2015 all completed questionnaires arrived in my email box. The response rate was thirty-four percent. After receiving the answered questionnaires, I contacted most of the respondents again, sometimes more than once, in order to clarify unclear points in their answers. Some respondents referred me to their published essays and interviews and in several cases I used these data as well.

---

14 See, e.g., Joly, "Preface"; Yves Gambier, "Translators and the Transmission of Cultural Values," in *Translators through History*, eds. Jean Delisle and Judith Woodsworth (Amsterdam: John Benjamins, 2012), 191–228; Sela-Sheffy, "Translators' Identity Work."; Roig-Sanz, D and Meylaerts, R., "General Introduction. Literary Translation and Cultural Mediators. Toward an Agent and Process-Oriented Approach." Through the vast body of their published works (such as translations, their own writings, and educational literature) and other cultural and educational activities (such as lectures, workshops, and interviews), the renown literary translator have an access to a broader audience and this means that their cultural impact as mediators is higher than in other cases of such mediation.

15 The Guild does not maintain a website at present; however, the archived version of the pages is available via the Internet Archive. The full list of the aims and objectives of the organization (in English) may be found on the website's thirteenth page and the English-language Articles of Association may be found by scrolling through the Russian text on a website's fourth page.

In total, forty-three Guild members assessed their professional and sociocultural position for the purposes of this study through the questionnaire-based survey with, for the most part, qualitative responses. The questionnaire contained open-ended questions that revolved around three main parameters:

1) sociocultural status (questions regarding additional roles of translators, importance of a translators' work, and the meaning of professional membership)
2) professional action (questions regarding selection process of what to translate and the overall influence of distance between cultures on translators' actions as professionals and as members of an occupational group)
3) self-conceptualization (questions regarding translators' own metaphors for their translating activity).

The analysis that follows is mainly qualitative. The descriptive approach I apply here draws upon the constructivist paradigm—espoused by such leading theorists as Jean Piaget and Lev Vygotsky—that assumes that an individual's perceptions of the world are constructed by language and discourse, or, in other words, by the way people talk about things and conceptualize them. This approach is associated with examining phenomena through the subjective voices of respondents.

3 Translator as Kulturträger: A Quest for Status Enhancement

As previous research shows, literary translators tend to mobilize and negotiate certain role-images (such as "cultural custodians" or "ambassadors of foreign culture") that highlight the importance and significance of their work within the target culture and society.[16] The present study supports these findings: in the answers of a majority of the respondents "translator" is referred to as a significant cultural agent: "disseminator of culture,"[17] "advocate of

16 See publications of Sela-Sheffy on literary translators and translators' "habitus": Rakefet Sela-Sheffy, "How to Be a (Recognized) Translator: Rethinking Habitus, Norms, and the Field of Translation." *Target* 17, no. 1 (2005): 1–26; Rakefet Sela-Sheffy, "The Pursuit of Symbolic Capital by a Semi-Professional Group: The Case of Literary Translators in Israel," in *Übersetzen–Translating–Traduire: Towards a "Social Turn"?*, ed. Michaela Wolf (Berlin: LIT, 2006), 243–252; Rakefet Sela-Sheffy, "The Translators' Personae: Marketing Translatorial Images as Pursuit of Capital," Meta 53, no. 3 (2008): 609–622; Sela-Sheffy, "Translators' Identity Work." Also see Sela-Sheffy and Shlesinger, "Strategies of Image-Making and Status Advancement."

17 Anonymous interviewee #1, written interview with author, July 9, 2015. When citing the interviews I use the names of the interviewees in the cases where I have permission to do

culture,"[18] "ambassador of one's own culture,"[19] "bridge that connects cultures,"[20] and as a "Kulturträger."[21] As such, the translator is seen to have a special mission of "shaping a cultural context,"[22] "launching not only cross-cultural but also cross-historical bridges,"[23] and "shedding light on long-forgotten cultural figures."[24] In social dimensions the translator also has the important tasks of "defending freedom of speech and possibilities for education,"[25] "to bring peace to the world through mutual understanding,"[26] "developing scientific and literary language,"[27] "creating a field of mutual understanding between people, languages, cultures, and histories,"[28] and "curing the fear of all things foreign."[29] Hence, literary translators construct the image of themselves as agents of cultural and social change *par excellence* in possession of potential social power.

Translators articulate the social and cultural importance of their agency via different communication channels on different public occasions. For example, twenty-five of my respondents (approximately sixty percent) signed a "Translators' Anti-war Petition" that was issued in September 2014 by the participants of the Third International Congress of Translators in Moscow.[30] Of course to sign an anti-war petition one does not have to be a translator—one may oppose war whether one is translator, teacher, or farmer. However, it is important to understand that many such petitions were initiated around that

so, and in the cases where I do not have such permission I am citing them as "anonymous interviewee #1," "anonymous interviewee # 2," and so forth.

18 Vladimir Babkov, written interview with author, July 9, 2015 (quote); Mikhail Yasnov, written interview with author, August 23, 2015.

19 Grigory Kruzhkov, written interview with author, March 1, 2015.

20 Olga Bukhina, written interview with author, March 16, 2015.

21 Olga Varshaver, written interview with author, February 25, 2015; Vyacheslav Kupriyanov, written interview with author, July 7, 2015. Kulturträger (German, lit. culture carrier) is someone or something that transmits cultural ideals, especially from one generation to the next.

22 Anton Nesterov, written interview, March 28, 2015.

23 Varshaver, written interview.

24 Alexey Prokopiev, written interview, March 11, 2015.

25 Lyubov Summ, written interview, May 26, 2015.

26 Varshaver, written interview.

27 Anonymous interviewee #2, written interview with author, July 2, 2015.

28 Nataliya Mavlevich, written interview with author, March 8, 2015.

29 Bukhina, written interview.

30 The document gathered more than three hundreds signatures, mostly from Russian and foreign translators. For the document in German and Russian and the full list of signatories see "Translators' Anti-war Petition." website.

time and translators who were "just against the war" could choose to sign any other anti-war petition not directly related to their profession. Their choice, though, was to support a petition that not only conveyed translators' collective protest against Russia's action in Ukraine, but also emphasized the concept of translators as cultural ambassadors and peace envoys. According to the petition:

> The duty of a translator as a cultural mediator is to promote and assist peace and freedom of speech, to openly stand out against violence and lies. Translation is possible only as free transfer of languages, ideas, cultures and worldviews.[31]

Why do translators stress their professional actions and outputs as culturally and/or socially significant? From a constructivist perspective that serves as an underlying worldview assumption for this study, discourse shapes the social world and relations within it. Occupying a marginal and relatively low-status occupational group, translators seek empowerment, professional prestige and status enhancement.[32] Literary translators, who "serve as the uncontested image brokers for the field at large,"[33] employ various tactics to change the profession's low-status image through that discourse: they publish essays and criticism, establish educational programs for translators and the general public, give interviews, talks, and lectures having in mind the popularization of the profession. As one interviewee commented:

> I am not obliged to popularize our profession, but I want (and I use every occasion) to assist spreading an interest in things that are important to me. I never refuse to participate in book presentations; I do take part in literary conferences and publish (rather seldom) academic papers on various authors. I also gladly join translators' meetings that involve mutual discussions of the works and [where] translators have a chance to really help each other.[34]

31 "A Labor of Love or a Science? Experts Gather in Moscow to Discuss Translation," *Russia Beyond the Headlines*, September 12, 2014.

32 Sela-Sheffy and Shlesinger, "Strategies of Image-Making and Status Advancement"; see also Dam, "The Translator Approach in Translation Studies."

33 Sela-Sheffy, "Translators' Identity Work", P. 51.

34 Tatyana Baskakova, written interview with author, March 10, 2015. Translation by the author.

Obviously, the recognition of translators as full-fledged professionals has not yet been achieved.[35] I believe the fact that many of my respondents serve in such roles as university lecturers, academic researchers, literary critics, editors, and language teachers is related to this lack of recognition. For some translators, it is reflected also in their rhetoric of the "secondariness" of material considerations.[36] Translators' experiences as "nameless anonyms"[37] and "invisible people"[38] whose work "brings neither fame nor money"[39] urges them to unite. And yet, paradoxically most of my respondents see the Guild not as a purely professional union that deals mostly with pragmatic issues, but rather as "members' social club" that promotes translators' social and cultural agendas. Other interviewees stated:

> This is our club. I enjoy being among friends who are not 'just friends' but people whose work I admire. It raises your own self-esteem too.[40]
>
> I was very glad and flattered to learn that I was accepted into this professional community composed of top-notch translators, who have justly earned an excellent reputation among their colleagues. I appreciate the efforts of the Guild's management to hold a high bar in spite of harsh conditions: they inform us about events, support the "sick and disabled," give a Master award for the best literary translation of the year. All these help us lonely artisans to maintain the feeling of fellowship and keen interest in what happens in our professional world.[41]

When it comes to the conceptualization of professional actions translators represent themselves as "lonely artisan,"[42] "one-man theater,"[43] and a creative individualist "whose work requires loneliness."[44] These expressions display a

35 See e.g., Sela-Sheffy and Shlesinger, "Strategies of Image-Making and Status Advancement."

36 For example, anonymous interviewee #2, written interview; Varshaver, written interview; Mark Grinberg, written interview with author, July 8, 2015; and Irina Volevich, written interview with author, July 3, 2015.

37 Anastasiya Starostina, written interview with author, July 8, 2015.

38 Anonymous interviewee #3, written interview with author, March 7, 2015; Anna Yampolskaya, written interview with author, July 7, 2015.

39 Azamat Rakhimov, "Alexander Livergant: Translating is [a] Humble Profession," (interview with Alexander Livergant), *Nasha Gazeta*, December 17, 2014.

40 Anonymous interviewee #4, written interview with author, July 4, 2015. Translation by the author.

41 Inessa Stam, written interview with author, July 5, 2015. Translation by the author.

42 Ibid.

43 Baskakova, written interview.

44 Yampolskaya, written interview.

working ethos of personal devotion and attachment, and they also stress the capacity of literary translators as people-of-art with strong personal creativity, as individual "agents" who construct and reconstruct their and others' worlds.

4 Individual Agency in the Professional Action of Translating

Within the limited scope of this study I examined translators' perceptions of their professional action within the paradigmatic context of intercultural borders and distance between cultures. The respondents were asked to specify criteria of selection of the text(s) for translation, to assess the distance between the cultures they work with and to describe their strategies in overcoming this distance.

Interestingly, eighty percent of my respondents (thirty-four of forty-three translators) mentioned their personal preferences ("I chose what is interesting for me," "I translate what I like myself") as the main criterion for the text selection. Personal preferences are so crucial that some literary translators, rather than translating something they do not like, might prefer not to translate at all:

> For me the possibility to choose [what to translate] is very important. Even though because of such "excessive discretion" some publishers have stopped working with me.[45]

Other frequently mentioned criteria were high degree of potential user appeal (six respondents), high artistic quality (five respondents), reputation and significance of the author (five respondents). Only three respondents mentioned social or cultural significance of the source text as an influential criterion.

The issue of cultural and social significance seems to be mediated differently when translators make representations of the conceptual level versus the operational level of translating. The vast majority of my respondents perceive their work as culturally important and sixty percent of them recognize it as socially significant. However, this significance is something that is visible to critics, readers, and translators themselves mostly externally, from the outside. One respondent remarked that as an insider of the translation process, the professional translator "should not think of himself as practitioner of [the socially significant] process of cross-cultural reception."[46] Indeed, some

45 Stam, written interview. Translation by the author.

46 Grinberg, written interview.

respondents reported that they perceive the concept of social significance as too comprehensive and encompassing,[47] and that usually during their daily work they do not engage conceptually with 'culture,'[48] are not interested in differences between cultures as such[49] and do not think of their professional action as "overcoming intercultural distance."[50]

In general, the notion of "intercultural distance" appeared to be highly subjective. For example, four different respondents—all of them translators from modern English into Russian—when describing the distance between contemporary British culture and Russian culture, referred to it as "close,"[51] "not close,"[52] "not far"[53] and "far."[54] There were respondents who spoke of overcoming in translation "temporal" rather than "cultural distance."[55] One respondent found the question on intercultural distance irrelevant and chose not to answer it at all.[56] Twenty-five respondents assessed the cultures they work with as "distant"(or "not close"); seventeen other respondents thought of the distance between their source and target cultures as rather "close" (or "not far"). However, some of those who defined the intercultural distance as "close" pointed out that this "proximity" might, in fact, be deceptive:

> One can say that Polish culture is close [to Russian culture], but this is an insidious 'closeness' that is full of temptations and, after all, it is not easier to translate from Polish than from English or French.[57]

The answers of my respondents also show that there are no significant differences in the strategies of overcoming "close" intercultural distance or "far" intercultural distance. "Deep understanding" of the source text's meaning and subsequent "explanation" and "transfer" of it through various intra- and

47 Anonymous interviewee #5, interview with author, August 16, 2015.
48 Alexander Yarin, written interview with author, July 3, 2015.
49 Babkov, written interview.
50 Vera Milchina, written interview with author, July 23, 2015.
51 Victor Sonkin, written interview with author, March 12, 2015.
52 Alexandra Borisenko, written interview with author, March 12, 2015.
53 Inna Streblova, written interview with author, July 12, 2015.
54 Anonymous interviewee #3, written interview.
55 Mavlevich, written interview; Baskakova, written interview; Milchina, written interview; and Yarin, written interview.
56 Nadezhda Buntman, written interview, June 30, 2015.
57 Marina Boroditskaya, written interview with author, February 28, 2015. Translation by the author.

extratextual means appeared to be the main strategy common to vast majority of my respondents, as one suggested:

> Translation itself, commentary to translation, translation criticism, discussions on specific translation phenomena, literary talks and meetings, translator's testimonies (including memoirs)—all these might serve as methods of overcoming "intercultural distance."[58]

Eventually, some of these methods are very similar to the tactics translators employ to enhance the low status of their profession (as mentioned above). This similarity is not accidental. According to a collection entitled *Translators Through History* (a comprehensive survey of the history of translation compiled by nearly fifty scholars from twenty different countries), ever since ancient times translators were those who held the key to most cultural and linguistic exchanges, and their potential social power is encapsulated in their work.[59] Therefore, translators' professional actions, the working methods translators report using to overcome intercultural distance, such as translation criticism, literary talks, and discussions, can at the same time serve as an instrument of their status enhancement.

The answers to the questions on text selection and intercultural distance (in other words, strategies of overcoming the distance and the social significance of such overcoming) can be summarized as follows: in representations of the conceptual level there is no objective and impartial notion of "intercultural distance," but the sociocultural significance of the translator's professional action is recognized by most of the respondents. When the operational level is represented, though, neither intercultural distance nor sociocultural significance is perceived by translators as a causal factor that influences their choices. Translators tend to represent their real-time professional action as one that is carried out not so much for the sake of society and culture (although, at the end of the day it does serve the society), but rather for the sake of professional and self-realization. After all, people feel good when doing what they love and know how to do best. Different methods and tactics can be effectively applied in every particular case, but in general all these tactics serve an underlying strategy of "understanding" that is subjective and individual. According to one of the most reflective respondents:

58 Kupriyanov, written interview. Translation by the author.

59 Jean Delisle and Judith Woodsworth, eds., *Translators through History* (Amsterdam: John Benjamins, 1995).

> When we talk about overcoming an "intercultural distance" within the particular text, there are many different tricks, such as intratextual explanations, usage of hidden quotations, etc. But I would prefer not to generalize about them as common principles. These are just several professional tricks among others. However, there is common sense, personal taste, sense of proportion and tactfulness—that's what rules in translating and not the theory.[60]

As Rakefet Sela-Sheffy, a prominent researcher into identity processes and self-representation among translators, points out, top literary translators tend to "stress inspiration and intuition … and are not simply unable to define translatorial competence, but rather take pains to *avoid* definition, evoking the vague idea of personal aptness instead."[61] Eventually, what matters in translating is the individual agency of translator, her ability to act independently and to make her own professional choices and decisions.

5 "Translating" as Reflected in Cognitive Metaphors

Exploring the professional choices of translators means investigating their way of translating (of doing translation) and their preferences in terms of translation norms (such as *domestication* or *foreignization*).[62] Analysis of the cognitive metaphors of "translating" sheds more light on the relations between "theoretical models and translation practice," as perceived by translators.[63]

According to George Lakoff, most famous for his theory of conceptual systems and cognitive metaphors, "the locus of metaphor is not in language at all, but in the way we conceptualize one mental domain in terms of another."[64]

60 Babkov, written interview. Translation by the author.

61 Sela-Sheffy, "Translators' Identity Work," 48.

62 Domestication and foreignization are strategies (or norms) in translation. These terms are used to characterize the degree to which translator makes a translation conform to the target culture. The former is the strategy of making translated text closely conform the target culture, while the latter is the strategy that involves breaking the conventions of the target language deliberately. See e.g., Daniel Gile, *Basic Concepts and Models for Interpreter and Translator Training* (Amsterdam: John Benjamins, 2009).

63 Celia Martin de Leon, "Metaphorical Models of Translation: TRANSFER VS. IMITATION and ACTION," in *Thinking through Translation with Metaphors*, ed. James St. André (Manchester: St. Jerome, 2010), 75–108.

64 Lakoff, "The Contemporary Theory of Metaphor," 203. Lakoff describes metaphor as "cross-domain mapping" that involves two domains: a source domain and a target domain. The target domain (TD) is understood in terms of the source domain (SD), thus

It means that metaphors are not only linguistic and rhetorical devices, but conceptual structures, and as such they "shape our thoughts, language, values, beliefs, and actions."[65]

Previous research offers several classifications of cognitive metaphors of "translation" and "translating." For the purposes of this study I will use two such classifications as an analytical frame for the further exploration of translators' self-conceptualizations and tendencies in their professional strategies. To explore the former subject, I will apply the detailed classification of metaphors by source domain,[66] and for the exploration of the latter the metaphorical models of Celia Martin de Leon, a Spanish researcher in a cross-field of translation studies and cognitive science, will be used.[67]

There are many metaphors of "translation" and "translating" that highlight different aspects of the translator's work. My respondents were not limited to selecting one choice; therefore, some answers contain several metaphors. Taking into consideration that the questionnaire brings up the issue of translation in the wider context of cross-cultural encounters/reception, intercultural distance/borders and intercultural communication, I assume the metaphors selected are perceived by the respondents as the most relevant to the implied context.

The most popular choice among my respondents was metaphors from the source domain of *performing/visual arts*. Twenty-seven translators (sixty-three percent) conceptualized "translating" as similar to such professions as stage acting, musical interpretation, dance, painting, and even the art of embroidery. Another frequently exploited metaphorical domain was that of

---

the cross-domain metaphorical mapping may appear in the following two forms: "TD is SD" or "TD as SD." For example, everyday English expressions such as "Look how far we've come" and "Our relationship has hit a dead-end street" are based on the metaphor LOVE IS A JOURNEY where the love relationship (TD) is regarded as a vehicle that allows lovers to move toward their common goals (SD). The cross-domain mapping for this metaphor is represented as follows: "THE "LOVE-AS-JOURNEY" MAPPING:

- The lovers correspond to travelers.
- The love relationship corresponds to the vehicle.
- The lovers' common goals correspond to their common destinations on the journey.
- Difficulties in the relationship correspond to impediments to travel.

Lakoff, "The Contemporary Theory of Metaphor," 207."

65 George Lakoff and Mark Johnson, "Conceptual Metaphor in Everyday Language," *The Journal of Philosophy* 77, no. 8 (1980): 464.

66 Dmitry Shatalov, *Metaphorical Conceptions of Translation* (PhD diss., Voronezh State University, 2014).

67 Martin de Leon, "Metaphorical Models of Translation: TRANSFER VS. IMITATION and ACTION".

caused motion (twelve respondents). This group of metaphors includes two sub-groups:

- metaphors of translator-as-carrier (Alexander Pushkin's famous metaphor of translator as the "post-horse of human civilization," translator-as-ferry metaphor and metaphor of translating as driving a bus)
- metaphors of translator-as-route-planner (metaphors of translator as a switchman or switchboard operator, translator-as-a-guide metaphor and an interesting metaphor of translating as a mole's subterranean movement).

Five respondents spoke of translating as a "philosophical art of interpretation" and of translator as a "philosopher-commentator."

According to Dmitry Shatalov, whose doctoral dissertation is focused on metaphorical conceptions of translation in England, Russia, and France, *performing/visual arts* metaphors represent translation as a new creation based on relative resemblance.[68] The stage-acting metaphor points out the necessity of adapting to the stylistic peculiarities of the original through the individual and creative understanding of an author's intention.[69] Similarly, the metaphors of painting/drawing and of musical interpretation illustrate the idea of re-creation of the original with new "insertions" and changes.[70] Thus, metaphors of translating as performing or visual arts are conceptualizations of the translation process as a creative process of achievement of partial and individually-perceived similarity. The same statement seems to be true for the translation-as-philosophical-art metaphor; but, the latter does not imply the emotional involvement of the translator, which appears to be an important characteristic of translators' professional activity as conceptualized through the *performing/visual arts* metaphor. And yet, both types of metaphors emphasize the manipulative role of the translator as an agent of change, and the purposefulness of her action.[71]

The "translating" (making of translation) is a purposeful action/activity, and as such it might be understood as motion. However, in *caused motion* metaphors the translator appears in the role of transportation device that is used to move/deliver cultural goods. In this case the cultural goods and meanings' motion is caused by the translator, who follows the existing trajectory of the

68 Shatalov, *Metaphorical Conceptions of Translation*, 224.

69 Ibid., 230.

70 Ibid., 223, 228.

71 Arts and crafts often involve processes of change and copying. The processes discussed here are not natural (as in genocopy) because they are being carried out purposely by humans. ibid., 135.

original. When a translator serves as a route planner he, eventually, also follows an existing route, but in this case he has to choose one of several possible trajectories tolerable to the source text. Through this kind of metaphor, the translator's active (though much less manipulative) role is accentuated.[72]

How does self-conceptualization of the translator correlate with the tendencies in her professional strategy? Drawing on the theory of conceptual metaphor, Celia Martin de Leon, through the cognitive analysis of metaphors, distinguished six metaphorical models: *transfer* model (e.g., translating as digging treasure out of the ground), *footsteps* model (e.g., translator as tracker who follows the footsteps of the source author), *target* model (e.g., translation is a motion to a destination), *assimilation* and *reincarnation* models (e.g. new recreation of the author's intention and translators as the "medium of the source author, who speaks through their mouths and writes through their pens"[73] respectively) and *projection* model (e.g., translation as conscious construction of the author's world in the translator's mind). Each model implies existence of a specific relation between source text (ST) and target text (TT) and, as the theory of cognitive metaphor states, shapes translators' actions.

Twenty-seven (63 percent) of my respondents used in their questionnaires more than one metaphor, or complex metaphors, thus creating synthetic metaphorical models of two types: *footsteps/reincarnation* (e.g., translator as switchboard operator, who connects different lines/translator as actor-elocutioner)[74] and *footsteps/assimilation* (e.g., translator as "post-horse of civilization"/translator as musician who interprets music in his own way),[75] including two cases of variation *footsteps/transformation* (e.g., translating as mole's digging that causes soil erosion).[76] The *footsteps* metaphor implies similarity between ST and TT and avoidance of change on translators' parts. At the same time, *assimilation* and *reincarnation* metaphors highlight differences between ST and TT and signalize that the translator most likely will tend to adapt ST to the target audience.[77] Usage of synthetic metaphorical models demonstrates aspiration

72 As opposed to a concept of *translatio studii* that was widespread in medieval times and later. According to this metaphorical concept of self-motion, "light of learning" or, in other words, knowledge, was moving from one country to another by itself much as the light of the sun or the blood in veins did. Ibid, 80–81.

73 Martin de Leon, "Metaphorical Models of Translation: TRANSFER vs. IMITATION and ACTION," 31.

74 Olga Maeots, written interview with author, March 15, 2015.

75 Bukhina, written interview.

76 Kupriyanov, written interview.

77 Martin de Leon, "Metaphorical Models of Translation: TRANSFER vs. IMITATION and ACTION," 37.

for the freedom of action: translators reserve the right to choose what strategy to apply in each particular case. This conclusion is supported by Sela-Sheffy's analyses of translators' identity discourses that reveal "the habitus-based range of translators' flexibilities in employing norms" and suggests that maneuvering between translation norms is a privilege of elite translators."[78]

Joined by eight respondents who used *projection* metaphors (e.g., translator as actor who focuses internally to portray a character's and an author's emotions onstage according to the Stanislavsky stage method),[79] the twenty-seven translators mentioned above are part of a larger group of thirty-five (eighty-one percent of respondents) whose metaphors correspond to models that hypothesize translator tendencies as attention to the different coexisting points of view.[80] Thus, the vast majority of my respondents conceptualize themselves as creative artists who act independently and have freedom to choose different ways of professional acting.

6 Acting at the Cultural Borders?

For a long time, the rhetoric of the cultural border was territory-based and focused on homogeneous, societal culture, suggesting that one culture represents one society and vice versa. However, in the current multicultural era, cultures have come to be seen as heterogeneous and dynamically-evolving open entities and the focus has switched from societal culture to cultures of individuals, who, as Heewon Chang points out, "serve as carriers, movers, consumers and inventors of a culture."[81] Through personal contacts, people invent and develop personal versions of a culture that are always carried with them. In a certain sense, each individual serves as a cultural mediator that communicates cultures through his or her individual agency, and each such contact appears to be intercultural.

78 Sela-Sheffy, "Translators' Identity Work," 52.

79 Anonymous interviewee #5, written interview.

80 Metaphors of the rest of the respondents fit into the *assimilation* (five respondents) or *reincarnation* (three respondents) categories of conceptual metaphorical models. The *transfer* model was not found in my respondents, supporting the assumption that proposing a simplified and all-encompassing view of the translation process *transfer* metaphor is usually exploited by novice translators. See, e.g., Celia Martin de Leon and Marisa Presas, "The Evolution of Translation Trainees' Subjective Theories: an Empirical Study of Metaphors about Translation," in *Metaphor and Intercultural Communication*, eds. Andreas Musolf, Fiona MacArthur and Giulio Pagani (London: Bloomsbury, 2014), 19–33.

81 Chang, "Re-examining the Rhetoric of the 'Cultural border'."

Seen from this perspective, translation may be understood as a mediated type of communication exercised by the individual agency of the translator and involving two different sides, such as source and target culture, and source and target language. These sides, supposedly, are separated by a cultural border. And translators, supposedly, act at this pre-existing border—crossing/breaking/eliminating or bridging it by their purposeful, culturally and socially significant professional actions. However, as the analysis in the previous sections shows, it is precisely the operational level that is represented by translators as one where they care less about cultural and social issues and more about personal and professional actualization. As one respondent put it:

> There are only a few cult [-classic] books. If you could translate two or three of them, you are lucky: your work is not for nothing. But you live every day, and you can't afford to wait until the opportunity to translate a masterpiece will turn up. You have to work on second rate novels too, after all they can also teach you something. At least you can get an idea of "their customs." And you always improve yourself; self-improvement is the meaning of life. Translation as a professional activity facilitates self-improving—you spend your working time on learning and self-actualization.[82]

Another respondent commented:

> You know, "work is just work, you'd better be strong" and so on. What is special about [translating], though, is that I really enjoy it and not every [other type of] work is enjoyable.[83]

My respondents, literary translators with strong professional profiles, are usually guided by their personal preferences, creativity, and inspiration. After all, they conceptualize "translating" as an artistic activity, as art in its own right.[84] This distinctive conceptualization gives us new insight or a different perspective on the cultural borders in translation. In the context of philosophy of art, a cultural border is understood as a "zone of most intensive intercultural communication ... where cultures not just share experience, but also hold a

82 Yulia Fokina, written interview with author, July 23, 2015. Translation by the author.

83 Anonymous interviewee #6, written interview with author, July 3, 2015. Translation by the author.

84 See also Sela-Sheffy, "Translators' Identity Work," 51.

dialogue."[85] So, rather than being a line, an intercultural border appears as a space where cultures actually meet and interact through mutual conversation. I believe the translators, whose profession is based on cultural overlaps, serve as precisely such spaces.[86] One respondent observed that:

> Both cultures, his own and the foreign one, are engaged in dialogue inside the head of the translator, a Kulturträger, while the quantitatively insignificant 'Present' along with an indeterminately better 'Future' are listening eagerly to their conversation.[87]

Rather than acting *at* cultural borders translators act *as* cultural borders and cultural spaces, exercising certain communicative practices that construct meanings through (on the operational level) and about (on the conceptual level) their professional action.[88]

7 Conclusion

The present study aims to explore the professional self-representations of Russian literary translators and to examine how they conceptualize their professional actions as intercultural communicative agents. A complex analytical framework of cognitive metaphor theory and the newly-emerging research perspective of "translator approach" are used to look closely at literary translators and the act of translating as a locus of intercultural communication.

It appears that literary translators in Russia share a working ethos of personal devotion and attachment, and tend to represent themselves as people-of-arts and creators. These representations strongly correlate with translators' conceptualization of their professional self: the conceptual analysis of metaphorical expressions used by translators shows that they conceptualize themselves as independent creative artists with a strong individual agency. Being put in a paradigmatic context of borders and distance between cultures, this

85 Dmitry Likhachev, "Dva tipa granits mezhdu kulturami" [Two types of intercultural borders] in *Ocherki po filosofii khudozhestvennogo tvorchestva* [Essays in philosophy of art], 2nd ed., ed. Dmitry Likhachev, (St. Petersburg: Blitz, 1999), 103–108.

86 Pym, "Alternatives to Borders in Translation Theory," 458.

87 Kupriyanov, written interview. Translation by the author.

88 Kathryn Sorrells defines cultural space as the communicative practices that construct meanings in, through, and about particular places. See Kathryn Sorrells, *Intercultural Communication: Globalization and Social Justice.* (Thousand Oaks, CA: Sage, 2013), ch. 4.

distinctive conceptualization gives a different perspective on the cultural borders in translation, which highlights the creative potential of translators as communicators. Through their individual agency literary translators play a manipulative role as agents of change within the wider context of intercultural communication. Holding positions with direct access to the literary and cultural world of a target culture—such as educators, university teachers, critics, editors, poets, and authors—they function as critical figures encompassing "cultural borders," multifaceted contact zones of communication between source and target culture, source and target language, source author and target reader, original and translated text.

Another finding of this study is that, as the analysis of translators' metaphors about "translating" revealed, the vast majority of Russian literary translators perceive their work as culturally important and socially significant; however, they rather see this significance as a byproduct of personal and professional actualization (the difference between the representations of the conceptual level of translation versus the operational level). Therefore, as this study shows, the working methods translators use as intercultural communicators to overcome distance between cultures can at the same time serve as an instrument of their status enhancement.

Although the limited scope of this chapter does not permit me to elaborate on gender issues in regard to translation, this paper still can give some insight into how these are connected to professional translating, bringing into discussion such topics as the prevalence of female translators over their male counterparts and the correspondence between the translator's effort to enhance their professional opportunities and the more general attempt to enhance women's professional status. Also, there are studies that investigate these issues from different perspectives, including research from such prominent figures in the field of translation studies as Brian Baer, Susan Bassnett and Luise von Flotow.[89]

---

89 Brian James Baer, *Translation and the Making of Modern Russian Literature* (New York: Bloomsbury, 2015), 87–114; Susan Bassnett, "Translation and Gender," in *Translation* (Abingdon: Routledge, 2014), 59–80; Luise von Flotow, *Translation and Gender: Translating in the "Era of Feminism"* (Ottawa: St. Jerome Publishing, 1997). For additional reading in this area see two recent collections edited by Eleonora Federici: *Translating Gender*, eds. Eleonora Federici, et al. (Bern: Peter Lang, 2011) and *Bridging the Gap between Theory and Practice in Translation and Gender Studies*, eds. Eleonora Federici and Vanessa Leonardi (Newcastle Upon Tyne: Cambridge Scholars Publishing, 2013). There is also relatively new research field focusing on effect of a translator's gender on her professional practice. See, e.g., Leila Amanati, "The Translator's Gender and its Impact on Translation Accuracy of Narrative Style," *The Social Sciences*, 11:9 (2016); Navid Hayeri, *Does Gender Affect*

Another research direction that has not been fully addressed in this chapter is the question of links between gender and metaphors for conceptualizing one's professional identity which has yet to be adequately examined in future studies.

Bibliography

Amanati, Leila. "The Translator's Gender and Its Impact on Translation Accuracy of Narrative Style." *The Social Sciences*, 11, no. 9 (2016): 2144–50.

Attolino, Paola et al., eds. *(Re)visiting Translation*. New York: Peter Lang, 2015.

Baibikov, Elena. "Revised Translations, Revised Identities: (Auto)biographical Contextualization of Translation." In *Identity and Status in the Translational Professions*, edited by Rakefet Sela-Sheffy and Miriam Shlesinger, 173–188. Amsterdam: John Benjamins, 2011.

Baer, Brian James. *Translation and the Making of Modern Russian Literature*, New York: Bloomsbury, 2015.

Bassnett, Susan. "The Translator as Cross-Cultural Mediator." In *The Oxford Handbook of Translation Studies*, edited by Kristen Malmkjær and Kevin Windle, K. 97–107. Oxford University Press Canada, 2011.

Bassnett, Susan. "Translation and Gender," in *Translation*, 59–80. Abingdon: Routledge, 2014.

Chang, Heewon. "Re-examining the Rhetoric of the 'Cultural Border'," *Electronic Magazine of Multicultural Education* 1, no. 1 (1999), accessed July 3, 2020, at https://www.researchgate.net/publication/280558629_Reexamining_the_Rhetoric_of_the_Cultural_Border.

Chesterman, Andrew. "The Name and Nature of Translator Studies," *Hermes* 42 (2009): 13–22.

Dam, Helle Vrønning. "The Translator Approach in Translation Studies—Reflections Based on a Study of Translators' Weblogs," in *Haasteena näkökulma, Perspektivet som utmaning* [Point of view as challenge], *Perspektivität als Herausforderung*. VAKKI-symposiumi XXXIII 7.–8.2.2013, edited by Maria Eronen and Marinella Rodi-Risberg, 16–35. Vaasa, Finland: *VAKKI Publications* 2, 2013.

Even-Zohar, Itamar. "Laws of Cultural Interference," in *Papers in Culture Research*, edited by Itamar Even-Zohar, 52–69. Tel Aviv: The Culture Research Laboratory, 2010.

Translation? Analysis of English Talks Translated to Arabic (PhD diss., University of Texas at Austin, 2014); and Jihan Mahmoud Sherbini, *Differences in Word Choice between Male and Female Translators: in Historical, Hostile and Romantic Texts* (MA thesis, An-Najah National University, 2014).

Federici, Eleonora et all, eds. *Translating Gender*. Bern: Peter Lang, 2011.

Federici, Eleonora and Vanessa Leonardi, eds. *Bridging the Gap between Theory and Practice in Translation and Gender Studies*. Newcastle Upon Tyne: Cambridge Scholars Publishing, 2013.

Gambier, Yves. "Translators and the Transmission of Cultural Values," in *Translators through History*, edited by Jean Delisle and Judith Woodsworth, 191–228. Amsterdam: John Benjamins, 2012.

Joly, Jean-François. "Preface," in *Translators through History*, edited by Jean Delisle and Judith Woodsworth, ix–xii. Amsterdam: John Benjamins, 1995.

Gile, Daniel., *Basic Concepts and Models for Interpreter and Translator Training*. Amsterdam: John Benjamins, 2009.

Guild of Literary Translators, "Aims and objectives of the organization," *Masters of Literary Translation Official Site* archived version, accessed July 3, 2020, at https://web.archive.org/web/20120817043340/http://www.lit-perevod.ru/index.php?page=13.

Guild of Literary Translators, "Articles of Association," *Masters of Literary Translation Official Site* archived version, accessed July 3, 2020, at https://web.archive.org/web/20120817043411/http://www.lit-perevod.ru/index.php?page=4.

Hayeri, Navid. *Does Gender Affect Translation? Analysis of English Talks Translated to Arabic*. PhD diss., University of Texas at Austin, 2014.

Katan, David. *Translating Cultures: An Introduction for Translators, Interpreters and Mediators* 2nd edition. Manchester: St Jerome, 2004.

Lakoff, George. "The Contemporary Theory of Metaphor," in Metaphor and *Thought*, 2nd edition, edited by Andrew Ortony, 202–251. Cambridge: Cambridge University Press, 1993.

Lakoff, George and Mark Johnson. "Conceptual Metaphor in Everyday Language," *The Journal of Philosophy* 77, no. 8 (1980): 453–486.

Likhachev, Dmitry. "Dva tipa granits mezhdu kulturami" [Two types of intercultural borders] in *Ocherki po filosofii khudozhestvennogo tvorchestva* [Essays in philosophy of art], 2nd edition, edited by Dmitry Likhachev, 103–108. St.Petersburg: Blitz, 1999.

MacShane, Frank. "The Fantasy World of Italo Calvino," *New York Times Magazine* (July 10, 1983): 23–50, accessed July 3, 2020, at http://www.nytimes.com/1983/07/10/magazine/the-fantasy-world-of-italo-calvino.html.

Martin de Leon, Celia. "Metaphorical Models of Translation: TRANSFER VS. IMITATION and ACTION," in *Thinking through Translation with Metaphors*, edited by James St. André, 75–108. Manchester: St. Jerome, 2010.

Martin de Leon, Celia and Marisa Presas. "The Evolution of Translation Trainees' Subjective Theories: an Empirical Study of Metaphors about Translation," in *Metaphor and Intercultural Communication*, edited by Andreas Musolf, Fiona MacArthur and Giulio Pagani, 19–33. London: Bloomsbury, 2014.

Munday, Jeremy. "Issues in Translation Studies," *The Routledge Companion to Translation Studies*, edited by Jeremy Munday, 1–19. London: Routledge, 2009.

Monticelli, Daniele and Anne Lange. "Translation and Totalitarianism: the Case of Soviet Estonia," *The Translator* 20, no. 1 (2014): 95–111.

Pym, Anthony. "Alternatives to Borders in Translation Theory," in *Translation Translation*, edited by Susan Petrilli, 451–63. Amsterdam/New York: Rodopi, 2003.

Rakhimov, Azamat. "Alexander Livergant: Translating is [a] Humble Profession," (interview with Alexander Livergant), *Nasha Gazeta*, December 17, 2014, accessed July 3, 2020, at http://nashagazeta.ch/news/peoples/18739.

Robinson, Douglas. *Becoming a Translator: an Introduction to the Theory and Practice of Translation*, 2nd edition. New York: Routledge, 2003.

Roig-Sanz, Diana and Reine Meylaerts. "General Introduction. Literary Translation and Cultural Mediators. Toward an Agent and Process-Oriented Approach," in *Literary Translation and Cultural Mediators in 'Peripheral' Cultures. Customs Officers or Smugglers?*, edited by Diana Roig-Sanz et al., 1–37. Palgrave Macmillan, 2018.

Rubel, Paula G. and Abraham Rosman. "Introduction: Translation and Anthropology," in *Translating Cultures: Perspectives on Translation and Anthropology*, edited by Paula G. Rubel and Abraham Rosman, 1–22. New York: Berg, 2003.

Russia Beyond the Headlines, "A Labor of Love or a Science? Experts Gather in Moscow to Discuss Translation," September 12, 2014, accessed July 3, 2020 at http://rbth.com/literature/2014/09/12/a_labor_of_love_or_a_science_experts_gather_in_moscow_to_discuss_t_39753.html.

Salama-Carr, Myriam. "Translators and the Dissemination of Knowledge," in *Translators through History*, edited by Jean Delisle and Judith Woodsworth, 101–127. Amsterdam: John Benjamins & Unesco Publishing, 1996.

Schäffner, Christina. "Action (Theory of "Translatorial Action")" in *Encyclopedia of Translation Studies*, edited by Mona Baker, 3–5. London: Routledge, 1998.

Schäffner, Christina. "Translation and Intercultural Communication: Similarities and Differences," *Studies in Communication Sciences*, 3, no. 2 (2003), 93.

Sela-Sheffy, Rakefet. "How to Be a (Recognized) Translator: Rethinking Habitus, Norms, and the Field of Translation," *Target* 17, no. 1 (2005), 1–26.

Sela-Sheffy, Rakefet. "The Pursuit of Symbolic Capital by a Semi-Professional Group: The Case of Literary Translators in Israel," in *Übersetzen—Translating—Traduire: Towards a "Social Turn"?*, edited by Michaela Wolf, 243–252. Berlin: LIT, 2006.

Sela-Sheffy, Rakefet. "The Translators' Personae: Marketing Translatorial Images as Pursuit of Capital," *Meta* 53, no. 3 (2008), 609–622.

Sela-Sheffy, Rakefet. "Translators' Identity Work: Introducing Micro-sociological Theory of Identity to the Discussion of Translators' Habitus," in *Remapping*

Habitus in Translation Studies, edited by Gisella M. Vorderobermeier, 43–55. Amsterdam: Rodopi, 2014.

Sela-Sheffy, Rakefet and Miriam Shlesinger. "Strategies of Image-Making and Status Advancement of Translators and Interpreters as a Marginal Occupational Group: A Research Project in Progress," in *Beyond Descriptive Translation Studies: Investigations in Homage to Gideon Toury*, edited by Anthony Pym, Miriam Shlesinger and Daniel Simeoni, 79–90. Amsterdam: John Benjamins, 2008.

Shatalov, Dmitry. *Metaphorical Conceptions of Translation*. PhD diss., Voronezh State University, 2014.

Sherbini, Jihan Mahmoud. *Differences in Word Choice between Male and Female Translators: in Historical, Hostile and Romantic Texts*. MA thesis, An-Najah National University, 2014.

"Translators' Anti-war Petition." Accessed July 3, 2020, at http://znn.info/petition.html.

Von Flotow, Luise. *Translation and Gender: Translating in the "Era of Feminism."* Ottawa: St. Jerome Publishing, 1997.

Von Flotow, Luise. *Translation and Gender: Translating in the "Era of Feminism."* Ottawa: St. Jerome Publishing, 1997.

Index

See entries under "Japan" for place names and locations in Japan

www.ingramcontent.com/pod-product-compliance
Lightning Source LLC
LaVergne TN
LVHW021725021026
849161LV00004BA/722